INTRODUCTION

Welcome to the world of digital publishing ~ the book you now hold in your hand, while unchanged from the original **1960's** edition, was printed using the latest state of the art digital technology. The advent of print-on-demand has forever changed the publishing process, never has information been so accessible and it is our hope that this book serves your informational needs for years to come. If this is your first exposure to digital publishing, we hope that you are pleased with the results. Many more titles of interest to the classic automobile and motorcycle enthusiast, collector and restorer are available via our website at **www.VelocePress.com**. We hope that you find this title as interesting as we do.

NOTE FROM THE PUBLISHER

The information presented is true and complete to the best of our knowledge. All recommendations are made without any guarantees on the part of the author or the publisher, who also disclaim all liability incurred with the use of this information.

TRADEMARKS

We recognize that some words, model names and designations, for example, mentioned herein are the property of the trademark holder. We use them for identification purposes only. This is not an official publication.

INFORMATION ON THE USE OF THIS PUBLICATION

This manual is an invaluable resource for the classic **Austin-Healey** automobile enthusiast and a must have for owners interested in performing their own maintenance. However, in today's information age we are constantly subject to changes in common practice, new technology, availability of improved materials and increased awareness of chemical toxicity. As such, it is advised that the user consult with an experienced professional prior to undertaking any procedure described herein. While every care has been taken to ensure correctness of information, it is obviously not possible to guarantee complete freedom from errors or omissions or to accept liability arising from such errors or omissions. Therefore, any individual that uses the information contained within, or elects to perform or participate in do-it-yourself repairs or modifications acknowledges that there is a risk factor involved and that the publisher or its associates cannot be held responsible for personal injury or property damage resulting from the use of the information or the outcome of such procedures.

It is important that the reader recognizes that any instructions may refer to either the right-hand or left-hand sides of the vehicle or the components and that the directions are followed carefully. One final word of advice, this publication is intended to be used as a reference guide, and when in doubt the reader should consult with a qualified expert.

HEALEY OWNERS HANDBOOK of Maintenance & Repair

By

Past & Present
Technical Editors of
Clymer Publications
and Floyd Clymer

Published by
FLOYD CLYMER PUBLICATIONS
World's Largest Publisher of Books Relating to
Automobile, Motorcycles, Motor Racing, and Americana
222 NO. VIRGIL AVENUE, LOS ANGELES 4, CALIFORNIA

ANNOUNCEMENT

The name Austin-Healey is a combination of words which have special significance in the field of automobiles and auto competition events. Austin, a marque which has been in existence for half a century, has always stood for a sound, conservative type construction yet with a sporting flavor. The little Austin Saloons were always great favorites for 'hot rodding' as we would say in this country, and the various models plentifully supplied builders of racing specials with strong, light components. Now a big portion of the giant British Motors Corporation, Austin still gives the firm's products much of their character. Healey, of course, is the surname of Donald Healey, a prominent and highly successful racing and rally competitor for many years. After building several cars for his own use, Healey turned to producing limited number of special interest sports cars using a variety of chassis and engines. The Nash-Healey, Healey Palm Beach (using Ford engines) and soon were fore runners of the most successful hyphenation of them all: the Austin-Healey.

Employing the four cylinder two-liter Austin engine, the first Healey 100 was a sensation, a slick, streamlined and racy two seater that went as well as it looked. From there to the present, comfortable, yet sporting convertible, was a logical evolution.

This book deals with the most popular and numerous Healeys — the sixes, and covers all models with those engines. It is designed to be as complete as the average owner ever finds necessary as a guide to maintenance and repair. Those operations beyond the scope of home workshop tools are best left to the experienced, factory trained mechanic, and in case of trouble, the best place for your Healey is an authorized service garage. Following the tips and hints in this book will, of course, make such visits far less frequent. We are happy to publish it and hope that it will make your use of Austin Healey more pleasant.

Floyd Clymer

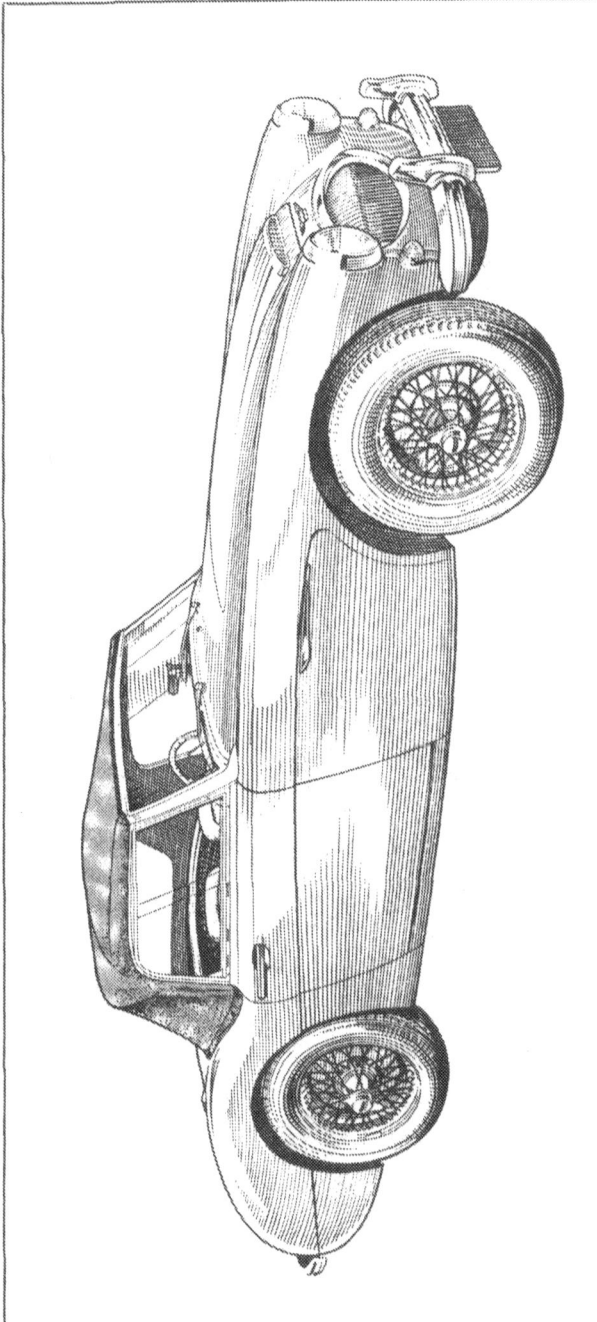

THE AUSTIN-HEALEY 3000 Mk. II SERIES BN7
(Two-seater Model)

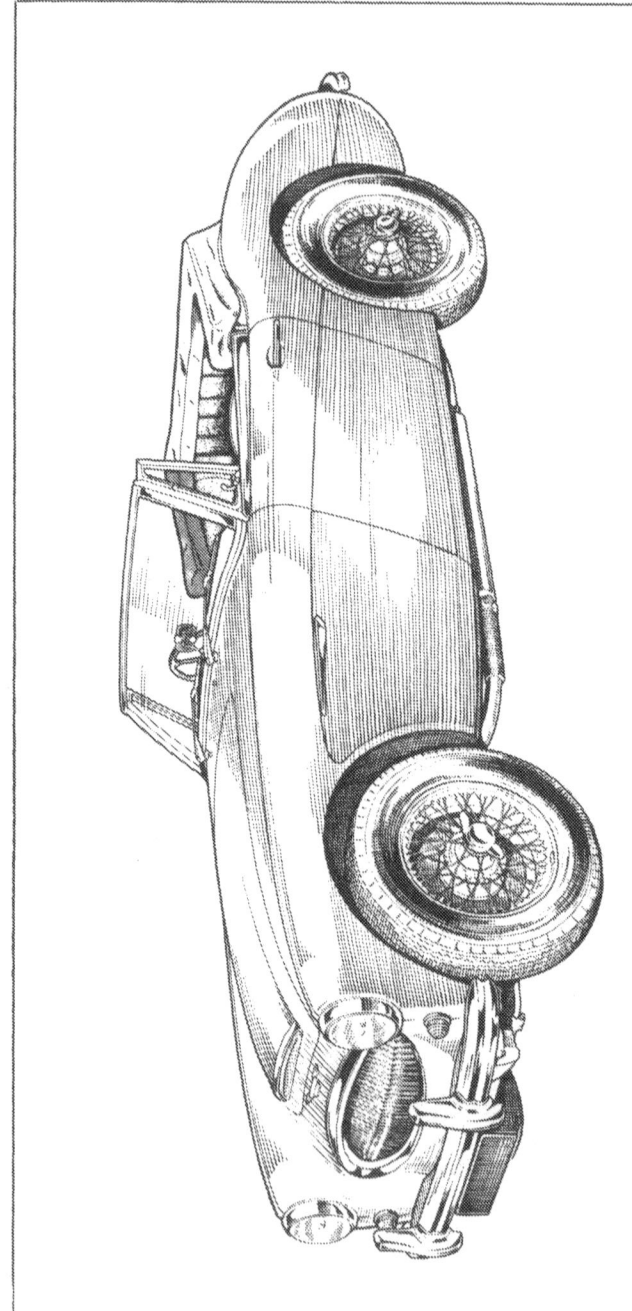

THE AUSTIN-HEALEY 3000 Mk. II SPORTS CONVERTIBLE
(Series BJ7)

CONTENTS

Topic	Page
GENERAL DATA	2
ENGINE	16
COOLING SYSTEM	49
IGNITION SYSTEM	54
FUEL SYSTEM	66
CLUTCH	90
GEARBOX	97
OVERDRIVE	108
DRIVESHAFT	126
REAR AXLE	130
STEERING	137
FRONT SUSPENSION	141
BRAKES	149
ELECTRICAL SYSTEM	163
MAINTENANCE	182

GENERAL DATA

Thorough and conscientious maintenance can prevent a great many minor and major problems encountered in the operation of a sports car. Those automobiles which are allowed to deteriorate through neglect call for the most expensive procedures when they are finally brought to the shop. A small amount of time spent by the owner in **routine** examination and attention will generally ensure having the best running and least costly machine. It is wise, therefore, to establish good habits in reference to visual inspection of the car and in giving it the proper care.

Cleanliness is the most important habit which can be cultivated. Not only for appearance sake, but for safety and prevention of more serious faults, the car should be kept as clean as possible in the area of engine and chassis (as well as exterior and interior which reflects pride of ownership). By such cleanliness, the less-obvious signs of wear or damage which precede more serious failures can often be determined. Allowing accumulations of grease and dirt to encrust steering arms, shock absorber links and so forth, will prevent good visual inspection which is the key to preventive maintenance. Likewise a dirty piece of metal does not invite close inspection and is apt to be looked over.

The second most important habit to be cultivated in the care of a sports car is that of listening to and recognizing the sounds of normal running and abnormal noises. Learn the sound your Healey makes when it is in prime tune and running well, then any variation which makes itself known to your ear will call for investigation. The experienced driver can sense when the engine begins to lose its sharpness, although it is quite a gradual process, and he is quick to spot any unusual click or rattle. Even if the noise cannot be identified at once, its presence can be accounted for by a little detective work.

Do not procrastinate. When some fault is noticed, correct it at once. This is not only the most economical method, but surely the one resulting in the least time lost and the least annoyance.

All cars are human. They will have problems in greater or lesser degree eventually. The Healey is a sturdy, rugged and thoroughly stressed automobile and its dependability is well known, but, like any other piece of machinery, it obeys certain physical laws. It requires lubrication, the correct maintenance of working clearances, proper tightening of nuts and bolts and replacement of components eroded by time and wear. If the maintenance and lubrication procedure advised here is followed and proper care given to whatever faults need correction, the Healey will prove to be one of the most faithful and enjoyable of sports cars. Abuse it, ignore its wants and leave it in the hands of the Gods and it will be as unsatisfactory as any other car.

As a Healey owner who has gone so far as to purchase this handbook, it is unlikely that you will abandon your car to such a routine of no maintenance. And if you want to extract the most pleasure from it, you may as well carry out maintenance properly. Therefore the first few pages are devoted to maintenance and lubrication.

In approaching the various parts of the Healey the following manner is used: First the function and operation of the component is described. Then, if it can be serviced in the vehicle, this procedure is described. If it must be removed or disassembled, these steps are next. Special hints in trouble shooting are given in graphic form at the end of the section.

It must be understood that this handbook is not a shop manual in that the full shop procedures and details of repairs which require the use of a great number of special service tools or professional equipment are not included. However, it is designed to enable the owner or enthusiast to diagnose and correct most faults. Or, in an emergency the book can be handed to a garage mechanic who is unfamiliar with the car and it will enable him to take care of nearly any problem. Truly major repairs such as replacing ring and pinion or a front suspension assembly are naturally best left to the trained BMC mechanic.

The complete set of specifications in the General Data section will be most appreciated by those who have occasion to replace components since the correct sizes and nomenclature are given. In addition it is a verified guide to torque wrench settings, clearances and wear limits.

GENERAL DATA

Data variations for cars fitted with the 6 port cylinder head are given on General Data page 9 and for Series BN6 and later Series BN4 cars on page 10. Data for Series BN7 and BT7 cars will be found on General Data page 10.

ENGINE

Type	BN4
Number of cylinders	6.
Bore	3·125 in. (79·375 mm.).
Stroke	3·5 in. (88·9 mm.).
Capacity	2639 c.c. (161 cu. in.)
B.H.P.	102 at 4600 r.p.m.
Compression ratio	8·25 : 1.
Bore, 1st Oversize	+·010 in. (·254 mm.).
Bore, 2nd Oversize	+·020 in. (·508 mm.).
Bore, 3rd Oversize	+·030 in. (·762 mm.).
Bore, 4th Oversize	+·040 in. (1·016 mm.).
Firing Order	1, 5, 3, 6, 2, 4
Cooling	Thermo-siphon; pump, fan, and thermostat.
Torque	142 lb./ft. (19·77 kg./m.) at 2,400 r.p.m.
B.M.E.P.	139 lb./sq. in. (9·77 kg./cm.^{2}).

Valves

Position	Overhead, push-rod-operated.
Lift	·3145 in. (8·054 mm.).
Diameter: Head: Inlet	1·693 to 1·683 in. (42·99 to 42·75 mm.).
Exhaust	1·420 to 1·415 in. (36·07 to 35·94 mm.).
Stem: Inlet	·34175 to ·34225 in. (8·68 to 8·69 mm.).
Exhaust	·34175 to ·34225 in. (8·68 to ·869 mm.).
Stem/guide clearance: Inlet	·0025 to ·0015 in. (·063 to ·038 mm.).
Exhaust	·002 to ·001 in. (·051 to ·025 mm.).
Valve rocker clearance	·012 in. (·305 mm.) hot.
Seat angle: Inlet	30°.
Exhaust	45°.
Seat face width: Inlet	·091 to ·097 in. (2·311 to 2·464 mm.).
Exhaust	·198 to ·217 in. (5·029 to 5·512 mm.).

Valve guides

Length: Inlet	2·266 in. (57·55 mm.).
Exhaust	2·578 in. (65·49 mm.).

Valve springs

Free length: Inner	1·969 in. (50 mm.).
Outer	2·047 in. (51·99 mm.).
Fitted length: Inner	1·517 in. (38·53 mm.) load 25·3 lb. (11·476 kg.).
Outer	1·607 in. (40·82 mm.) load 54·2 lb. (24·58 kg.)

Tappets

Type	Cylindrical, spherical foot.
Diameter	·93725 in. (23·81 mm.).
Length	2·548 in. (64·72 mm.).

Rockers

Bushes	Steel and white metal.
Outside diameter (before fitting)	·913 in. (23·17 mm.).
Inside diameter (reamed in position)	·8115 to ·8125 in. (20·62 to 20·65 mm.).
Clearance	·0025 to ·0005 in. (·063 to ·012 mm.).
Bore of arm	·909 to ·910 in. (23·076 to 23·101 mm.).

Pistons

Material	Low expansion aluminium alloy.
Clearance at skirt (right angles to gudgeon pin)	·0226 to ·0008 in. (·066 to ·020 mm.).
Width of ring groove: Compression	·0952 to ·0962 in. (2·410 to 2·436 mm.).
Oil	·189 to ·190 in. (4·81 to 4·83 mm.).
Oversizes	+·010 in.; +·020 in.; +·030 in.; +·040 in. (+·254 mm.; +·508 mm.; +·762 mm.; +1·016 mm.).

Piston rings

Number	3 compression (2 taper), 1 oil control.
Width: Compression	·0938 to ·0928 in. (2·383 to 2·357 mm.).
Oil	·1865 to ·1875 in. (4·737 to 4·762 mm.).
Clearance in groove: Compression	·0034 to ·0014 in. (·086 to ·036 mm.).
Oil	·0015 to ·0035 in. (·038 to ·088 mm.).
Ring gap (compression and oil)	·009 to ·014 in. (·23 to ·35 mm.).

Gudgeon pins
Type ... Clamped in rod. Fully floating from Engine No. 40501.
Fit ... Selective; push in piston.
Diameter ... ·8748 to ·8750 in. (22·215 to 22·220 mm.).

Crankshaft
Journal diameter ... 2·3742 to 2·3747 in. (60·305 to 60·317 mm.).
Crankpin diameter ... 2·0000 to 2·0005 in. (50·80 to 50·8127 mm.).
Undersizes (journals and crankpins) ... —·010 in.; —·020 in.; —·030 in.; —·040 in.
(—·254mm.; —·508 mm.; —·762 mm.; —1·016 mm.).
End-float ... Taken on thrust washer at front middle (No. 2) main bearing; ·0025 to ·0055 in. (·063 to ·140 mm.).
Thrust washer: Standard ... ·091 to ·093 in. (2·315 to 2·366 mm.).
+·0025 in. (+·063 mm.) ... ·0935 to ·0955 in. (2·378 to 2·429 mm.).
+·005 in. (+·127 mm.) ... ·0960 to ·0980 in. (2·442 to 2·493 mm.).
+·0075 in. (+·190 mm.) ... ·0985 to ·1005 in. (2·505 to 2·556 mm.).
+·010 in. (+·254 mm.) ... ·1000 to ·1030 in. (2·569 to 2·620 mm.).

Main bearings
Number ... 4.
Type ... White-metalled steel shell.
Length ... 1·495 to 1·505 in. (37·973 to 38·227 mm.).
Running clearance ... ·0013 to ·0028 in. (·033 to ·071 mm.).
Sizes for reground journals ... ·010 in. U/S; ·020 in. U/S; ·030 in. U/S; ·040 in. U/S. (·254 mm.; ·508 mm.; ·762 mm.; 1·016 mm.).

Connecting rods
Length (centres) ... 6·601 to 6·605 in. (167·665 to 167·767 mm.).
Side clearance ... ·007 to ·004 in. (·178 to ·102 mm.).
Big-ends: Type ... White-metalled steel shells.
Diametrical clearance ·0005 to ·002 in. (·0127 to ·051 mm.).
Small-end bush ... ·8750 to ·8755 in. (22·225 to 22·328 mm.).
Sizes for reground crankpins ... ·010 in. U/S; ·020 in. U/S; ·030 in. U/S; ·040 in. U/S. (·254 mm.; ·508 mm.; ·762 mm.; 1·016 mm.).

Camshaft
Journal diameters: Front ... 1·78875 to 1·78925 in. (45·434 to 45·447 mm.).
Middle front ... 1·76875 to 1·76925 in. (44·926 to 44·939 mm.).
Journal diameters: Middle rear ... 1·74875 to 1·74925 in. (44·418 to 44·431 mm.).
Rear ... 1·72875 to 1·72925 in. (43·910 to 43·923 mm.).
End-float ... Taken on thrust plate at front end: ·003 to ·006 in. (·076 to ·152 mm.).

Camshaft bearings
Number and type ... 4 thin-wall rolled bush.
Outside diameter (before fitting): Front ... 1·9205 in. (48·780 mm.).
Middle front ... 1·9005 in. (48·272 mm.).
Middle rear ... 1·8805 in. (47·762 mm.).
Rear ... 1·8605 in. (47·252 mm.).
Inside diameter (reamed in position): Front ... 1·79025 to 1·79075 in. (45·472 to 45·485 mm.).
Middle front ... 1·77025 to 1·77075 in. (44·964 to 44·977 mm.).
Middle rear ... 1·75025 to 1·75075 in. (44·456 to 44·469 mm.).
Rear ... 1·73025 to 1·73075 in. (43·946 to 43·959 mm.).
Clearance ... ·002 to ·001 in. (·051 to ·025 mm.).

Valve timing
Marking ... Adjoining gear teeth are marked.
Chain pitch and number of pitches ... ·375 in. (9·525 mm.). 62.
Rocker clearance for valve ... ·0234 in. (·610 mm.).
Inlet valve: Opens ... 5° B.T.D.C.
Closes ... 45° A.B.D.C.
Exhaust valve: Opens ... 40° B.B.D.C.
Closes ... 10° A.T.D.C.

Lubrication
System ... Pressure.
Pump type ... Rotor.
External filter ... Full flow; Tecalemit.
Oil pressure: Running ... 55 to 60 lb/sq. in. (3·9 to 4·2 kg/cm²).
Idling ... 25 to 30 lb/sq. in. (1·758 to 2·109 kg/cm²).
Release valve spring, free length ... 2·562 in. (65·09 mm.).
Release valve: Number of coils ... 13.
Diameter ... ·484 in. $\pm \frac{·000 \text{ in}}{·015 \text{ in}}$ (12·30 mm. $\pm \frac{·000 \text{ mm}}{·381 \text{ mm}}$).

Flywheel
    Diameter ... 12·8125 in. (325·45 mm.).
    Number of teeth on starter ring ... 106.

Torque wrench settings
    Cylinder head studs ... 400 lb. in. (4·6 kg. m.).
    Cylinder head nuts ... 900 lb. in. (10·4 kg. m.).
    Main bearing nuts ... 900 lb. in. (10·4 kg. m.).
    Connecting rod set screws ... 600 lb. in. (6·91 kg. m.).
    Front cover screws ... $\frac{7}{16}$ in. (11·11 mm.) less than 150 lb. in. (1·73 kg. m.), $\frac{1}{2}$ in. (12·70 mm.) less than 150 lb. in. (1·73 kg. m.).
    Front mounting plate screws ... 200 lb. in. (2·30 kg. m.).
    Rear mounting plate screws ... 600 lb. in. (6·91 kg. m.).
    Flywheel bolts ... 600 lb. in. (6·91 kg. m.).
    Rocker shaft bracket nuts ... 300(324 lb. in. (3·45/3·72 kg. m.).

IGNITION

Type ... Lucas 12-volt coil
Distributor type ... Lucas DM6A
Direction of rotation ... Anti-clockwise at rotor arm
Contact breaker gap ... ·014 in. to ·016 in. (·356 to ·406 mm.).
Static setting ... 6° (Crankshaft) B.T.D.C.
Maximum advance ... 35° (Crankshaft) B.T.D.C.
Coil type ... Lucas type HA 12
Sparking plug type ... Champion N5—14 mm. Long Reach
Sparking plug gap ... ·024 in. (·6096 mm.) to ·026 in. (·660 mm.).

COOLING SYSTEM

Capacity ... 20 Imp. pints (24 U.S. pints, 10·8 litres)
Circulation ... Pump and thermostat

FUEL SYSTEM

Fuel delivery ... S.U. electric, type H.P.
Carburetter type ... Twin S.U. horizontal H.4.
Needle (normal) ... A.J.
Jet size ... ·090 in. (2·286 mm.).
Tank capacity ... 12 Imp., 14·4 U.S. gallons (54·5 litres)
Air cleaner ... Twin "Pancake" type

CLUTCH

Make ... Borg and Beck
Type ... Single dry plate
Diameter ... 9 in. (229 mm.)
Total friction area ... 36·5 sq. in. (235 cm.^{2}) × 2
Thickness of friction linings ... ·150 (3·81 mm.)
Release bearings ... Special carbon graphite or copper carbon graphite
Number of springs ... 9
Total axial spring pressure ... 1215 to 1305 lb. (551 to 592 kg.)
Distance thrust race to thrust plate ... ·10 in. (2·54 mm.)
Thrust plate travel to fully released position ... ·42 to ·47 in. (10·66 to 11·93 mm.)

GEARBOX

Type ... Synchromesh on 2nd, 3rd and top
Type of gear ... Helical constant mesh
Type overdrive (optional extra) ... Laycock de Normanville electrically controlled
Gear ratios :
    First ... 3·076 : 1
    Second ... 1·913 : 1
    Third ... 1·333 : 1
    Overdrive, third ... 1·037 : 1
    Fourth ... Direct
    Overdrive, fourth ... ·778 : 1
    Reverse ... 4·16 : 1
Overall Gear Ratios—
Standard Box :
    First ... 12·027 : 1
    Second ... 7·48 : 1
    Third ... 5·212 : 1
    Fourth ... 3·91 : 1
    Reverse ... 16·4 : 1

Including overdrive :
- First ... 12·6 : 1.
- Second ... 7·84 : 1.
- Third ... 5·47 : 1.
- Third and overdrive ... 4·24 : 1.
- Fourth ... 4·1 : 1.
- Fourth and overdrive ... 3·19 : 1.
- Reverse ... 17·1 : 1.

Layshaft bearing :
- Type ... Needle roller.
- Number of rollers ... 46.
- Length of roller ... 1·551 in. (39·6 mm.).
- Diameter of roller ... 3·118 in. (3 mm.).

Mainshaft bearing :
- Make ... R. & M.
- Type ... MJ.35.
- Size ... 1·39 × 3·15 × ·827 in. (35 × 80 × 21 mm.).

First motion shaft bearing :
- Make ... R. & M.
- Type ... IM J40G.
- Size ... 1·58 × 3·55 × ·905 in. (40 × 90 × 23 mm.).

Oil capacity (standard box) ... 5 pints (6 U.S. pints, 2·84 litres).
Oil capacity (overdrive fitted) ... 6¼ Imp. pints (7·5 U.S. pints, 3·55 litres).

REAR AXLE

Type ... ¾ floating.

Ratio :
- Standard ... 3·91 : 1.
- With overdrive ... 4·1 : 1.

Final drive ... Hypoid bevel.

Teeth on crown wheel :
- Standard ... 43
- With overdrive ... 41

Teeth on pinion :
- Standard ... 11
- With overdrive ... 10

Crown wheel/pinion backlash ... Marked on crown wheel.
Oil capacity ... 3 Imp. pints (1·704 litres, 3·6 U.S. pints).

REAR SPRINGS

- Type ... Semi-elliptic.
- Number of leaves ... 7
- Thickness of leaves ... 6 at $\frac{7}{32}$ in. (4·76 mm.) and 1 at $\frac{5}{32}$ in. (3·97 mm.).
- Width ... 1¾ in. (44·45 mm.).
- Deflection ... 4 in. (101·6 mm.) ± ¼ in. (6·35 mm.).
- Loaded camber ... ½ in. (12·70 mm.) ± ⅛ in. (3·18 mm.).
- Number of zinc leaves ... 3 ($\frac{1}{32}$ in. (·80 mm) thickness).

STEERING

- Make ... Cam gears.
- Ratio ... 14 : 1.
  15 : 1. from Car Nos. BN4 68960 and BN6 1995
- Track toe-in ... $\frac{1}{16}$ in. to ⅛ in. (1·58 to 3·17 mm.).

SUSPENSION

Front :
- Type ... Independent by coil spring and wishbones
- Castor angle ... 2°.
- Camber angle ... 1°.
- Swivel pin inclination ... 6½°.

Rear :
- Type ... Semi-elliptic underslung leaf-springs with Panhard rod.

Shock absorbers :
- Type ... Lever hydraulic.

BRAKES

- Type ... Girling hydraulic two leading shoes front.
- Drum diameter ... 11 in. (280 mm.).
- Total frictional area ... 188 sq. in. (1213 sq. cm.).
- Shoe lining width ... 2¼ in. (57 mm.).

Shoe lining length :
    Front ... ... 10·4 in. (265·6 mm.).
    Rear ... ... 10·4 in. (265·6 mm.).
Shoe lining thickness ... ... ·167 to ·174 in. (4·24 to 4·42 mm.).
Pedal free movement ... ... ⅛ in. (3·175 mm.).
Handbrake ... ... Mechanical, rear wheels only.

ELECTRICAL

Battery
  Type :
    Home (standard) ... ... GTW 9A.
    Dry charged (export) ... ... GTZ 9A.
  Voltage ... ... 12.
  Capacity :
    10 hour rate ... ... 51 amp. hr.
    20 hour rate ... ... 58 amp. hr.
  Electrolyte to fill one cell ... ... 1 pint (·57 litres).
  Initial charging current ... ... 3·5 amp.
  Normal recharge current ... ... 5 amp.
  Master switch ... ... Lucas type ST330.
Generator
  Type ... ... Lucas C45 PV-5
  Cutting-in speed ... ... 1,100 to 1,250 generator r.p.m.
  Maximum output ... ... 22 amps., 13·5 volts at 1700 to 1900 generator r.p.m.
  Field resistance ... ... 6 ohms.
Starting motor :
  Type ... ... Lucas M418 G.
  Lock torque ... ... 17 lb. ft. (1·2858 kg.m.) at 440 to 460 amps. and 7·0 to 7·4 volts.
  Light running current ... ... 45 amps. at 7,400 to 8,500 r.p.m.
  Solenoid switch ... ... Lucas type, ST 950.
Overdrive (optional extra) :
  Control switch ... ... Lucas type 2TS.
  Transmission gear solenoid ... ... Lucas type TGS1.
  Relay—overdrive ... ... Lucas type SB 40—1.
  Interrupter switch ... ... Lucas type 5510—1.
  Rotary throttle switch ... ... Lucas type RTS1.
Control box :
  Type ... ... Lucas RB 106/2.
  Cut-out :
    Cut-in voltage ... ... 12·7 to 13·3 volts.
    Drop off voltage ... ... 8·5 to 11 volts
    Reverse current ... ... 3·5 to 5 amps.

Regulator :
  Setting on open circuit at 68°F. (20°C.) ... ... 16·0 to 16·6 volts at 3,000 generator r.p.m.
  Note : For circuit temperature other than 20°C. the following allowances should be made to the above setting.
  For every 10°C. (18°F.) above 20° subtract 0·1 volt.
  For every 10°C. (18°F.) below 20° add 0"1 volt.

Windscreen wiper :
  Type ... ... Lucas DR2.
  Normal running current ... ... 2·3 to 3·1 amp. at 12 volts.
  Stall current (motor hot) ... ... 8 amp.
  Stall current (motor cold) ... ... 14 amp.
  Armature resistance (adjacent commutator segments) ... 0·34 to 0·41 ohms.
  Field resistance ... ... 12·8 to 14·00 ohms.
  N.B.—On some high output motors usually identified by a red insulating piece above the terminals, the field resistance is 8·0 to 11·5 ohms.

Fuse Unit :
  Type (two live and two spare fuses) ... ... Lucas SF6.

Fuses :
  A1—A2 ... ... 50 amp.
  A3—A4 ... ... 35 amp.

Sidelamps :
    Type ... ... Lucas model 594.

Headlamps :
    Type ... ... Lucas model F700

Stop-tail lamps :
    Type ... ... Lucas model 594.

Number plate illumination :
    Type ... ... Lucas model 467/2.

Flashing indicator unit :
    Type ... ... Lucas FL.5.

TYRE SIZES AND INFLATION PRESSURES

Tyre sizes ... ... 5·90—15 tubeless or 5·90—15 road speed (optional alternative).

Pressures :
    Front ... ... 20 lb./sq. in. (1·41 kg./cm.^{2}).
    Rear ... ... 23 lb./sq. in. (1·62 kg./cm.^{2}).

WHEELS

Type ... ... 15 × 4J ventilated steel disc or 15 × 4J wire (optional alternative).

DIMENSIONS

Wheelbase ... ... 7 ft. 8 in. (2·34 m.).
Overall length ... ... 13 ft. 1½ in. (4·00 m.).
Overall height (hood raised) ... ... 4 ft. 1 in. (1·24 m.).
Overall height (hood lowered) ... ... 3 ft. 10 in. (1·17 m.).
Overall width ... ... 5 ft. 0½ in. (1·54 m.).
Height over scuttle ... ... 2 ft. 11⅞ in. (0·91 m.).
Ground clearance ... ... 5½ in. (0·14 m.).
Track, front ... ... 4 ft. 0¾ in. (1·24 m.).
Track, rear ... ... 4 ft. 2 in. (1·27 m.).
Turning circle ... ... 35 ft. 0 in. (10·67 m.).
Approximate weight (with overdrive and wire wheels) ... ... 2,436 lb. (1105 kg.).

The following are the differing details of vehicles fitted with the 6 port cylinder head engine and should therefore be used in conjunction with the preceding specification.

ENGINE

Engine type ... ... BN6.
B.H.P. ... ... 117 at 5,000 r.p.m.
Torque ... ... 150 at 3,000 r.p.m.
Compression ratio ... ... 8·7 : 1.

Piston rings :
    1st ring ... ... Taper

Connecting rod, type of bearing ... ... Steel backed lead indium.
Standard journal diameter ... ... 2·3742 in. (60·3047 mm.) to 2·3747 in. (60·3174 mm.).

Exhaust valve :
    Throat diameter ... ... 1·3125 in. (33·3375 mm.).
    Head diameter ... ... 1·5625 in. (39·6875 mm.) to 1·5575 in. (39·5605 mm.).

Inlet valve :
    Throat diameter ... ... 1·5 in. (38·1 mm.).
    Head diameter ... ... 1·750 in. (44·45 mm.) to 1·745 in. (44·323 mm.).

Valve seat angles :
    Inlet ... ... 45°.
    Exhaust ... ... 45°.

Valve spring :
    Outer ;
        Fitted length ... ... 1·504 in. (38·20 mm.) load, 55·7 lb. (25·27 kg.).
    Inner :
        Fitted length ... ... 1·594 in. (40·488 mm.) load, 43·6 lb. (19·776 kg.).

IGNITION

Distributor	Lucas DM6.
Static setting	6° (crankshaft) B.T.D.C.
Maximum advance	36° (crankshaft) B.T.D.C.

CARBURATION

Carburetter type	Twin S.U. H.D.6.
Needle (normal)	C.V.
Jet size	·100 in. (2·54 mm.).
Angle of fitting	30° semi-downdraught.
Spring colour code	Yellow.

The following information is applicable to the Austin-Healey Series BN6 and later BN4 cars, and should be used in conjunction with the preceding specifications.

FUEL SYSTEM

Fuel delivery	S.U. Electric, type LCS.
Fuel pipe	Outside diameter ⅜ in. (9·52 mm.).
Maximum output per hour	12¼ gall. (56 litres).
Maximum suction lift (approx.)	33 in. (81 cm.).
Maximum output lift (approx.)	48 in. (122 cm.).

The following information is applicable to the Austin-Healey BN6 and should be used in conjunction with the preceding specifications.

ELECTRICAL

Battery
   Type :

Home (standard)	SLG 11E
Export (dry charged)	SLGZ 11E.
Voltage	(2) 6 volt.
Capacity :	
10 hour rate	50 amp. hr.
20 hour rate	58 amp. hr.
Electrolyte to fill one cell	1 pint (·57 litres).

The following information is applicable to the Austin-Healey 3000 (Series BN7 and BT7).

ENGINE

Type	29D.
Number of cylinders	6.
Bore	3·28 in. (83·34 mm.).
Stroke	3·5 in. (88·9 mm.).
Capacity	2912 c.c. (177·7 cu. in.).
B.H.P.	130 at 4,750 r.p.m.
Compression ratio	9 : 1.
Bore, 1st Oversize	+·010 in. (·254 mm.).
Bore, 2nd Oversize	+·020 in. (·508 mm.).
Bore, 3rd Oversize	+·030 in. (·762 mm.).
Bore, 4th Oversize	+·040 in. (1·016 mm.).
Firing order	1, 5, 3, 6, 2, 4.
Cooling	Thermo-siphon; pump, fan, and thermostat.
Torque	167 lb./ft. (23·14 kg./m.) at 2,700 r.p.m.
B.M.E.P.	142 lb./sq. in. (9·98 kg./cm²) at 2,700 r.p.m.

Valves
Position	Overhead, push-rod operated.
Lift	·3145 in. (8·054 mm.).
Diameter : Head : Inlet	1·750 to 1·745 in. (44·45 to 44·32 mm.).
Exhaust	1·5625 to 1·5575 in. (39·69 to 39·56 mm.).
Stem : Inlet	·34175 to ·34225 in. (8·68 to 8·69 mm.).
Exhaust	·34175 to ·34225 in. (8·68 to 8·69 mm.).
Stem/guide clearance : Inlet	·0025 to ·0015 in. (·063 to ·038 mm.).

Exhaust...	·002 to ·001 in. (·051 to ·025 mm.).
Valve rocker clearance	·012 in. (·305 mm.) hot.
Seat angle : Inlet...	45°.
Exhaust	45°.
Seat face width : Inlet	·091 to ·097 in. (2·311 to 2·464 mm.).
Exhaust	·198 to ·217 in. (5·029 to 5·512 mm.).

Valve guides

Length : Inlet	2·266 in. (57·55 mm.).
Exhaust..	2·578 in. (65·49 mm.).

Valve springs

Free length : Inner	1·969 in. (50 mm.).
Outer	2·047 in. (51·99 mm.).
Fitted length : Inner	1·504 in. (38·2 mm.) load 26 lb. (11·8 kg.).
Outer	1·594 in. (40·49 mm.) load 55·7 lb. (25·2 kg.).

Tappets

Type	Cylindrical, spherical foot.
Diameter	·93725 in. (23·81 mm.).
Length	2·548 in. (64·72 mm.).

Rockers

Bushes	Steel and white metal.
Outside diameter (before fitting)	·913 in. (23·17 mm.).
Inside diameter (reamed in position)	·8115 to ·8125 in. (20·62 to 20·65 mm.).
Clearance	·0025 to ·0005 in. (·063 to ·012 mm.).
Bore of arm	·909 to ·910 in. (23·076 to 23·101 mm.).

Pistons

Material	Low expansion aluminium alloy.
Clearance at skirt : Top	·0032 to ·0043 in. (·081 to ·109 mm.).
Bottom	·0010 to ·0016 in. (·025 to ·040 mm.).
Width of ring groove : Compression	·1417 to ·1482 in. (3·599 to 3·764 mm.).
Oil	·1567 to ·1632 in. (3·98 to 4·137 mm.).
Oversizes	+·010 in.; +·020 in.; +·030 in.; +·040 in. (+ ·254 mm.; + ·508 mm.; + ·762 mm.; + 1·016 mm.).

Piston rings

Number	3 compression (2 taper), 1 oil control.
Width : Compression and oil	3·2055 to 3·3832 mm.
Clearance in groove: Compression and oil	·0015 to ·0035 in. (·038 to ·088 mm.).
Ring gap (compression and oil)	·009 to ·014 in. (·23 to ·35 mm.)

Gudgeon pins

Type	Fully floating.
Fit	Selective; push in piston.
Diameter	·8748 to ·8750 in. (22·215 to 22·220 mm.).

Crankshaft

Journal diameter	2·3742 to 2·3747 in. (60·305 to 60·317 mm.).
Crankpin diameter	2·0000 to 2·0005 in. (50·80 to 50·8127 mm.).
Undersizes (journals and crankpins)	—·010 in.; —·020 in.; —·030 in.; —·040 in. (—·254 mm.; —·508 mm.; —·762 mm.; —1016 mm.).
End-float	Taken on thrust washer at front middle (No. 2) main bearing; ·0025 to ·0055 in. (·063 to ·140 mm.).
Thrust washer: Standard	·091 to ·093 in. (2·315 to 2·366 mm.).
+·0025 in. (+·063 mm.)	·0935 to ·0955 in. (2·378 to 2·429 mm.).
+·005 in. (+·127 mm.)	·0960 to ·0980 in. (2·442 to 2·493 mm.).
+·0075 in. (+·190 mm.)	·0985 to ·1005 in. (2·505 to 2·556 mm.).
+·010 in. (+·254 mm.)	·1000 to ·1030 in. (2·569 to 2·620 mm.).

Main bearings

Number	4.
Type	White metalled steel shell, lead indium plated.
Length	1·495 to 1·505 in. (37·973 to 38·227 mm.).
Running clearance	·0013 to ·0028 in. (·033 to ·071 mm.).
Sizes for reground journals	·010 in. U/S; ·020 in. U/S; ·030 in. U/S; ·040 in. U/S. (·254 mm.; ·508 mm.; ·762 mm.; 1·016 mm.).

Connecting rods

Length (centres)	6·601 to 6·605 in. (167·665 to 167·767 mm.).
Side clearance	·005 to ·009 in. (·127 to ·229 mm.).
Big-ends : Type	White metalled steel shells, lead indium plated.
Diametrical clearance	·002 to ·0035 in. (·051 to ·089 mm.).
Small-end bush	·8749 to ·8752 in. (22·22 to 22·23 mm.).
Sizes for reground crankpins	·010 in. U/S; ·020 in. U/S; ·030 in. U/S; ·040 in. U/S. (·254 mm.; ·508 mm.; ·762 mm.; 1·016 mm.).

Camshaft
Journal diameters : Front ... ... 1·78875 to 1·78925 in. (45·434 to 45·447 mm.).
         Middle front ... ... 1·76875 to 1·76925 in. (44·926 to 44·939 mm.).
Journal diameters : Middle rear ... ... 1·74875 to 1·74925 in. (44·418 to 44·431 mm.).
         Rear ... ... 1·72875 to 1·72925 in. (43·910 to 43·923 mm.).
End-float ... ... Taken on thrust plate at front end: ·003 to ·006 in. (·076 to ·152 mm.).

Camshaft bearings
Number and type ... ... 4 thin-wall rolled bush.
Outside diameter (before fitting) : Front ... ... 1·9205 in. (48·780 mm.).
          Middle front ... ... 1·9005 in. (48·272 mm.).
          Middle rear ... ... 1·8805 in. (47·762 mm.).
          Rear ... ... 1·8605 in. (47·252 mm.).
Inside diameter (reamed in position) : Front ... ... 1·79025 to 1·79075 in. (45·472 to 45·485 mm.).
          Middle front ... 1·77025 to 1·77075 in. (44·964 to 44·977 mm.).
          Middle rear ... 1·75025 to 1·75075 in. (44·456 to 44·469 mm.).
          Rear ... ... 1·73025 to 1·73075 in. (43·946 to 43·959 mm.).
Clearance ... ... ·002 to ·001 in. (·051 to ·025 mm.).

Valve timing
Marking ... ... Adjoining gear teeth are marked.
Chain pitch and number of pitches ... ... ·375 in. (9·525 mm.). 62.
Rocker clearance for valve ... ... ·0234 in. (·610 mm.).
Inlet valve : Opens ... ... 5° B.T.D.C.
     Closes ... ... 45° A.B.D.C.
Exhaust valve : Opens ... ... 40° B.B.D.C.
      Closes ... ... 10° A.T.D.C.

Lubrication
System ... ... Pressure.
Pump type ... ... Gear.
External filter ... ... Full flow; Tecalemit or Purolator.
Oil pressure : Running ... ... 50 lb./sq. in. (3·52 kg./cm²) at 40 m.p.h.
      Idling ... ... 20 lb./sq. in. (1·4 kg./cm²) at 600 r.p.m.
Release valve spring, free length ... ... 2·687 in. (68·26 mm.).
Release valve : Number of coils ... ... 13.
      Diameter ... ... ·484 in. $^{+·008}_{-·015}$ in. (12·30 mm. $^{+·000}_{-·318}$ mm.).

Flywheel
Diameter ... ... 12·8125 in. (325·45 mm.).
Number of teeth on starter ring ... ... 106.

Torque wrench settings
Cylinder head studs ... ... 400 lb. in. (4·6 kg. m.).
Cylinder head nuts ... ... 900 lb. in. (10·4 kg. m.).
Main bearing nuts ... ... 900 lb. in. (10·4 kg. m.).
Connecting rod set screws ... ... 600 lb. in. (6·91 kg. m.).
Front covers screws ... ... $\frac{1}{4}$ in. (11·11 mm.) less than 150 lb. in. (1·73 kg. m.)
               $\frac{1}{2}$ in. (12·70 mm.) less than 150 lb. in. (1·73 kg. m.)
Front mounting plate screws ... ... 200 lb. in. (2·30 kg. m.).
Rear mounting plate screws ... ... 600 lb. in. (6·91 kg. m.).
Flywheel bolts ... ... 600 lb. in. (6·91 kg. m.).
Rocker shaft bracket nuts ... ... 300/324 lb. in. (3·45/3·72 kg. m.)

IGNITION
Type ... ... Lucas 12-volt coil.
Distributor type ... ... Lucas DM6A.
Direction of rotation ... ... Anti-clockwise at rotor arm.
Contact breaker gap ... ... ·014 in. to ·016 in. (·356 to ·406 mm.).
Static setting ... ... 5° (Crankshaft) B.T.D.C.
Maximum advance ... ... 35° (Crankshaft) B.T.D.C.
Coil type ... ... Lucas type HA 12.
Sparking plug type ... ... Champion N5—14 mm. Long Reach
               Champion N3—14 mm. (High speed work).
Sparking plug gap ... ... ·024 in. (·6096 mm.) to ·026 in. (·660 mm.).

COOLING SYSTEM
Capacity ... ... 18 Imp. pints (21·6 U.S. pints, 10·2 litres).
Circulation ... ... Pump and thermostat.

FUEL SYSTEM
Fuel delivery ... ... S.U. electric, type LCS.
Carburetter type ... ... Twin S.U. type HD6, semi-downdraught.
Needle (normal) ... ... CV.
Jet size ... ... ·100 in. (2·54 mm.).

Tank capacity ... ... 12 Imp., 14·4 U.S. gallons (54·5 litres).
Air cleaner ... ... Oil wetted.

CLUTCH

Make ... ... Borg and Beck.
Type ... ... Single dry plate.
Diameter ... ... 10 in. (25·4 cm.).
Total friction area ... ... 39 sq. in. (241·5 cm²)×2.
Thickness of friction linings ... ... ·150 (3·81 mm.).
Release bearings ... ... Special carbon graphite or copper carbon graphite.
Number of springs ... ... 12.
Total axial spring pressure ... ... 1,620 to 1,740 lb. (735 to 789 kg.).
Distance thrust race to thrust plate ... ... ·10 in. ·2·54 mm.).
Thrust plate travel to fully released position ... ... ·42 to ·47 in. (10·66 to 11·93 mm.).

GEARBOX

Type ... ... Synchromesh on 2nd, 3rd and top.
Type of gear ... ... Helical constant mesh.
Type overdrive (optional extra) ... ... Laycock de Normanville electrically controlled.
Gear ratios :
    First ... ... 2·93 : 1.
    Second ... ... 2·053 : 1.
    Third ... ... 1·309 : 1.
    Fourth ... ... Direct.
        Overdrive ... ... ·822 : 1.
    Reverse ... ... 3·78 : 1.
Overall Gear Ratios—
Standard Box: (3·545 : 1 axle)
    First ... ... 10·386 : 1.
    Second ... ... 7·877 : 1.
    Third ... ... 4·640 : 1.
    Fourth ... ... 3·545 : 1.
    Reverse ... ... 13·400 : 1.
Including overdrive (3·909 : 1 axle) :
    First ... ... 11·453 : 1.
    Second ... ... 8·025 : 1.
    Third ... ... 5·116 : 1.
    Third and overdrive ... ... 4·195 : 1.
    Fourth ... ... 3·909 : 1.
    Fourth and overdrive ... ... 3·205 : 1.
    Reverse ... ... 14·776 : 1.
Layshaft bearing:
    Type ... ... Needle roller.
    Number of rollers ... ... 46.
    Length of roller ... ... 1·551 in. (39·6 mm.).
    Diameter of roller ... ... 3·118 in. (3 mm.).
Mainshaft bearing:
    Make ... ... R. & M.
    Type ... ... MJ.35.
    Size ... ... 1·39×3·15×·827 in. (35×80×21 mm.).
First motion shaft bearing:
    Make ... ... R. & M.
    Type ... ... IM J40G.
    Size ... ... 1·58×3·55×·905 in. (40×90×23 mm.)
Oil capacity (standard box) ... ... 5 pints (6 U.S. pints, 2·84 litres).
Oil capacity (overdrive fitted) ... ... 6¼ Imp. pints (7·5 U.S. pints, 3·55 litres).

REAR AXLE

Type ... ... ⅜ floating.
Ratio :
    Standard ... ... 3·545 : 1.
    With overdrive ... ... 3·909 : 1.
Final drive ... ... Hypoid bevel.
Teeth on crown wheel :
    Standard ... ... 39.
    With overdrive ... ... 43.
Teeth on pinion :
    Standard ... ... 11.
    With overdrive ... ... 11.
Crown wheel/pinion backlash ... ... Marked on crown wheel.
Oil capacity ... ... 3 Imp. pints (1·704 litres, 3·6 U.S. pints).

REAR SPRINGS

Type ... ... Semi-elliptic.
Number of leaves ... ... 7.

Thickness of leaves ... ... 6 at $\frac{7}{32}$ in. (4·76 mm.) and 1 at $\frac{5}{32}$ in. (3·97 mm.).
Width ... ... 1¾ in. (44·45 mm.).
Deflection ... ... 4 in. (101·6 mm.) ± ¼ in. (6·35 mm.).
Loaded camber ... ... ½ in. (12·70 mm.) ± ⅛ in. (3·18 mm.).
Number of zinc leaves ... ... 3 ($\frac{1}{32}$ in. (·80 mm.) thickness).

STEERING

Make ... ... Cam gears
Ratio ... ... 15 : 1.
Track toe-in ... ... $\frac{1}{16}$ in. to $\frac{1}{8}$ in. (1·58 to 3·17 mm.).

SUSPENSION

Front :
   Type ... ... Independent by coil spring and wishbones.
   Castor angle ... ... 2°.
   Camber angle ... ... 1°.
   Swivel pin inclination ... ... 6½°.
Rear :
   Type ... ... Semi-elliptic underslung leaf-springs with Panhard rod.
Shock absorbers :
   Type ... ... Lever hydraulic.

BRAKES

Type ... ... Girling hydraulic.
Front ... ... Disc.
Rear ... ... Drum. One leading, one trailing shoe.
Disc diameter ... ... 11¼ in. (28·57 cm.).
Drum diameter ... ... 11 in. (28·0 cm.).
Total frictional area (rear) ... ... 95 sq. in. (612·75. cm².).
Shoe lining width ... ... 2¼ in (57 mm.).
Shoe lining length ... ... 10·53 in. (267·4 mm.).
Shoe lining thickness ... ... ·187 in. (4·76 mm.).
Pedal free movement ... ... ⅛ in. (3·175 mm.).
Handbrake ... ... Mechanical, rear wheels only.

ELECTRICAL

Battery
   Type (Series BN7—two seater) :
      Standard ... ... SLG11E (two).
      Dry-charged (export only). ... ... SLGZ11E (two).
   Type (Series BT7—four seater) :
      Standard BT9A
      Dry-charged (export only) ... ... BTZ9A.
   Voltage ... ... 12.
   Capacity, 20 hour rate : ... ... 58 amp. hr.
   Electrolyte to fill one cell ... ... 1 pint (·57 litres).
   Initial charging current ... ... 3·5 amp.
   Normal recharge current ... ... 5 amp.
   Master switch ... ... Lucas type ST330.
Generator
   Type ... ... Lucas C45 PV-6.
   Cutting-in speed ... ... 1,100 to 1,250 generator r.p.m.
   Maximum output ... ... 22 amps., 13·5 volts at 1,700 to 1,900 generator r.p.m.
   Field resistance ... ... 6 ohms.
Starting Motor
   Type ... ... Lucas M418 G.
   Lock torque ... ... 17 lb. ft. (1·2858 kg.m.) at 440 to 460 amps. and 7·0 to 7·4 volts.
   Light running current ... ... 45 amps. at 7,400 to 8,500 r.p.m.
   Solenoid switch ... ... Lucas type, ST 950.
Overdrive (optional extra)
   Control switch ... ... Lucas type 2TS.
   Transmission gear solenoid ... ... Lucas type TGS1.
   Relay—overdrive ... ... Lucas type SB 40—1.
   Interrupter switch ... ... Lucas type 5S10—1.
   Rotary throttle switch ... ... Lucas type RTS1.

Control Box
   Type ... ... Lucas RB 106/2.
   Cut-out :
      Cut-in voltage ... ... 12·7 to 13·3 volts.
      Drop off voltage ... ... 8·5 to 11 volts.
      Reverse current ... ... 3·5 to 5 amps.

Regulator
Setting on open circuit at 68°F. (20° C). ... ... 16·0 to 16·6 volts at 3,000 generator r.p.m.
Note: For circuit temperature other than 20·C, the following allowances should be made to the above setting.
For every 10°C. (18°F.) above 20° subtract 0·1 volt.
For every 10°C. (18°F.) below 20° add 0·1 volt.

Windscreen Wiper
Type ... ... Lucas DR2.
Normal running current ... ... 2·3 to 3·1 amp. at 12 volts.
Stall current (motor hot) ... ... 8 amp.
Stall current (motor cold) ... ... 14 amp.
Armature resistance (adjacent commutator segments) ... 0·34 to 0·41 ohms.
Field resistance ... ... 12·8 to 14·00 ohms.
N.B.—On some high output motors usually identified by a red insulating piece above the terminals, the field resistance is 8·0 to 11·5 ohms.

Fuse Unit
Type (two live and two spare fuses) ... ... Lucas SF6.

Fuses
A1—A2 ... ... 50 amp.
A3—A4 ... ... 35 amp.

Sidelamps
Type ... ... Lucas model 594.

Headlamps
Type ... ... Lucas model F700.

Stop-Tail Lamps
Type ... ... Lucas model 594.

Number Plate Illumination
Type ... ... Lucas model 467/2.

Flashing Indicator Unit
Type ... ... Lucas FL5.

Replacement Bulbs :	Watts	B.M.C. Part No.
Headlamp—R.H.D.	50/40	13H140
Headlamp L.H.D. (not Europe)	50/40	13H141
Headlamp L.H.D. (Europe, except France)	45/40	13H138
Headlamp L.H.D. (France)	45/40	13H139
Sidelamps (combined flashing indicators)	6/21	1F9026
Stop/tail Lamp	6/21	1F9026
Number Plate Lamp	6	2H4817
Ignition, Main Beam Warning and Panel Lights	2·2	2H4732

TYRE SIZES AND INFLATION PRESSURES
Tyre sizes ... ... 5·90—15 road speed (with tubes).

Pressures:
Front ⎫ two up ... ... 20 lb./sq. in. (1·41 kg./cm²).
Rear ⎭   ... ... 23 lb./sq. in. (1·62 kg./cm²).
Rear, full load ... ... 26 lb./sq. in. (1·83 kg./cm²).

WHEELS
Type ... ... 4J × 15 ventilated steel disc or 4J × 15 wire (optional alternative).

DIMENSIONS
Wheelbase ... ... 7 ft. 7½ in. (2·33 m.).
Overall length ... ... 13 ft. 1½ in. (4·00 m.).
Overall height (hood raised) ... ... 4 ft. 1 in. (1·24 m.).
Overall height (hood lowered) ... ... 3 ft. 10 in. (1·17 m.).
Overall width ... ... 5 ft. 0 in. (1·52 m.).
Height over scuttle ... ... 2 ft. 11⅞ in. (0·91 m.).
Ground clearance ... ... 4¾ in. (0·17 m.).
Track, front ... ... 4 ft. 0½ in. (1·24 m.).
Track, rear ... ... 4 ft. 2 in. (1·27 m.).
Turning circle ... ... 35 ft. 7 in. (10·84 m.).
Approximate weight ... ... 2,465 lb. (1117·5 kg.).

ENGINE

GENERAL DESCRIPTION
The Engines fitted to Series BN4, BN6, BN7, BJ7 and BT7 cars are all serviced and repaired in the same manner with a few variations which will be detailed in the appropriate places. In general the engine is a six cylinder unit with the bores cast integral with the crankcase. Adequate cooling under the most arduous operating conditions is ensured by the provision of large area water circulating passages, and full length water jackets.

The detachable cylinder head is of cast iron and carries the overhead push rod operated valve gear.

Forged steel is used for the counter balanced crankshaft which is supported by four large diameter main bearings of the preformed "Thinwall" type. The same type of bearings are used for the connecting rod big end assemblies.

Particular attention has been paid to the design of the lubrication system to ensure that the moving parts of the engine are adequately supplied with oil at all times. The choice of oils is of great importance and those recommended on page 229 have been tested under various running conditions.

Regular Visual Inspection Is Important
Examine the engine for any signs of oil leakage, with particular attention to the sump drain plug the joint between the oil filter bowl and its head casting, and the rocker cover to cylinder head joint.

The connections to the distributor should be checked occasionally for tightness, and any perished or cracked high tension leads renewed.

Tune Up
The purpose of the following adjustments is to maintain the performance of the engine at its maximum, and consists of a series of cleaning, inspecting and adjusting operations. A compression test of each cylinder should first be made to determine the general condition of the engine before proceeding with any adjustments. If a compression gauge is not available, a simple method to test the compression is to remove all the spark plugs with the exception of one in the cylinder being tested, and then rotate the engine with the starting handle through at least two complete revolutions. If the cylinder compression is satisfactory, proceed as detailed below, otherwise the specific fault should be diagnosed by referring to "Fault Diagnosis".

  1 — Clean the engine generally and lubricate as indicated by maintenance instructions.

  2 — Adjust the fan belt tension.

  3 — Remove the valve gear cover and test the cylinder head studs

for tightness, using a torque wrench set to the figures quoted under "General Data".

4 — Check and adjust the valve and rocker clearances.

5 — Check for evidence of cracked valve springs or scored or worn stems.

6 — Replace the valve gear cover, using a new gasket if necessary.

7 — Disconnect the high-tension cables and remove the spark plugs.

8 — Check to make sure that the correct type of spark plug is being used.

9 — Clean the spark plugs and examine the insulation for breaks or cracks.

10 — Adjust the spark plug gaps as specified.

11 — Test the spark plugs and renew any found to be unfit for further service.

12 — Refit the spark plugs, using new copper washers.

13 — Check the high tension cables for wear and deterioration before refitting.

14 — Remove the distributor head cover and clean it inside and out. Examine it for cracks and burned contacts and renew if necessary.

15 — Inspect the contact breaker points to determine whether new points are needed.

16 — Check the distributor rotor arm, making sure the carbon brush makes contact. Check the capacitor terminal to make sure it is clean and tight.

17 — Check the ignition timing.

18 — Clean the air cleaners.

19 — Make sure the fuel system is operating properly and clean all filters in the system.

20 — Check the carburetor flange gaskets for evidence of leakage.

21 — Adjust the carburetors if necessary.

ENGINE REMOVAL
(without gearbox)

1 — Remove the radiator as described under Cooling and detach the fan by unscrewing the four securing setpins.

2 — Disconnect the throttle linkage and choke control cable. The throttle linkage is freed by unclamping the throttle control rod at its projection from the bulkhead.

3 — Unscrew the four setpins securing the air cleaners to the carburetor inlets and remove the air cleaners.

4 — Disconnect the fuel feed pipe at its carburetor union.

5 — The battery master switch, which is situated inside the luggage compartment, should be turned to the "off" position.

6 — Remove the high tension cables from their connections at the coil and the spark plugs.

7 — Release the generator, distributor and coil low tension cables,

and place the complete harness to one side.

8 — Release the heater inlet and outlet hoses from their connections at the rear of the cylinder head and the heater outlet pipe.

9 — Remove the distributor.

10 — Remove the generator, complete with coil.

11 — Remove the external oil filter.

12 — Release the oil pressure flexible pipe at its upper connection.

13 — Remove the starter motor.

14 — Withdraw the four setpins which secure each engine mounting bracket to the chassis frame. Detachment of the left-hand bracket is facilitated by a slit in the carburetor heat shield.

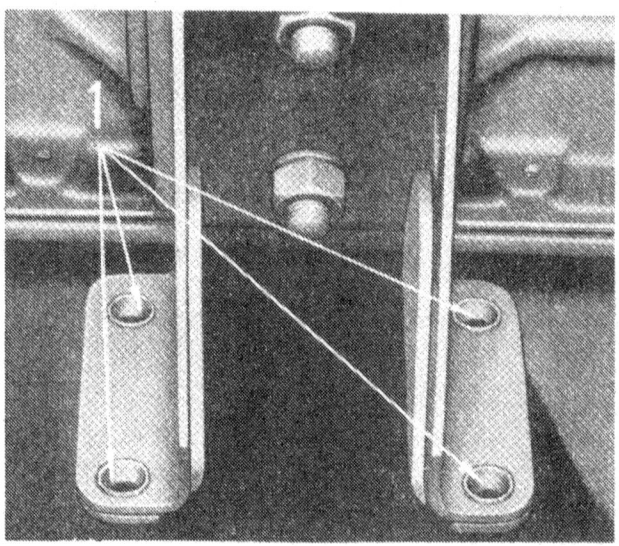

The engine left-hand front mounting bracket showing the four setpin holes at 1.

15 — Unscrew the six brass nuts securing the exhaust down pipe to the exhaust manifolds, and pull the down pipe away from the manifold studs.

16 — Remove the valve rocker and secure two suitable lifting brackets.

17 — By means of lifting tackle, similar to that illustrated, support the engine so that the engine mounting brackets are just clear of their chassis mountings.

18 — Unscrew the four setpins securing the right-hand engine mounting bracket to the cyinder block and withdraw the mounting.

19 — Place a suitable support underneath the gearbox bell housing and unscrew the nuts, bolts and setpins securing the bell housing to the engine backplate.

20 — Hoist the engine to give clearance between the crankshaft damper and the chassis cross member and pull the engine forward

Showing the engine being removed at the correct lifting angle.

so that the clutch driven plate slides off the first motion shaft splines when the engine can be lifted through the bonnet opening and clear of the car.

21 — Replacing the engine is the reverse of the procedure.

Engine and Gearbox Removal

To avoid possible damage, either to individual components or to the car, removal of the generator, distributor and right-hand mounting bracket is advised.

1 — Follow the instructions 1 to 10 and 12 to 18 as detailed in the engine removal less gearbox.

2 — Inside the car remove the seat cushions and release the clips securing the padded arm rest to the central tunnel.

3 — Unclip and roll back the carpet over the short gearbox tunnel to expose the twelve screws securing the tunnel to the body of the car. Unscrew the setscrews and remove the tunnel and its carpeting.

4 — Unscrew the six setscrews, three either side, which secure the carpet covered bulkhead and remove the bulkhead.

5 — Using a suitable tool tap back the locking washers on the propeller shaft flange bolts and remove the bolts.

6 — Unscrew the four setpins from the gearbox mounting brackets, also unscrew the speedometer cable at its connection to the gearbox.

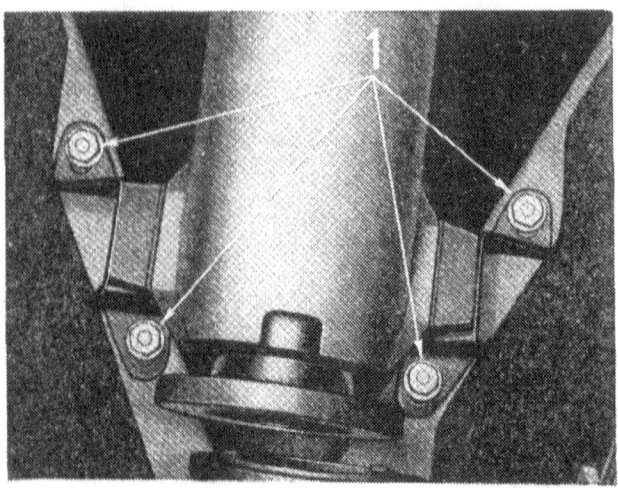

The gearbox rear upper securing bracket showing the four setpins at 1.

The gearbox lower securing points showing 1, Setpins; 2, Stabiliser Adjusting Nut; 3, Securing Pin.

Note.—When an overdrive gearbox is fitted it will also be necessary to unclip the cable to the gearbox switch and release it at its terminal on the switch.

7 — Working beneath the vehicle remove setpins 1 and unscrew the nuts 2 and 3 to release the stabilizer bar.

8 — Detach the clutch slave cylinder from the gearbox bell housing by removing the two securing setpins. The slave cylinder push rod is released from the clutch operating lever by the removal of the securing clevis pin.

9 — Hoist the engine complete with gearbox through the bonnet

opening as shown, ascertain that no damage is done by the gearbox when maneuvering it through the bulkhead aperture.

LUBRICATION

The oil supply is carried in the sump below the cylinder block and the filler cap is fitted on the forward end of the rocker cover. The dipstick is on the right-hand side of the engine and is marked to indicate the maximum and minimum levels. The eccentric rotor type oil pump driven by the camshaft is mounted below the crankcase and is partially submerged in the oil reservoir.

Oil is drawn through a gauze strainer secured to the oil pump and passes through a drilling up the right-hand side of the crankcase to the oil filter, passing the non-adjustable pressure relief valve. After leaving the full flow filter the oil-way divides, one drilling passing up the right-hand side of the cylinder block through the cylinder head to a pipe feeding oil to No. 4 rocker shaft bracket. From here, oil passes through the hollow center of the rocker shaft to lubricate all rocker bearings, and through drillings in the rockers, to lubricate the valve gear. Oil returning to the sump from the rockers lubricates the tappets. The second oilway from the oil filter passes around No. 3 camshaft bearing (lubricating this bearing as it does so), to the oil gallery on the left-hand side of the engine. From the gallery, drillings in the cylinder block take oil to each main bearing and through the crankshaft to the big ends. Oil-ways from the main bearings also supply the camshaft bearings. The connecting rods have jet holes to deliver oil to the cylinder walls.

A vent pipe is attached to the rear tappet chamber cover and a breather in the valve rocker cover is connected to the rear air cleaner. An oil pipe connects the rear end of the main oil gallery on the left-hand side of the engine with the oil gauge on the instrument panel.

Draining the Sump

The sump on new and reconditioned engines must be drained and filled with new oil after the first 500 miles (800 km.) and at intervals of 3,000 miles (4800 km.).

The hexagon-headed sump drain plug is at the rear on the right-hand side.

The sump should be allowed to drain for at least ten minutes before the drain plug is replaced. The oil will flow more readily if it is drained while the engine is hot. When the sump has been drained, approximately 10¼ pints (12.3 U.S. pints, 5.85 litres) of oil are required to fill it. The capacity of the filter is approximately 1¼ pints (1.5 U.S. pints, .84 litres), giving a total of 11½ pints (13.8 U.S. pints, 6.55 litres). Do not forget to replace the sum drain plug.

Never use gasoline, kerosene or solvent for flushing purposes. Such cleaning mediums are never completely dispersed from the engine lubrication system, and will remain to contaminate any fresh oil. This may cause premature bearing failure. Use flushing oil only.

At every alternate oil change, or every 6,000 miles (9600 km.), a new external oil filter element should be fitted.

Refilling

When refilling the sump do not pour the oil in too quickly, as it may overflow from the filler orifice and mislead the operator as to the quantity of lubricant in the engine.

Before testing the level of the oil, ensure that the vehicle is as near level as possible. Always wipe the dipstick clean with a non-fluffy cloth before taking the reading. It should be remembered that time must be allowed for new oil to reach the sump before reading the dipstick.

Oil Pressure

The pressure indicated by the gauge may rise to 60 lb. per sq. in. when the engine is started up from cold, but after the oil has circulated and becomes warm, the pressure will drop to approximately 55 lb. per sq. in., with a proportionately lower idling pressure (about 25 lb. per sq. inch). **If no oil pressure is registered by the gauge, stop the engine at once and investigate the cause.**

NOTE: The automatic relief valve in the lubrication system deals with any excessive oil pressure when starting from cold.

Continuous running with unnecessary use of a rich mixture is often the cause of serious oil dilution by fuel, and a consequent drop in pressure.

Check for Low Oil Pressure

Check the level of oil in the engine sump by means of the dipstick and top up if necessary. Ascertain that the gauze strainer in the sump is clean and not choked with sludge, also that there is no air leakage at the strainer union on the suction side of the pump.

In the unlikely event of the oil pump being defective, remove the unit and rectify the fault. The oil relief valve should be examined. If the engine bearings are worn the oil pressure will be reduced A complete bearing overhaul and the fitting of replacement parts is the only remedy, necessitating the removal of the engine from the chassis.

OIL FILTER

The external filter is a full flow type thus ensuring that oil in the lubrication system passes through the filter before reaching the bearings.

The element of the filter is of star formation in which a special quality felt, selected for its filtering properties, is used.

Oil is passed to the filter from the pump at a pressure controlled at 50/55 lb. per sq. inch by the engine oil relief valve. Some pressure is lost in passing the oil through the filter element; this will only be a pound or two per square inch with a new element, but will increase as the element becomes progressively contaminated by foreign matter removed from the oil.

Should the filter become completely choked due to neglect, a balance valve is provided to ensure that oil will still reach the bearings. This valve, set to open at a pressure difference of 15/20 lbs. per square inch, is non-adjustable and is located in the filter head cast-

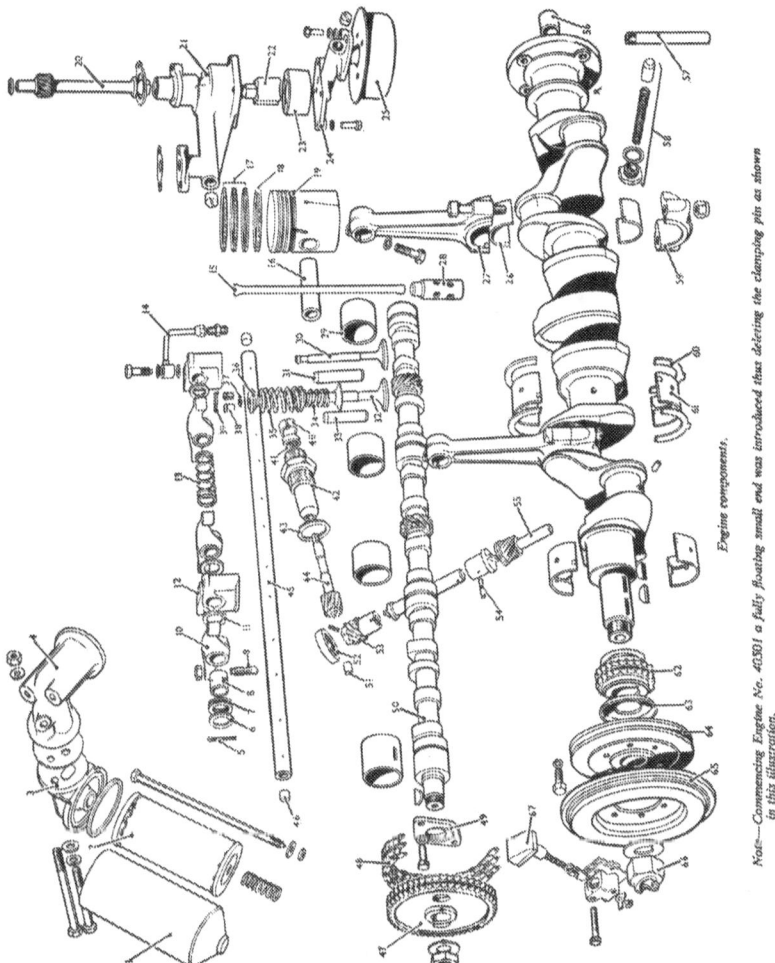

Note—Commencing Engine No. 46381 a fully floating small end was introduced thus deleting the clamping pin as shown in this illustration.

Engine components.

1. Filter bowl.
2. Element.
3. Head casting.
4. Filter extension bracket.
5. Split pin.
6. Plain washer.
7. Spring washer.
8. Rocker bush.
9. Rocker adjusting screw.
10. Rocker.
11. Spacing washer.
12. Rocker shaft bracket.
13. Spacing spring.
14. Rocker oil feed pipe.
15. Push rod.
16. Gudgeon pin.
17. Compression rings.
18. Oil control ring.
19. Piston.
20. Oil pump drive spindle.
21. Oil pump body.
22. Inner rotor.
23. Outer rotor.
24. Bottom cover.
25. Pick-up stainer.
26. Shell bearing big end.
27. Connecting rod.
28. Tappet.
29. Camshaft bearings.
30. Exhaust valve.
31. Exhaust valve guide.
32. Inlet valve.
33. Inlet valve guide.
34. Inner valve spring.
35. Outer valve spring.
36. Spring cap.
37. Oil seal.
38. Collets.
39. Split pin.
40. Bush.
41. Oil seal.
42. Spindle housing.
43. Washer.
44. Tachometer spindle.
45. Rocker shaft.
46. Rocker shaft plug.
47. Camshaft gear.
48. Timing chain.
49. Camshaft location plate.
50. Camshaft.
51. Plug.
52. Oil seal.
53. Tachometer gear.
54. Securing pin.
55. Distributor drive.
56. First motion shaft bush.
57. Drain pipe.
58. Relief valve assembly.
59. Big end cap.
60. Thrust washer.
61. Centre front main bearing.
62. Crankshaft gear.
63. Oil thrower.
64. Crankshaft pulley.
65. Vibration damper.
66. Starter dog.
67. Timing chain tensioner.

ing. When the valve is opened, unfiltered oil can by-pass the filter element and reach the bearings.

To renew the filter element proceed as follows:

1 — Unscrew and remove the tachometer drive from the distributor housing.

2 — Remove the two setpins securing the filter bracket to the crankcase.

3 — Unscrew the center fixing bolt, and the container complete with element can be removed.

4 — Withdraw the contaminated element and carefully cleanse the container of all foreign matter that has been trapped.

5 — After ensuring that no fibres from the cleansing operation have been left in the container, put in a new element, prime the filter and refit to the head casting, tightening the center fixing bolt sufficiently to make an oil-tight joint.

6 — Replace the filter and bracket complete by means of the two setpins.

7 — Refit the tachometer drive to the distributor housing.

8 — Check the level of oil in the sump by means of the dipstick. It is recommended that the filter container should not be disturbed other than for cleaning and the fitting of a new element at the recommended mileages; to do so invites the hazard of added contamination from accumulated dirt on the outside of the filter entering the container, and thus being carried into the bearings on restarting the engine.

SUMP AND GAUZE STRAINER
Removing

1 — Drain off the oil into a suitable container then extract the setscrews and washers, thus enabling the sump to be removed.

2 — Detach the bottom of the strainer by removing the nut, washer and distance piece. Take out the three setpins holding the strainer to the pump, so allowing the body of the gauze strainer to be removed. The pump and strainer can be swilled out with solvent and thoroughly dried with a non-fluffy rag.

3 — Inspect the two joint washers and renew if they are damaged in any way.

Refitting the Sump

Clean out the sump by washing it in solvent. Take care to remove any traces of the solvent before refitting the sump to the engine. Pay particular attention to the sump and crankcase joint faces, and remove any traces of old jointing material. Examine the joint washer and renew it if necessary. The old joint washer can be used again if it is sound, but it is advisable to fit a new one.

Smear the faces of the joint with grease and fit the joint washer. Lift the sump into position and insert the setscrews into the flange tightening them up evenly.

Removing the Oil Pump (Rotary Vane Type)

1 — Remove the sump and pick up strainer.

2 — Take off the nuts and spring washers from the three studs which secure the oil pump assembly to the crankcase, when the pump can be withdrawn.

If the pump is removed with the engine still in the car, the drive shaft will be free to disengage from the camshaft, and care must be taken to prevent it falling out. Note also the thrust washer fitted on the drive shaft above the gear.

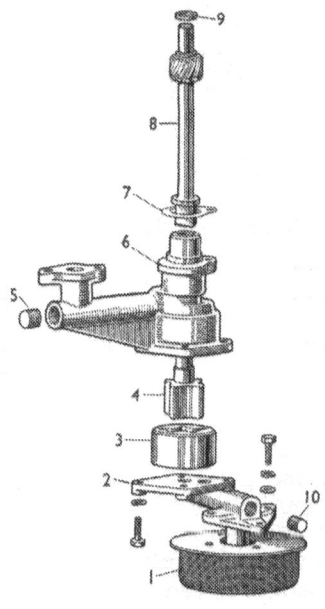

1. *Pick-up strainer.*
2. *Bottom lower plate.*
3. *Outer rotor.*
4. *Inner rotor.*
5. *Screw plug.*
6. *Pump body.*
7. *Joint washer.*
8. *Drive spindle.*
9. *Drive spindle thrust washer.*
10. *Screw plug.*

Dismantling the Oil Pump

Mark the flange and pump body to assist reassembly. Separate the body from the bottom flange. The outer rotor can then be lifted out of the body.

Replacing the Oil Pump

Insert the pump from below and push the shaft right home until the driving gear is meshed with the gear on the camshaft.

GEAR TYPE OIL PUMP

The oil pump fitted to early engines is of the Hobourn Eaton rotary vane type, the service procedure for which is detailed above. Later engines, however, are equipped with a gear type pump and instructions for servicing this type of pump are given below. Removal is the same as for the older type.

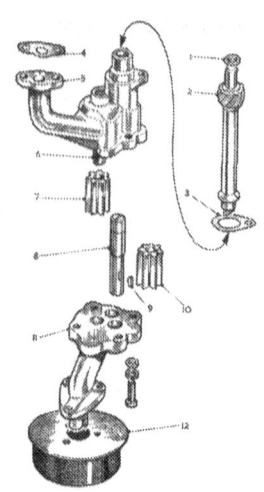

Components of the oil pump.

1. Thrust washer.
2. Drive spindle.
3. Joint washer.
4. Joint washer.
5. Pump body.
6. Driven gear spindle.
7. Driven gear.
8. Drive gear spindle.
9. Key.
10. Drive gear.
11. Pick up.
12. Pick up strainer

Dismantling the Oil Pump

1 — Mark the flange and pump body to assist reassembly and remove the four retaining bolts with their spring and plain washers.

2 — Separate the pick-up from the pump body, withdraw the drive gear and spindle and the driven gear from its fixed spindle.

Thoroughly clean all parts in solvent and dry off.

3 — Replace the gears and check for wear.

(a) The radial clearance between the gears and the pump body should not exceed .00125 in. to .0025 in. (.032 mm. to .063 mm.).

(b) Check the clearance between the gears and the end cover by placing a straight edge across the pump body and checking with a feeler gauge. End float should be between .0005 in. and .002 in. (.013 mm. and .051 mm.).

Renew worn parts as necessary. The pump driving gear is a press fit on its shaft and is keyed in position. The spindle should protrude .312 in. (7.94 mm.) from the gear face.

Replacing the Oil Pump

Care should be taken to see that the abutting faces of the cylinder block and the pump are clean before replacing and that the joint washers are in good condition. Insert the pump from below ascertaining that the driving gear is in mesh with the gear on the camshaft. Secure the pump with the three nuts and spring washers. Replace the pick-up strainer and sump.

1. *Feeler gauge.*   2. *Rocker.*   3. *Lock nut.*
4. *Adjusting screw.*

ADJUSTING VALVE CLEARANCE

Lift off the valve cover after removing the two flat and two dome cap nuts.

Between the rocker arm and the valve stem there must be a clearance of .012 (.305 mm.) for both inlet and exhaust, clearance being set with the engine hot.

1 — If adjustment is necessary, slacken the locknut while continuously applying sufficient pressure to the adjusting screw with a heavy screwdriver, and raise or lower the adjusting screw in the rocker arm. Check the clearance with a feeler gauge.

2 — Tighten the locknut when the adjustment is correct, but always check it again afterwards in case the adjustment has been disturbed during the locking process.

3 — When replacing the valve cover, take care that the joint washer (using a new one if necessary) is properly in place to ensure an oil tight joint.

ROCKER SHAFT ASSEMBLY

The valve rocker shaft on the cylinder head is hollow. It is supplied with oil by a pipe connection and is drilled for lubrication to each rocker bearing.

This shaft is plugged at each end, one of these being screwed in order that the shaft may be cleaned internally.

Removal

1 — Disconnect the breather pipes at their rocker cover terminals.

2 — Unscrew the two flat and two dome nuts securing the rocker cover to the cylinder head, taking care not to damage the cork gasket, and remove the rocker cover.

3 — Detach the oil feed pipe at the union on the cylinder head.

4 — Unscrew and remove the twelve nuts and spring washers which hold the rocked shaft brackets to the cylinder head.

5 — Remove the rocker assembly, complete with brackets, rockers and oil feed pipe.

Dismantling

1 — Unscrew and remove the oil feed pipe banjo from its bracket noting its corresponding position on the shaft.

2 — Remove the split pins from the end of the rocker shaft to release thrust washers and double coil springs.

3 — Withdraw rocker, rocker shaft brackets, thrust washers and springs, retaining them in their original order for reassembly.

Reassembling

When reassembling the rocker gear, commence with No. 4 bracket and secure the oil feed pipe with the washers in position, ensuring that the dowel on the banjo bolt locates in the rocker shaft.

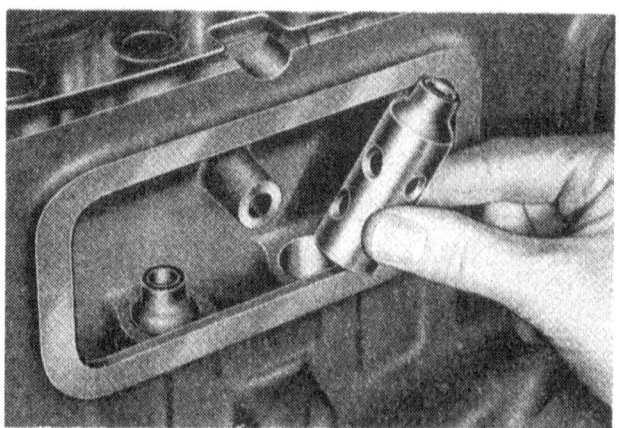

Removing a tappet.

Tappets Removal

1 — Remove the valve rocker shaft assembly.

2 — Disconnect the dynamo terminals and remove the set bolt securing the dynamo to the slotted link. Take out the bolts on which the dynamo pivots and remove the dynamo and coil.

3 — Release the front tappet chamber cover by removing the five securing bolts. The center and rear tappet chamber covers give access to the valves for No. 3, 4, 5 and 6 cylinders when the single retaining bolts are removed.

4 — Withdraw the push rods, keeping them in their respective positions to ensure replacement onto the same tappets. Lift out the tappets, keeping them in the same respective locations. Inspect the tappet cam contacting surfaces for wear. New tappets should be fitted by selective assembly so that they just fall into their guides under their own weight when lubricated.

Replacement

Assembly is a reversal of the above procedure, but care should be taken to see that the tappet cover joints are oil-tight and that the rockers are adjusted to give the correct valve clearance.

Renewing Valve Spring in Position

1 — In an emergency a new valve spring(s) can be fitted without lifting the cylinder head, but it is advisable first to bring the piston to top dead center, to ensure that the valve cannot fall into the cylinder during the process.

2 — Remove the spark plug, and by means of a length of copper tubing or similar tool inserted through the plug hole, the valve can be held on its seat while the spring is compressed. The valve rocker shaft can be used as a fulcrum point using two screwdrivers to bear on the valve spring cap each side of the valve stem, while the cotters are removed.

INLET MANIFOLD
Removal and Replacement

1 — Detach the air cleaners from the carburetors by unscrewing the four setpins and releasing the breather pipe attached to the air cleaner.

2 — Disconnect the heat shield by removing the two securing nuts and washers.

3 — Unscrew and remove the six brass nuts and plain washers which secure the exhaust manifold to the down pipes.

4 — Disconnect the throttle and choke linkages to the carburetors, together with the vacuum control pipe and feed pipe.

5 — Unscrew and remove the 14 nuts and washers which secure the exhaust manifold and carburetors to the cylinder head (four on the carburetor flanges, ten on the exhaust manifold). These will be removed together with the vacuum control pipe and feed pipe.

6 — The exhaust manifold and carburetors can then be drawn off their respective studs and lifted clear of the engine.

7 — Reassembly is the reverse of the above procedure; always use a new joint washer for the exhaust manifold to ensure an air tight joint.

CYLINDER HEAD
Removing

1 — Drain all water from the cooling system, if the water contains anti-freeze mixture, it should be run into a clean container and used again.

2 — Detach the top water hose from the cylinder head.

3 — Disconnect the high tension wires from the spark plugs and remove the plugs.

4 — Detach the exhaust manifold, complete with carburetors.

5 — Remove rocker cover and breather pipes.

6 — Release the vacuum advance pipe clip from its securing point on the cylinder head. Also slacken the retaining clip and detach the heater inlet hose.

7 — Remove the rocker assembly.

8 — Withdraw the push rods, keeping them in order of removal taking care not to pull the tappets out of their guides in the block.

9 — Remove the sixteen cylinder head nuts together with their flat washers and lift off the cylinder head.

Replacing

1 — Replace the cylinder head joint washer with the side marked "Top" uppermost, it is not necessary to use jointing compound or grease for the gasket.

2 — Having slipped the gasket over the studs, next lower the cylinder head into position and position the cylinder head stud nut washers. Ensure that a bronze washer is fitted below the steel washer on each stud which passes through the inlet manifold on the left-hand side of the head; also ensure that the suction advance pipe clip is replaced in its original position on the cylinder head.

3 — Fit the nuts finger tight and then tighten them a turn at a time, in the order given in the illustration, to the recommended torque readings.

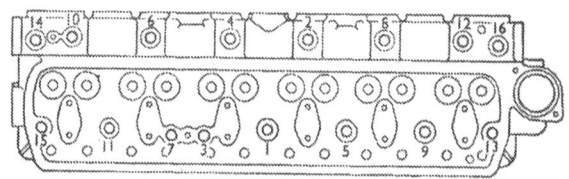

The order of tightening for the cylinder head nuts.

4 — Insert the push rods, ensuring that the ball ends are correctly located in the tappets.

5 — Replace the rocker gear and connect the oil feed pipe.

6 — Reset the valve clearance, and replace the rocker cover using a new joint washer if the old one is damaged in any way.

7 — Replace the exhaust manifold and carburetors and connect up the fuel pipe, throttle and choke controls and heater outlet pipe. Tighten the manifold nuts evenly ensuring that a good joint is made.

8 — Reconnect heater inlet pipe, water hose from the thermostat housing to the radiator, and breather pipes.

9 — Refill the cooling system, replace the spark plugs and their washers, and the high tension wires to their respective plugs.

10 — Check the valve clearance again after the vehicle has run about 100 miles (160 km.) as the valves have a tendency to bed down. At the same time it is advisable to test the cylinder head nuts for tightness. Tightening the cylinder head nuts may affect valve clearances, although not usually enough to justify resetting.

6 PORT CYLINDERHEAD

The Austin-Healey C-Series engine was modified by the introduction of an entirely new cylinder head, together with a detachable induction manifold.

Two S.U. HD6 carburetors with 1¾ inch throats replace the two S.U. H4 type used in the normal "C" type engine.

New features of the head include modified combustion chambers, larger inlet and exhaust valve head diameters and re-shaped inlet and exhaust ports to provide an even more efficient gas-flow.

The introduction of solid skirt, flat topped pistons increased the compression ratio from 8.25:1 to 8.7:1.

Dimensional and power changes brought about by these modifications are given in the General Data.

REMOVING AND REFITTING VALVES

With the cylinder head removed, a valve lifting tool can be used to compress the springs. Take away the circlip, split covers, and valve stem caps, so releasing the springs and allowing the valve to be removed.

1 — When removing the valves, place them in a rack, thus enabling them to be paired up with their correct cylinders. The valve springs should be tested and their free length checked, the correct length being approx. 1.969 in. (50.03 mm.) for the inner spring and 2.047 in. (52 mm.) for the outer spring.

2 — Clean the carbon from the top and bottom of the valve heads, as well as any deposit that may have accumulated on the stems. The valve heads should, if necessary, be refaced at an angle of 45° for the exhaust valve and 30° for the inlet valve. If the valve seats show signs of excessive pitting it is advisable to reface these also.

3 — The valves are made without any indentures or slots in the head, this necessitates the use of a rubber suction valve grinding tool.

4 — Reassembly is a reversal of the operations for removal.

VALVE GRINDING

1 — For valve grinding a little grinding paste should be smeared evenly on the valve face, and the valve rotated backwards and forwards against its seat, advancing it a step at short intervals until a clean and unpitted seating is obtained. The cutting action is facilitated by allowing a light spring situated under the valve head, to periodically lift the valve from its seat. This allows the grinding compound to re-penetrate between the two faces after being squeezed out.

2 — On completion, all traces of compound must be removed from the valve and seating. It is essential that each valve is ground-in and refitted to its own seating.

3 — It is also desirable to clean the valve guides; this can be done by dipping the valve stem in solvent, and moving it up and down in the guide until it is free.

VALVE GUIDES

1 — The valve guides are of a one-piece design. They are pressed into the cylinder head to allow .859 to .875 in. (21.8 to 22.23 mm.)

of the guide to protrude above the machined face when fitted.

2 — To position each valve spring on the cylinder head, a stepped pressed steel seating collar is fitted over the part of the guide protruding from the cylinder head.

3 — Valve guides should be tested for wear whenever valves are removed, and if excessive side play is present, a close check should be made of the valve stem and the guide. In the event of wear being noticeable, the defective components should be renewed. If a valve is at fault the wear will be evident on the stem. It should be borne in mind that the valve stem and guide should be a running fit to avoid the possibility of an air leak.

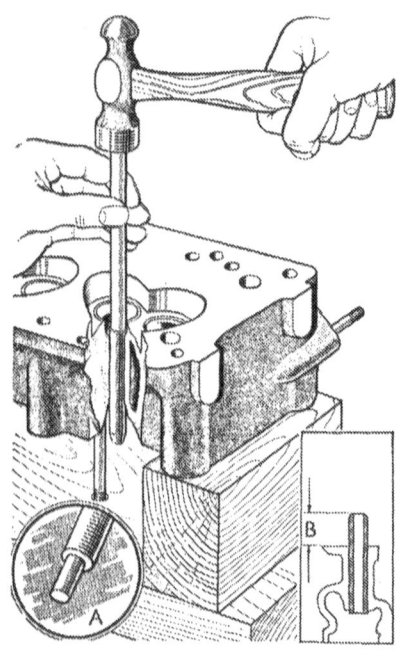

Removing a valve guide.
A shows the stepped end of the tool. B indicates the portion of the guide which must stand above the surface.

4 — If renewal is necessary due to wear, the valve guide may be driven out after removal of the valve.

5 — The drift is stepped from a ½ in. (12.7 mm.) diameter to a 5/16 in. (7.9 mm). diameter locating spigot in order to obviate it slipping off the guide and damaging the port. Knock out the guide in the direction shown.

6 — A new guide should be driven into position in the same direction, that is inserting it through the valve seating and driving towards the top of the cylinder head.

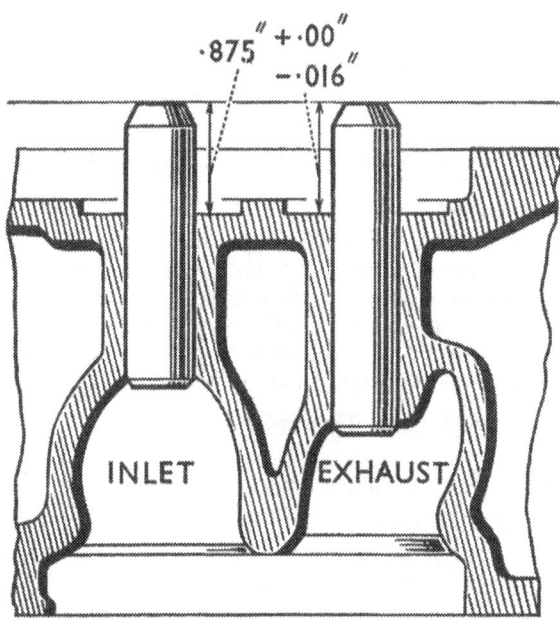

Showing the position of the valve guides after fitting.

DECARBONIZING

1 — Remove the cylinder head.

2 — Scrape off all carbon deposits from the cylinder head and ports. Clean the carbon deposit from the cylinder head and ports. Clean the carbon from the piston crowns, care being taken not to damage the pistons, and not to allow dirt or carbon deposit to enter the cylinder barrels or push rod compartment.

When cleaning the top of the pistons do not scrape right to the edge as a little carbon left on the chamfer assists in keeping down oil consumption; with the pistons cleaned right to the edge or new pistons, oil consumption is often slightly though temporarily increased.

3 — Blow out the oil passages and swill out the water passages using a water hose. The gasket contacting surfaces of the head should be checked for flatness with a straight-edge and the surfaces examined for scores. If the cylinder head is found to be badly out of true it should be renewed.

4 — Remove all carbon accumulation from the valves and thoroughly clean them. Inspect the valve bases and seats and if they are slightly pitted or rough, grind them in. If the valves and seats show signs of excessive pitting, or the faces are not flat, the valves and seats should be replaced.

5 — Examine the valve guides.

6 — Broken or weak valve springs should be renewed. The other valve springs should be tested and the results compared with

figures under "General Data".

7 — Clean the rocker shaft gear and blow out the oil passages.

8 — Inspect the rocker shaft, rockers and bushes for wear.

9 — Reassemble and install the cylinder head assembly.

The following operations should be carried out with the engine removed, although in some cases it is possible to perform them with the engine in position.

Before removing or replacing any component it is important to ensure that all surrounding surfaces are perfectly clean, to prevent the entry of foreign matter into the engine. This can best be accomplished by the use of a solvent bath and brush, and it is also important to note that fluffy rags should never be used, as there is danger of causing obstruction to small oil ways.

CONNECTING RODS AND BEARINGS
Removal

1 — Remove the cylinder head assembly.

2 — Drain and remove the sump.

3 — Remove the self-locking nuts. Secure the caps and bearings to the connecting rods. Remove the caps and bearings.

4 — Withdraw the pistons and connecting rods upwards through the cylinder bores.

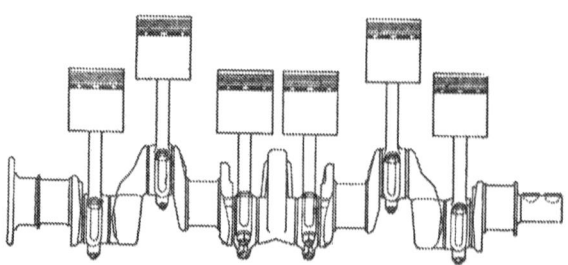

Showing the positions of connecting rod off-sets.

5 — It may be necessary to remove the carbon or ridge from the top of the bores prior to pushing the pistons upwards, to avoid piston-ring fracture.

6 — Remove the pistons from the connecting rods by unscrewing the clamp bolt from the small end of the connecting rod and pushing the pin out.

7 — Ensure that each connecting rod, cap and bearing is marked with the cylinder number from which it was removed.

8 — The big ends are offset, and rods in numbers 1, 3 and 5 cylinders are offset towards the front, with 2, 4 and 6 cylinders offset towards the rear.

9 — The alignment of the connecting rods should be checked on an alignment fixture. On no account must the rods or caps be filed.

10 — Examine the bearing shells for wear and pits. Renew the bearing shell if necessary. Bearings are pre-finished with the correct diametrical clearance and do not require bedding in.

1 — Check the crankpins with a micrometer if they are worn or are scored, the crankshaft will have to be removed for regrinding.

Replacing

Before installing the connecting rods and bearings it is assumed that the pistons and rings have been serviced.

The pistons and connecting rods must be fitted in the same cylinder bores and the same way around as when removed.

1 — Assemble the piston and the connecting rod to the pin, so that the split in the piston skirt is adjacent to the split in the top of the connecting rod.

2 — Refit the piston rings very carefully, make quite sure that the pistons and bores are perfectly clean and smear the bores with clean engine oil.

3 — Use a piston ring clamp when replacing the pistons from the top of the bore, and make sure that the split in the piston faces away from the camshaft.

4 — Clean the crankpins and both sides of the shell bearings, locate the feathered ends in the connecting rod and its cap, and smear the crank pins with engine oil.

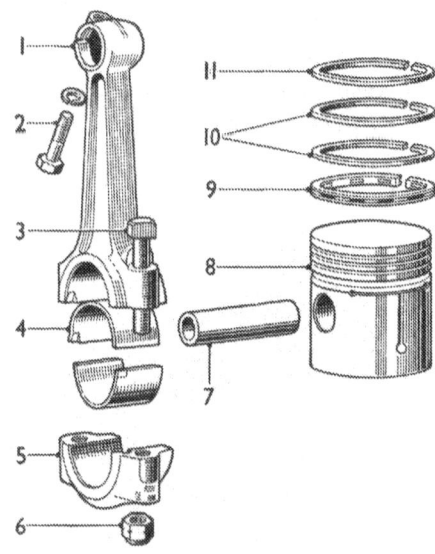

Connecting rod and piston assembly.

1. Connecting rod.
2. Small end clamping screw.
3. Big end bolt.
4. Sell bearing.
5. Big end cap.
6. Big end nut.
7. Gudgeon pin.
8. Piston.
9. Oil control ring.
10. Taper compression rings.
11. Plain compression ring.

5 — Before fitting the cap, check that the number stamped on the rod is the same as that on the cap. Note that the recesses in the cap and rod must be on the same side. Tighten the nuts. Turn the crankshaft after fitting each rod, to ensure that the bearing is not binding on the crankpin. Also check the side clearance of each rod, as given under "General Data".
6 — Refit the cylinder head assembly.
7 — Refit the sump and refill with recommended grade of oil.

PISTONS, RINGS AND PINS
Removal
The split-skirt pistons are of aluminum alloy material. Four rings are fitted above the pin, the bottom ring being of the oil-control type. The pistons are fastened to the connecting rods by pins which are clamped rigidly in the small ends of the connecting rods. Bushings are not needed in the pin bosses of the pistons because the aluminum alloy material serves as a suitable bearing for the pins, the bearing surfaces of which are lubricated by means of splash through the two holes drilled in each boss.

To view and overhaul
1 — Remove the rings over the tops of the pistons.
2 — Scrape all accumulation of carbon off the piston heads and, using a piston ring groove-cleaning tool or an old ring section, carefully scrape all carbon out of the ring grooves of the pistons. Clean the carbon out of the oil holes in the piston ring grooves.
3 — Thoroughly clean all the dismantled components in solvent.
5 — If cylinder reconditioning is required refer to "General Data" concerning oversize pistons available.

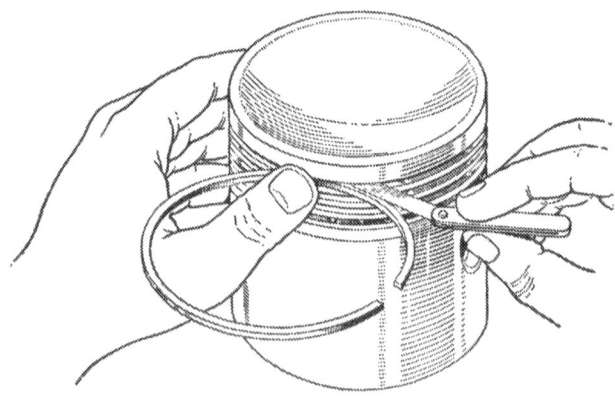

Checking piston ring and groove clearance.

6 — When fitting new or oversize pistons and rings to reconditioned cylinder bores, the clearances should be controlled within the limits given under "General Data".

Selective assembly is necessary, and for this purpose pistons are stamped with distinguishing symbols of grade and oversize.

7 — Piston rings should have a gap clearance (see "General Data") when installed in the cyinder bores. If new rings are being installed, each ring should be checked in the cylinder bore to determine whether its gap clearance is within the range specified. To do this, use the bottom of a piston to insert the ring part way into the bore. The ring will be squared up in the bore to measure the gap clearance as shown. To check the ring clearance in the piston grooves, install the rings on the pistons and determine the clearances with a feeler gauge. If the piston ring grooves are worn excessively, as indicated when comparing the actual clearance with those given under "General Data", renew the rings and pistons.

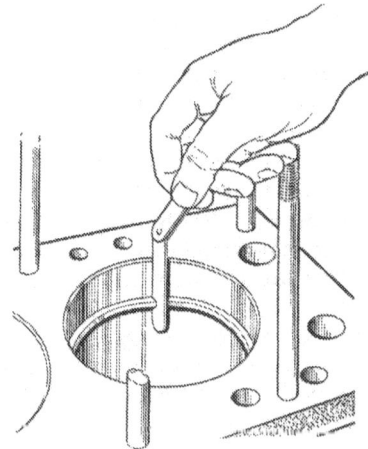

Checking piston ring gap.

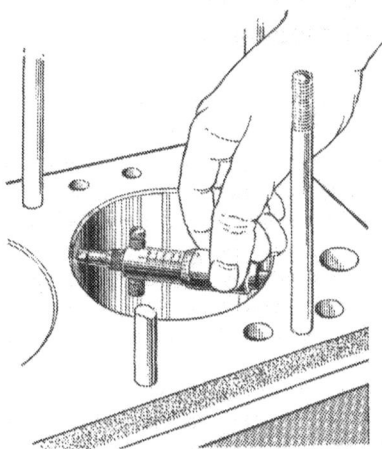

Checking bore wear.

8 — Pins should be a hand-push fit in the piston. The fit can be checked after the rod has been assembled by holding the piston with the connecting rod in an approximately horizontal position. The weight of the large end of the connecting rod should be just insufficient to turn the pin in the piston. On no account must pin piston bosses be reamed out as oversize pins are not supplied or permitted.

MODIFIED CONNECTING RODS

Connecting rods with fully floating pins were fitted from Engine No. 40501. They are interchangeable only in sets of six. The dismantling procedure is as follows.

Remove the two circlips securing each pin in its piston and press the pin out. Mark the pins and pistons for reassembly to their original positions and to their original connecting rods.

Check the pin and the connecting rod little-end bearings for wear, with the dimension given in the General Data section. If the bush is worn it should be removed and a new bush fitted. A light press is most suitable for this operation.

When pressing in the new bush ensure that the oil hole in the bush is in line with the oil hole in the connecting rod.

Replacement bushes must be finish reamed to size after pressing into the connecting rod (see the General Data section for the correct dimensions). The piston pin bosses must not be reamed as oversize pins are not supplied.

Assemble the pistons to the connecting rods by inserting the pins, which should be a hard hand-push fit at a room temperature of 68°F. (20°C.). Secure each pin in position with the two circlips, ensuring that they fit well into their grooves.

IMPORTANT.—When assembling the piston to the connecting rod make certain that the slot in the piston will be on the opposite side to the camshaft when the assembly is fitted to the cylinder block.

TIMING CHAIN AND SPROCKETS
Removal

1 — Remove the radiator as described in Section C, if the removal is to be done with the engine in position.

2 — Slacken the generator fixing bolts and take off the fan belt. Unscrew the starter dog nut using Austin Service Tool No. 18G 391. Before doing this the tab washer must be knocked back.

3 — In some cases it may now be possible to remove the crankshaft damper and pulley complete as one unit. If, however, the pulley is tight on the crankshaft, it will be necessary to undo the six nuts securing the damper, and with this component removed, draw off the pulley with Service Tool No. 18G 2.

4 — Take out the five ¼ in. and the seven 5/16 in. setpins from the timing cover flange, taking care to retrieve the special elongated washers fitted under the heads. The cover can now be removed and the joint washer separated, taking care to remove and retain the oil thrower.

5 — Remove the automatic chain tensioner.

6 — Unlock and remove the camshaft sprocket nut and remove the nut and lockwasher. Note that the locating tag on the lockwasher fits into the keyway of the camshaft sprocket.

7 — The camshaft and crankshaft sprockets may now be removed, together with the timing chain, by easing each wheel forward a fraction at a time, with suitable small levers or Service Tool No. 18G 58. As the crankshaft gear wheel is withdrawn care must be taken not to lose the gear packing washers immediately behind it.

The timing chain showing bright links opposite spot marks on gears. 'A' shows the position of the short run of chain between the bright links.

8 — Clean and examine the joint faces of the timing cover and front mounting plate.

9 — Examine the felt oil seal for signs of wear, hardening or damage. If the slightest wear or damage is apparent the timing cover and seal must be renewed as an assembly.

10 — Inspect sprockets for worn, broken or chipped teeth.

11 — Inspect the timing chain for excessive wear or stretch.

12 — Examine the timing chain tensioner.

Reassembling

The installation of the timing chain and sprocket is the reversal of the removal procedure but for the following points:

1 — Replace the same number of washers as was found when dismantling, unless new camshaft or crankshaft components have been fitted, which will disturb the alignment of the two sprockets. To determine the thickness of washers required, place a straight-edge across the sides of the camshaft sprocket teeth and measure with a feeler gauge the gap between the straight-edge and the crankshaft gear.

2 — When replacing the timing chain and gears, set the crankshaft and camshaft with the keyways approximately at T.D.C. when seen from the front. Double the timing chain, bringing both bright links together. This gives a long and short portion of the chain on either side of the bright links. With the shorter part of the chain on the **Right**, (the bright links facing the operator), and the longer on the **Left**, engage the marked camshaft sprocket tooth with the top bright link, and the crankshaft sprocket with the marked tooth coinciding with the other bright link.

Place the sprockets in their respective positions on the camshaft and crankshaft, complete with the chain, and push the assembly home. Carefully keep the sprockets in line with each other all the time to avoid straining the chain.

When replaced on the engine, the bright links and the marked teeth should take up the position shown in the illustration.

3 — Replace the camshaft chain wheel locking washer and nut.

4 — Apply engine oil to the timing chain and wheels before installing the cover.

5 — Replace the oil thrower, concave side towards the front of the engine.

6 — Use camshaft pulley boss, or Service Tool No. 18G 3 to locate the timing cover felt washer before the timing cover flange bolts are tightened.

NOTE: A new joint washer should be fitted between the timing cover and the front mounting plate.

AUTOMATIC CHAIN TENSIONER

The timing chain tensioner is secured to the engine front mounting plate by two bolts and a locking plate. When the tensioner is in operation and the engine is running, oil from the lubrication system enters the spigot on the back face under pressure and lubricates the bearing surface through a hole in the tensioner slipper pad.

The tensioner consists of a cylinder with a helical slot which moves in a plunger by the action of a compressed spring in the tensioner body. The helical slot has a recessed lower edge. Should the chain wear through use, the spring pushes the plunger and pad outwards against the chain. A limiting peg in the plunger, bearing on the upper edge of the helical slot, rotates the cylinder until the next recess in the lower edge engages it, and the plunger is prevented from returning to its original position and allowing the chain to become slack.

To Remove

1 — Unlock the tab washer fitted to the tensioner bottom plug and remove the plug from the body.

2 — Insert a ⅛ in. (3 mm.) Allen key into the plug hole to engage the cylinder, and turn the key in a clockwise direction (viewed from the opposite end to the slipper), until the rubber slipper is completely free of spring pressure. Between a half and one full turn is necessary.

3 — Unlock and remove the bolts to release the chain tensioner assembly and back plate.

To Dismantle.

1 — Withdraw the plunger and slipper assembly from the tensioner body and engage the lower end of the cylinder with the Allen key.

2 — Turn the key in an anti-clockwise direction, gripping the plunger and key securely, until the cylinder and spring are released from inside the plunger.

To View and Overhaul

1 — Clean the components thoroughly in solvent.

2 — The oil in the spigot, and outlet oil hole in the slipper should be blown out by compressed air before reassembly.

3 — Check the tensioner spring and examine the slipper pad for wear. Renew as an assembly if necessary.

To Reassemble

1 — Insert the spring in the plunger and place the cylinder on the other end of the spring.

2 — Compress the spring until the cylinder enters the plunger bore and engages with the peg in the bore.

3 — Hold the assembly compressed in this position and engage the Allen key. Turn the cylinder in a clockwise direction until the end of the cylinder is below the peg, thus fully compressing the spring and locking cylinder.

4 — Withdraw the key and insert the plunger assembly into the body.

To Replace

1 — Position the back plate and secure the assembly to the cylinder block.

Engine exploded.

1. Generator pulley.
2. Generator fan.
3. Dipstick.
4. Tachometer housing.
5. Tachometer oil feed pipe.
6. Heater pipe.
7. Oil filler cap.
8. Rocker cover.
9. Breather pipe.
10. Balance plug.
11. Balance plug cover.
12. Inlet manifold joint.
13. Exhaust manifold joint.
14. Exhaust manifold.
15. Deflector plate.
16. Engine back plate.
17. Oil gauge pipe connection.
18. Plug, oil filter feed hole.
19. Cylinder block drain tap.
20. Welch plug.
21. Cylinder block.
22. Tappet cover joint.
23. Engine front plate joint washer.
24. Tappet cover.
25. Generator mounting.
26. Generator mounting stud.
27. Generator swinging link.
28. Timing pointer.
29. Front cover.
30. Felt washer.
31. Engine front plate.
32. Seal for main bearing.
33. Front main bearing stud.
34. Front main bearing cap.
35. Sump joint washer.
36. Centre front main bearing cap.
37. Centre rear main bearing cap.
38. Rear main bearing cap.
39. Sump.
40. Engine mounting bracket.
41. Bracket carrying mounting rubber.
42. Bracket for mounting rubber.
43. Engine mounting rubber.

THE ENGINE

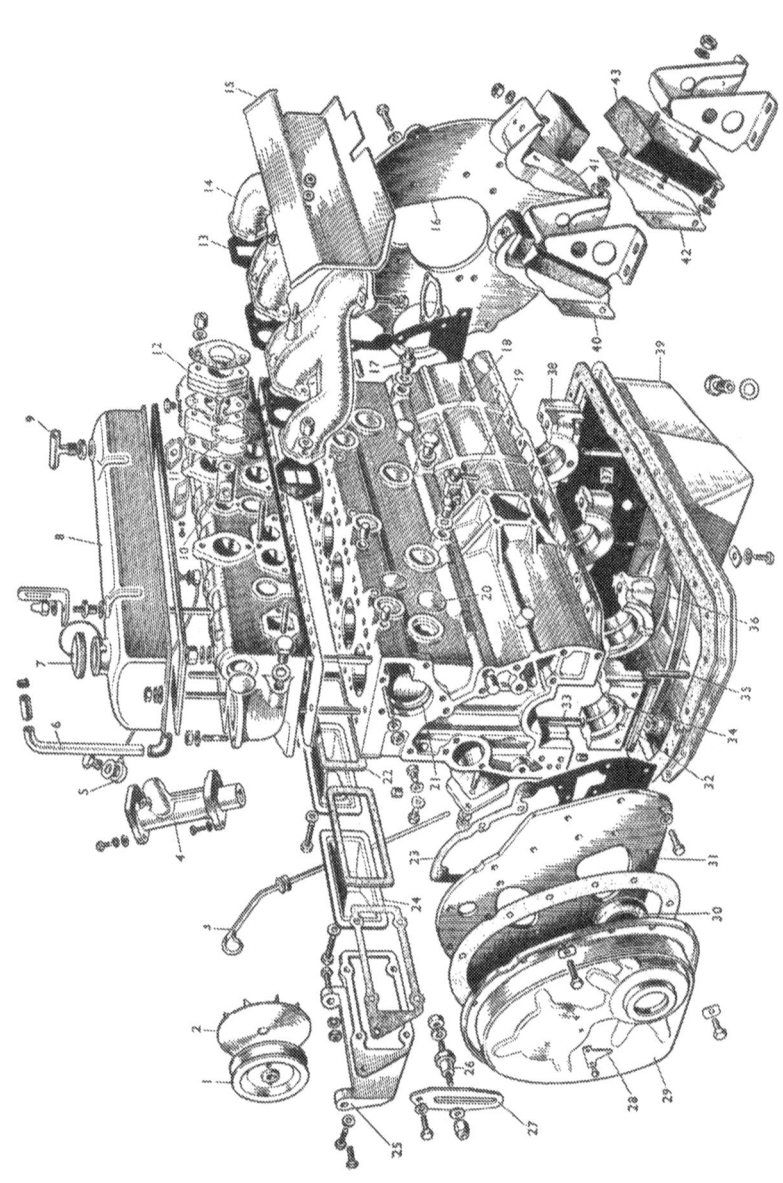

2 — Move the timing chain into position and release the tensioner for operation by inserting the Allen key and turning it in an anti-clockwise direction as far as possible, assisting the slipper to rise initially with the finger.

3 — Secure the bolts into their locking plate,, replace the bottom-plug, and lock it with a tab washer.

CAMSHAFT AND BEARINGS
Removal
1 — Drain the sump and release it from the engine. Remove the oil pump, and then take off the rocker assembly.

2 — Remove the push rods and take out the tappets.

3 — Remove the timing cover, timing chain tensioner, chain and gears.

4 — Remove the distributor and spindle drive. Do not slacken the clamping plate bolt or the ignition timing setting will be lost.

5 — Take out the two setscrews which secure the camshaft locating plate to the cylinder block.

6 — Withdraw the camshaft forward rotating it slowly to assist the withdrawal.

7 — Inspect the camshaft bearing journals and cams for signs of scoring. If the journals are not within the required diameter limits (see under "General Data"), the camshaft should be renewed.

8 — Examine the camshaft bearings for scores, pits or evidence of failure. If the bearings have to be renewed it will necessitate the removal of the engine back plate and the use of a number of special service tools. This operation is best referred to a professional or authorized service garage.

9 — Inspect the tappet cam contacting surfaces for wear. New tappets should be installed wherever evidence of unusual wear is found.

10 — The installation of the camshaft and tappets is a reversal of the procedure **"Removal"**. Lubricate the camshaft journals with engine oil.

FLYWHEEL AND ENGINE REAR PLATE
To Remove
The flywheel complete with starter ring is secured to the flange on the rear of the crankshaft by four set bolts, which are locked in position by three lockplates. The engine rear plate is secured to the crankcase by set bolts and lockwashers. To remove the flywheel and rear plate, after the engine is removed from the vehicle, proceed as follows:

1 — Remove the gearbox from the engine.

2 — Remove the clutch.

3 — Knock back the tabs of the lockplates, unscrew the bolts and withdraw the flywheel.

4 — Unscrew the set bolts and withdraw the engine rear plate. Note the cork sealing strip behind the engine rear plate under the crankshaft flange.

5 — Examine the flywheel teeth and friction face for excessive wear. If the teeth on the starter ring are damaged or badly worn, a replacement flywheel and ring may be fitted.

6 — Examine the engine rear plate for distortion and damage and clean the joint faces of the plate and crankcase and check for scores.

To Install

1 — Refit the engine rear plate to the crankcase, using a new joint washer. Tighten the securing bolts evenly and firmly.

2 — Place the flywheel over the flange and flange bolts of the crankshaft so that the timing mark "1" is at T.D.C. when the first throw of the crankshaft is at T.D.C. The joint faces should be perfectly clean. Fit the lockplates and nuts on the bolts and tighten them in diagonal sequence.

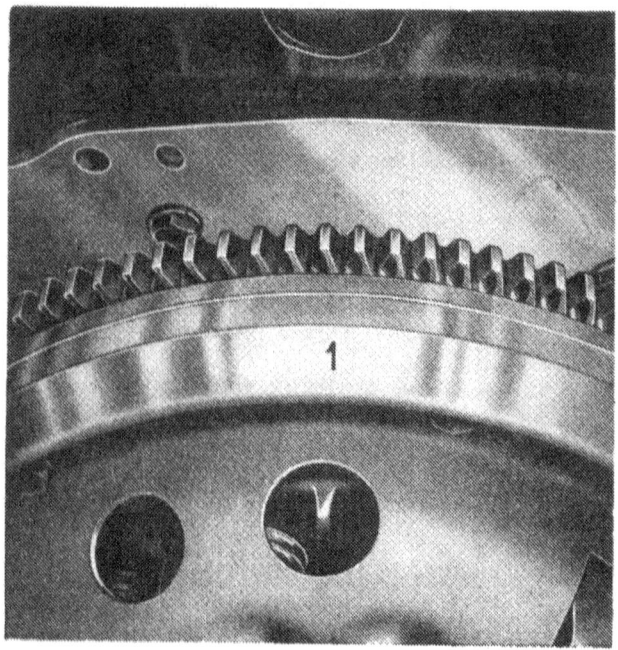

Flywheel T.D.C. mark.

CRANKSHAFT AND MAIN BEARINGS

To Remove

The forged-steel crankshaft is statically and dynamically balanced and is supported in the crankcase by three renewable main bearings of the sintered copper and lead steel-backed type. Crankshaft end float is controlled by thrust washers fitted on both sides of the center main bearing.

1 — Remove the engine from the vehicle and place it upside-down in a dismantling fixture.

2 — Remove the sump and oil strainer.
3 — Remove the timing chain.
4 — Remove the flywheel and engine rear plate.
5 — Check the crankshaft end float to determine whether the renewal of the thrust washers is necessary.
6 — Remove the connecting rod bearing caps and shells, keeping the shells with their respective caps for correct replacement, and release the connecting rods from the crankshaft. Remove the spark plugs from the cylinder head to facilitate the turning of the crankshaft.
7 — Withdraw the main bearing caps complete with bearing bottom shells. Caps and both bearing half-shells should be kept together. Remove the screwed plug from the rear bearing cap oil return pipe and withdraw the pipe in order to use the extractor. Note that each main bearing is stamped with a common number, which is also stamped on the center web of the crankcase near the main bearing. The bottom halves of the two thrust washers will be removed with the entire main bearing cap.
8 — Remove the crankshaft, the two remaining halves of the thrust washers and the top half-shells of the main bearings from the crankcase.
9 — Inspect the crankshaft main journals and crankpins for wear, scores, scratches and ovality. If necessary the crankshaft may be re-ground to the minimum limits shown under "General Data".
Main bearings for re-ground crankshafts are available in sizes shown under General Data".
10 — Clean the crankshaft thoroughly, ensuring that the connecting oilways between the journals and crankpins are perfectly clear. They can be cleaned out by applying a pressure gun containing solvent. When clean, inject a thin oil in the same manner.
11 — Thoroughly clean the bearing shells, caps and housings above the crankshaft.
2 — Examine the bearing shells for wear and pitting, and look for evidence of breaking away or picking-up. Renew the shells if necessary.
13 — Bearings are pre-finished with the correct diametrical clearance, and do not require bedding in. New bearings should be marked to match up with the marking on the cap, and **on no account should they be filed to take up wear or to reduce running clearance.**
14 — Check the thrust washers for wear on their bearing surfaces, and renew if necessary to obtain the correct end float.

To Install
The installation of the crankshaft and main bearings is a reversal of the procedure **"To Remove"**, noting the following points:
1 — Ensure that the thrust washers are replaced the correct way around and locate the bottom half tab in the slot in the bearing cap.
2 — The bearing shells are notched to fit the recesses machined in the housing and cap.
3 — In the case of the front and rear main bearing caps, install new

cork or felt sealing strips.

4 — The rear main bearing cap horizontal joint surfaces should be thoroughly cleaned and lightly covered with Wel-Seal (manufactured by Messrs. Wellworthy Ltd.) sealing compound (or equivalent) before the cap is fitted to the cylinder block. This will ensure a perfect oil seal when the cap is bolted down to the block.

5 — Lubricate the bearings freely with engine oil.

6 — Tighten the main bearing nuts, see "General Data" for torque settings.

CYLINDER BLOCK

To Remove and Dismantle

1 — Remove and dismantle the engine.

2 — Remove all studs, unions and screwed plugs, etc., if neccesary.

3 — If an expansion plug has blown, or leaks, remove the plug by drilling a hole in its center and lever it out with a screwdriver or other suitable tool.

To View and Overhaul

1 — Scrape as much sediment as possible from the water passages and thoroughly swill out with a water hose.

2 — Clean all gasket surfaces.

3 — Inspect for cracks and scores on gasket surfaces.

4 — It may be advisable to remove the ridge above the ring travel at the top of the cynder bores before checking the fit of the pistons.

5 — Wipe the cylinder bores clean and examine them for scores, out-of-round and taper. If the cylinders are found to be out-of-round or excessively tapered when measured with a dial indicator, they should be reconditioned.

6 — If cylinder reconditioning is required, determine accurately the amount of material to be removed (refer to "General Data" concerning oversize pistons available).

7 — Make sure that all traces of abrasives are cleaned from all parts of the cylinder block after the cylinder reconditioning operation is completed.

8 — Check the camshaft bearings.

To Reassemble and Install

1 — Install all studs, unions and screwed plugs, etc.

2 — When installing new expansion plugs, coat the edge of the plug with a sealing compound and insert the plug with the "bulge" on the outside. A carefully aimed blow at the center of the plug with a small hammer direct or with a blunt punch will expand the plug sufficiently to make a water-tight joint. If too heavy a blow is used, the plug will be useless and must be replaced by another new one.

3 — Reassemble, install and test the engine.

FAULT DIAGNOSIS

Symptom	No.	Possible Fault
(a) Will Not Start	1	Defective coil
	2	Faulty condenser
	3	Dirty, pitted, or incorrectly set contact breaker points
	4	Ignition wires loose or leaking
	5	Water on sparking plug leads
	6	Corrosion of terminals or discharged battery
	7	Faulty starter
	8	Wrongly connected plug leads
	9	Vapour lock in fuel line
	10	Defective fuel pump
	11	Over-choking
	12	Under-choking
	13	Choked petrol filter or jets
	14	Valves leaking
	15	Sticking valves
	16	Valve timing incorrect
	17	Ignition timing incorrect
(b) Engine Stalls		In (a), check 1, 2, 3, 4, 10, 11, 12, 13, 14 and 15
	1	Plugs defective or incorrect gap
	2	Retarded ignition
	3	Mixture too weak
	4	Water in fuel system
	5	Petrol tank breather choked
	6	Incorrect valve clearance
(c) Poor Idling		In (b), check 1 and 6
	1	Air leak at manifold joints
	2	Incorrect slow running adjustment
	3	Air leak in carburetter(s)
	4	Slow running jet choked
	5	Over-rich mixture
	6	Worn piston rings
	7	Worn valve stems or guides
	8	Weak exhaust valve springs
(d) Misfiring		In (a), check 1, 2, 3, 4, 5, 8, 10, 13, 14, 15, 16 and 17
		In (b), check 1, 2, 3 and 6
	1	Weak or broken valve springs
(e) Overheating		See cooling system
(f) Low Compression		In (a), check 14 and 15
		In (c), check 6 and 7
		In (d), check 1
	1	Worn piston ring grooves
	2	Scored or worn cylinder bores

FAULT DIAGNOSIS

Symptom	No.	Possible fault
(g) Lack of Power	1 2 3	In (a), check 3, 10, 11, 13, 14, 15 and 16 In (b), check 1, 2, 3 and 6 In (c), check 6 and 7 In (d), check 1 Check (e) and (f) Leaking joint washers Fouled sparking plugs Automatic advance not functioning
(h) Burnt Valves or Seats	1	In (a), check 14 and 15 In (b), check 6 In (d), check 1 Check (e) Excessive carbon around valve seat and head
(j) Sticking Valves	1 2 3	In (d), check 1 Bent valve stem Scored valve stem or guide Incorrect valve clearance
(k) Excessive Cylinder Wear	1 2 3 4 5 6	Check 11 in (a) Check (e) Lack of oil Dirty oil Dirty air cleaner Gummed up or broken piston rings Badly fitting piston rings Misalignment of conrods
(l) Excessive Oil Consumption	1 2 3 4 5 6	In (c), check 6 and 7 Check (k) Ring gap too wide Oil return holes in pistons choked with carbon Scored cylinders Oil level too high External oil leaks Ineffective valve oil seal
(m) Crankshaft and Connecting Rod Bearing Failure	1 2 3 4 5	In (k), check 1 Restricted oilways Worn journals on crankpins Loose bearing caps Extremely low oil pressure Bent connecting rod
(n) Internal Water Leakage		See cooling system

COOLING SYSTEM

RADIATOR
To Remove
1 — Drain the cooling system.
2 — Slacken the hose clip, on the upper water hose, at the thermostat housing and with the aid of a screwdriver ease the pipe off the housing extension.
3 — Take off the radiator bottom hose by releasing the clips on the water pump and the heater outlet pipe.
4 — Disconnect the thermometer element from the radiator header tank.
5 — Take off the six nuts (three on each side) which secure the radiator to the mounting flanges and remove the radiator.
6 — Inspect the radiator core for damage and test it for water leaks. Solder at the points where leakage occurs or renew the core if necessary.
7 — Inspect the flexible mountings for wear.
8 — Inspect the drain tap for leaks and renew it if necessary.
9 — Test the filler cap.
10 — Inspect the hose connections for deterioration and renew them if necessary.

To Replace
Installation is a reversal of the procedure **"To remove"**.

THERMOSTAT
To Remove
1 — Drain the cooling system.
2 — Disconnect the water outlet hose from the outlet elbow.
3 — Remove the two nuts securing the outlet elbow to the cylinder head and lift off the outlet elbow.
4 — Remove the outlet elbow to cylinder head joint.
5 — Lift out the thermostat.

To Replace
The installation of the thermostat is a reversal of the procedure **"To remove"**. Fit a new joint gasket between the outlet elbow and the cylinder head. In an emergency the engine can be run with the thermostat removed.

TEMPERATURE GAUGE
A temperature gauge unit, consisting of a thermal element and dial indicator is fitted to the vehicle. The thermal element is held in the radiator header tank by a gland nut. On later engines the thermal capillary is fitted to the engine. The dial indicator is situated in the instrument panel and is connected to the element by a capillary tube filled with mercury.

Damage to any of the above mentioned parts will necessitate the renewal of the complete temperature gauge unit.

FAN AND PUMP ASSEMBLY
To Remove
1 — Remove the radiator

2 — Remove the generator

3 — Unscrew the four set bolts securing the water pump to the crankcase. Withdraw the fan and pump assembly and remove the fan belt.

Test the thermostat opening temperature by immersing it in water heated to 70° to 75°C (158°–168°F) for engines prior to No. 3099; 68°C (154°F) for later engines. If the thermostat valve does not start to open or sticks in the fully open position, it should be replaced. The 68° thermostat for the 7 psi pressure cap is part No. 11K399.

DRAINING AND FLUSHING THE SYSTEM
To Drain the System
When the vehicle is to be stored, the entire cooling system should be drained to protect against corrosion and, in certain instances, freezing. To drain the system proceed as follows:

1 — With the vehicle standing on level ground, remove the radiator filler cap.

2 — Open the cylinder block and radiator drain taps. If the system contains anti-freeze mixture it should be drained into clean containers, strained and preserved for re-use.

3 — Insert a length of wire into the open taps to disturb any sediment, etc., that may block the flow.

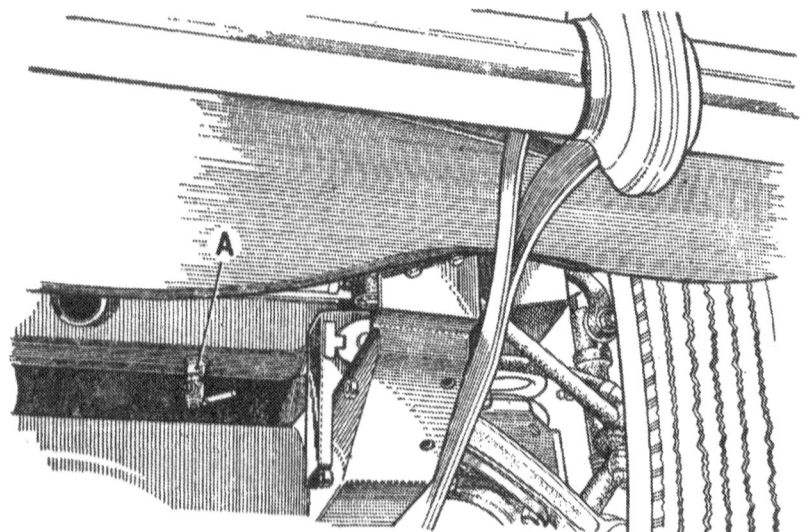

Showing the radiator drain tap A in the open position. Turn the tap lever down to close.

4 — To prevent the possibility of operating the vehicle with the system drained, make sure that a suitable notice is placed on the vehicle, or other suitable precautions taken.

To Flush the System

If an inhibitor is not used, the cooling system should be drained, cleaned and flushed at intervals depending upon the type of vehicle operation and the local water conditions. Do not use strong caustic or acid solutions for cleaning purposes because they have a detrimental effect on various parts of the system. To clean and flush the system, proceed as follows:

1 — Drain the system completely as described above.

2 — With a hose or fresh quantities of clean water, flush the system through until water issuing from the drain taps appear to be clean.

3 — Allow the system to drain completely, then close the drain taps.

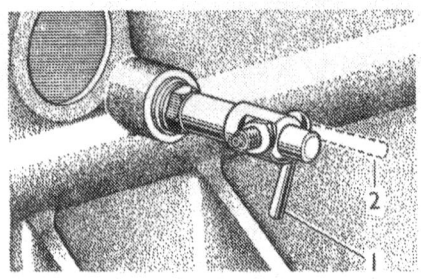

1. Closed position.   2. Open position.

4 — Fill the system with clean water (or anti-freeze solution), slowly, to allow air to escape past the thermostat valve, up to the bottom of the filler neck.

5 — Replace the filler cap by turning it approximately $90°$ in a clockwise direction.

FROST PRECAUTIONS

Care should be taken to see that the water is drained off completely, for in case of freezing it will do harm by expansion taking place, and fracture of the cylinder block may result. There are two drain taps, one of them on the right-hand side of the cylinder block, and the other at the base of the radiator. Both taps must be opened to drain the system and the vehicle must be on level ground while draining.

Freezing may occur first at the bottom of the radiator or in the lower hose connection. Ice in the hose will stop water circulation, and may cause boiling.

A muff can be used to advantage, but care must be taken not to run with the muff fully closed, or boiling will result.

Fan belt adjustment.
1 and 2. Generator securing bolts.
3. Swinging link.   4. Locknut.

When filling or topping-up the radiator, do so when the engine is cold, and if possible use rain water or clean soft water. Fill up to the filler plug orifice.

Overheating may be caused by a slack fan belt, excessive carbon deposit in the cylinders, running with the ignition too far retarded, improper carburetor adjustment, a partially choked radiator causing failure of the water to circulate, or loss of water due to leakage or evaporation.

The belt should be sufficiently tight to prevent slip, yet it should be possible to move it laterally about 1 in. (2.54 cm.). To make an adjustment, slacken the bolts which hold the generator in position, then raise or lower the generator until the desired tension of the belt is obtained. Securely lock the generator in position again when the adjustment has been made. It must be understood that there is a correct and incorrect method of fitting fan blades. The blades are not flat, but shaped, and the concave or hollow side should be the leading one, thus, when fitting to an engine the convex or arched side must always face the radiator. This convex side is further easily identified as stiffeners are pressed into the blades; they project on the concave face.

In cases of overheating, the position of the fan blades should at once be examined; make sure, after dismantling, that the fan is fitted the right way around.

If a heater is fitted to the car do not resort to draining the cooling system as an alternative to the use of anti-freeze. It is not possible to drain the heater unit completely by means of the cooling system drain taps.

Protection by Use of Anti-Freeze Mixture

When frost is expected or when the vehicle is to be used in very low temperatures, make sure that the strength of the solution is up to the strength recommended by the manufacturers, for the conditions likely to be encountered.

Only anti-freeze solutions of the ethylene glycol type are suitable for use in the cooling system. Bluecol, Shell Snowflake, and Esso Anti-freeze are recommended.

The strength of the solution must be maintained by topping-up with anti-freeze solution as necessary. Excessive topping-up with water will reduce the degree of protection afforded.

Showing location of the oiling plug on the water pump body.
1. Thermostat cover bolts.   2. Thermostat outlet.
3. Water pump oiling plug.

IGNITION SYSTEM

The ignition system consists of two circuits—primary and secondary. The primary circuit includes the battery, ignition switch, the primary or low-tension circuit of the coil and the distributor contact breaker and capacitor. The secondary circuit includes the secondary or high-tension circuit of the coil, the distributor rotor and cover segments, the high-tension cables and the spark plugs.

The ignition coil, which is mounted on the right-hand side of the engine, consists of a soft iron core around which is wound the primary and secondary windings. The coil carries at one end a center high-tension terminal and two low-tension terminals marked (SW) (switch) and (CB) (contact breaker) respectively.

The ends of the primary windings are connected to the (SW) and (CB) terminals and the secondary winding to the (CB) terminals and the high-tension terminal.

The distributor is mounted on the right-hand side of the engine and is driven by a shaft and helical gear from the camshaft. Automatic timing control of the distributor is controlled by a centrifugal mechanism and a vacuum-operated unit each operating entirely independently of each other. The centrifugal mechanism regulates the ignition advance according to engine speed, while the vacuum control varies the timing according to engine load. The combined effect of the two mechanisms gives added efficiency over the full operating range of the engine. A micrometer adjuster is provided to give a fine timing adjustment to allow for the engine condition and the grade of fuel used.

A keyed molded rotor with a metal electrode is mounted on top of the cam. Attached to the distributor body above the centrifugal advance mechanism is a contact breaker plate carrying the contact breaker points and a capacitor connected in parallel. A cover is fitted over the distributor body and retained by two spring clips attached to the body.

Inside the cover is a center electrode and spring-loaded carbon brush which makes contact with the rotor. The brush is of composite construction, the top portion being made of a resistive compound, while the lower portion is made of softer carbon to prevent wear of the rotor electrode. Under no circumstances must a short non-resistive brush be used to replace this long resistive type. A measure of radio interference suppression is given by this brush.

Spaced circumferentially around the center electrode are the spark plug high-tension cable segements. The distributor is secured in position on the cylinder block by a clamp plate.

The plugs are located on the right-hand side of the engine and have a 14 mm. thread with a ¾ in. reach.

When the ignition is switched on, the current from the battery flows through the primary circuit, and a magnetic field is built up around the core of the coil. When the contact breaker points are opened by rotation of the distributor cam, the current flow is interrupted, causing a high voltage to be induced in the secondary winding of the coil by sudden collapse and consequent change in the magnetic field. The high-tension current thus generated in the secondary winding of the coil is conveyed by the coil high-tension cable to the center terminal of the distributor cover. From here the current passes through the carbon brush to the rotor, where the high-tension current passes along the rotor electrode and is distributed to the segments and thence to the spark plugs via the high-tension cables.

TUNE UP

1 — Adjust the spark plugs at the recommended intervals as follows: The gap of the plug points should be within the limits of .024 to .026 in. (.61 to .66 mm.). Gap adjustment should be made by bending the side electrode only. Never bend the central electrode. If the plugs are dirty, damaged or excessively burned replace them.

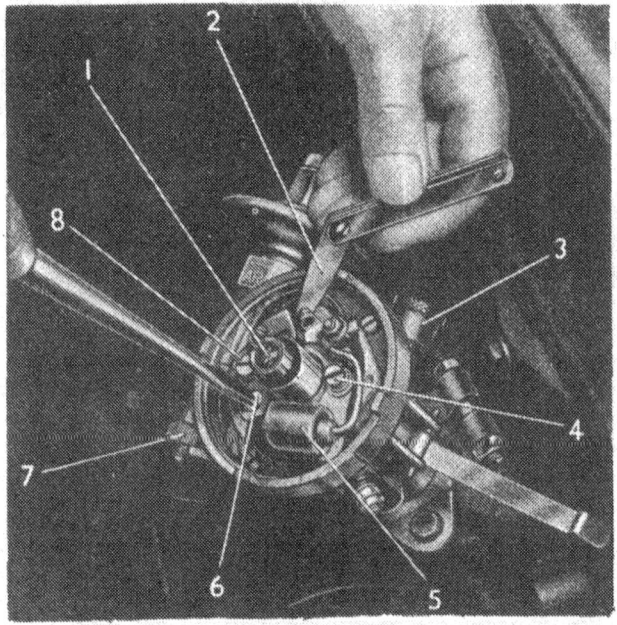

Contact breaker adjustment.

1. *Oiling point.*
2. *Feeler gauge.*
3. *Shaft lubricator.*
4. *Contact locking screws.*
5. *Condenser.*
6. *Contact adjusting screw.*
7. *Micrometer adjuster.*
8. *Contact locking screws.*

2 — Adjust the contact breaker points at the recommended intervals as follows:

Remove the distributor cover and rotor. Rotate the engine with the starting handle until the fibre heel of the rocker is on the peak of one of the cam lobes. The gap of the contact breaker points should be within .014 to .016 in. (.36 to .40 mm.).

Gap adjustment should be made by slackening the fixed contact plate securing screws and moving the plate until the gap gauge is a sliding fit between the two contacts. Tighten the securing screws and recheck the gap. Replace the rotor and cover. If the points are dirty or pitted, true or replace them.

3 — Adjust the ignition timing, if the distributor has been disturbed, as follows:

Remove the valve rocker cover so that the valve action can be observed. Rotate the engine with the starting handle until No. 1 piston is at the top of its compression stroke (i.e. the exhaust valve of No. 6 cylinder is just closing and the inlet valve just opening). Turn the crankshaft until the recess in the crankshaft pulley flange is in line with the pointer on the timing chain cover. If the timing chain cover has been removed, align the bright links on the timing chain with the marked teeth on the camshaft and crankshaft sprockets when No. 6 and No. pistons will be at T.D.C. Set the micrometer adjustment on the distributor to its central position. The crankshaft should now be rotated backwards to obtain its correct position before setting the distributor points, this setting is correct for premium grade fuels only. With the cover removed the distributor body must be rotated until the rotor arm is pointing to the position of No. 1 electrode in the cover. With the contact points just opening, tighten the clamp plate bolt.

Showing the timing pointer set opposite to the notch in the crankshaft pulley. (Number 1 piston at T.D.C.)

Finer adjustments can be obtained under road conditions, by means of the micrometer adjustment. Note this adjustment should not be used for initial setting of the ignition; it is only altered if the main setting requires adjustment to meet the characteristics of the grades of fuel being used. There is a considerable amount of latitude for adjustment, but only extremely small movement of the adjustment knob should be made at one time.

Replace the distributor cover and cylinder head cover.

TESTING

If the ignition system fails, or misfiring occurs, first make sure that the trouble is not due to defects in the engine, carburetor or fuel supply. Faults should be diagnosed by applying the following tests:

1 — Examine the high-tension cables, the cables from the coil to the distributor and from the distributor to the plugs. If the rubber insulation shows signs of deterioration or cracking, the cable should be removed.

2 — Test the plugs and high-tension cables by removing the plugs in turn and allowing them to rest on the cylinder head or other convenient ground point, and observing whether a spark occurs at the points when the engine is turned by hand. It should, however, be noted that this is only a rough test, since it is possible that a spark may not take place when the plug is under compression. If necessary, clean and test the plugs.

3 — To trace a fault in the low-tension circuit, release the instrument panel from the dash, switch on the ignition, and turn the engine until the distributor contacts are opened. Refer to the wiring diagram, and, with the aid of a voltmeter (0 to 20), check the circuit as follows:

(a) **Cable—Battery to starter switch**
Connect the voltmeter between the supply terminal of the starter switch and a ground point. No reading indicates a faulty cable or loose connection.

(b) **Cable (brown)—Starter switch to two-way fuse unit A.1 terminal**
Connect the voltmeter between the fuse unit A.1 terminal and ground. No reading indicates a faulty cable or loose connection.

(c) **Control box**
Connect the voltmeter between the control box terminal (A.1) and ground. No reading indicates a faulty control box.

(d) **Cable (brown and blue)—Control box to lighting and ignition switch**
Connect the voltmeter between the lighting switch terminal (A) and ground. No reading indicates a faulty cable or loose connection.

(e) **Ignition switch**
Connect the voltmeter between the ignition switch (white cable terminal) and ground. No reading indicates a faulty ignition switch.

(f) **Cable (white)—Ignition switch to fuse unit A.3 terminal**
Connect the voltmeter between the fuse unit A.3 terminal and ground. No reading indicates a faulty cable or loose connection.

(g) **Cable (white)—Fuse unit A.3 terminal to ignition coil**
Connect the voltmeter between the ignition coil terminal (SW) and ground. No reading indicates a faulty cable or loose connection.

(h) **Ignition coil**
Connect the voltmeter between the ignition coil terminal (CB) and ground. No reading indicates a faulty ignition coil.

(i) **Cable (white and black)—Ignition coil to distributor**
Connect the voltmeter between the distributor terminal and ground. No reading indicates a faulty cable or loose connection.

(j) **Distributor**
Connect the voltmeter across the distributor contacts. If no reading is given, remove the condenser and test again. If a reading is given, the capacitor is faulty.

5 — If, after carrying out the foregoing tests, the fault has not been located, remove the high-tension cable from the center terminal of the distributor. Switch on the ignition and crank the engine until the contacts close. Flick the contact breaker lever open while the high-tension cable from the ignition coil is held about 3/16 in. (5 mm.) away from the cylinder block. If the ignition equipment is in order a strong spark should be obtained. If no spark is given, it indicates a faulty ignition coil.

IGNITION COIL
To remove

1 — Disconnect the high-tension cable from the coil center terminal.

2 — Disconnect the low-tension cables from the (SW) and (CB) terminals of the coil.

3 — Unscrew the bolts fastening the coil to the generator strap, and remove the coil.

The installation of the ignition coil is a reversal of this procedure.

DISTRIBUTOR
To remove

1 — Disconnect the high-tension cables from the spark plugs.

2 — Disconnect the high-tension cable from the center terminal of the ignition coil.

3 — Disconnect the low-tension cable from the terminal on the side of the distributor.

4 — Disconnect the vacuum control pipe at the union.

5 — Unscrew and remove the tachometer drive and tachometer drive oil feed pipe.

6 — Remove the two set bolts attaching the clamp plate to the tachometer drive housing and withdraw the distributor from the tachometer housing. **Do not loosen the clamp plate.**

To dismantle

1 — Spring back the two securing clips and remove the distributor cover.

2 — Unscrew the terminal screws from the distributor cover and withdraw the high-tension cables.

3 — Remove the rotor.

4 — Take out the split pin securing the vacuum link to the sliding contact breaker plate and remove the two screws at the edge of the contact breaker base.

5 — Slacken the two nuts on the low tension terminal and pull the connection on the contact breaker away from the terminal block. Lift

out the contact breaker assembly.

6 — Remove the nut, insulating piece and connections from the pillar on which the contact breaker spring is anchored, and lift off the contact breaker lever and the insulating washers beneath it.

— Remove the two screws securing the fixed contact plate, together with their spring and plain washers and take off the plate.

8 — Withdraw the single screw securing the condenser and contact breaker ground lead. The contact breaker base assembly can be dismantled by removing the circlip and star washer located under the lower plate.

9 — Remove the circlip on the end of the micrometer timing screw and turn the micrometer nut until the screw and vacuum assembly are freed, take care not to loosen the ratchet and coil springs located under the micrometer nut.

10 — Tap out the parallel pin securing the driving dog and tachometer gear to the lower end of the spindle. The driving dog and tachometer gear can be removed.

11 — Unscrew and remove the lubricator from the distributor body together with its spring and felt washer.

12 — The distributor shaft, cam and centrifugal timing control can be pressed upwards through the distributor body.

13 — Remove the cam fixing screw from the top of the driving shaft and withdraw the cam and centrifugal timing control.

Note: A spacer is fitted on the shaft underneath the action plate.

14 — Clean the distributor cover and examine it for signs of cracks and evidence of "tracking", i.e. a conducting path may have formed between adjacent segments. This is indicated by a thin black line between segments; when this has occurred the cover should be renewed.

15 — Ensure that the carbon brush moves freely in the distributor cover.

16 — Examine the attachment of the metal electrode to the rotor moulding. If slack or abnormally burned, renew the rotor.

17 — The contact face of the contact breaker points should present a clean, greyish, frosted appearance. If burned or blackened, renew the contact set or polish the contact face of each point with a fine oil-stone, working with a rotary motion. Care should be taken to maintain the faces of the points flat and square, so that when reassembled full contact is obtained. Clean the points thoroughly in solvent.

18 — Check that the movable contact arm is free on its pivot without slackness.

19 — Check the centrifugal timing control balance weights and pivot pins for wear and renew the cam assembly or weights if necessary.

20 — The cam assembly should be a free sliding fit on the driving shaft. If the clearance is excessive, or the cam face is worn, renew the cam assembly or shaft as necessary.

21 — Check the fit of the shaft in the body bearing bushes. If slack, renew the bushes and shaft, as necessary.

Press out the old bushes. The new bushes should be allowed to stand completely immersed in thin engine oil for twenty-four hours, or alternatively for two hours in oil which has been heated to 212° F. (100° C.), before pressing them into the distributor body.

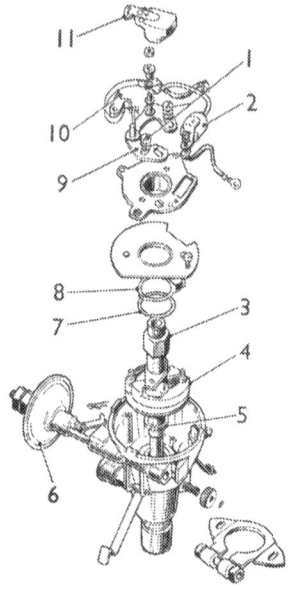

1. *Screws for contact plate.*
2. *Condenser.*
3. *Cam.*
4. *Automatic timing contact.*
5. *Distance collar.*
6. *Vacuum control.*
7. *Felt ring.*
8. *Spring.*
9. *Fixed contact plate.*
10. *Moving contact.*
11. *Rotor.*

To reassemble

Reassembly of the distributor is a reversal of the procedure **"To dismantle"**, noting the following points: —

1 — Apply a few drops of engine oil to the centrifugal timing control mechanism and cam bearing.

2 — Lightly smear the cam surface with engine oil.

3 — Apply a drop of engine oil to the top of the pivot on which the moving contact fibre rocker arm works.

4 — Secure the distributor driving dog to the driving spindle with a new peg, ensuring that the small offset of the driving tongue is on the right when the rotor arm driving slot is downwards.

5 — Connect the internal cables as follows: —

(a) Red cable, condenser to contact breaker spring anchor post.

(b) Cable, low-tension terminal to contact spring anchor post.

(c) Cable, base plate locating screw to condenser locating screw.

6 — Adjust the contact breaker points to proper specifications.

7 — Reassemble the high-tension cables.

8 — Turn the vacuum control adjusting nut to the half-way position when refitting the unit.

To Install

Replacing the distributor to the reverse of the procedure **"To Remove"**, noting the following points: —

1 — Insert the assembled distributor, with its cap removed, into the tachometer housing and turn the rotor arm until the driving slot on the distributor engages with the dog in the housing.

2 — Turn the distributor body to align the clamping plate holes with their respective holes on the tachometer housing and refit the set bolts.

DISTRIBUTOR DRIVING SPINDLE

Removal

1 — Remove the distributor.

2 — Release the three setscrews which secure the tachometer housing to the cylinder block and withdraw the housing.

3 — By using a 5/16 in. U.N.F. bolt approximately 3¼ in. long, screwed into the tapped end of the drive spindle, the spindle can be withdrawn.

4 — Examine the drive gear for worn teeth.

To Replace

1 — Remove the valve rocker cover.

2 — Crank the engine until No. 1 piston is at the top of its compression stroke (i.e. the exhaust valve of No. 6 cylinder is just closing and the inlet valve just opening).

3 — Turn the crankshaft until the recess in the crankshaft pulley flange is in line with the (T.D.C.) indicating pointer on the timing chain cover.

4 — Screw the 5/16 in. U.N.F. bolt into the threaded end of the distributor drive and replace the drive in the block so that the centrally cut slot takes up the position shown (i.e. "twenty-to-two" position).

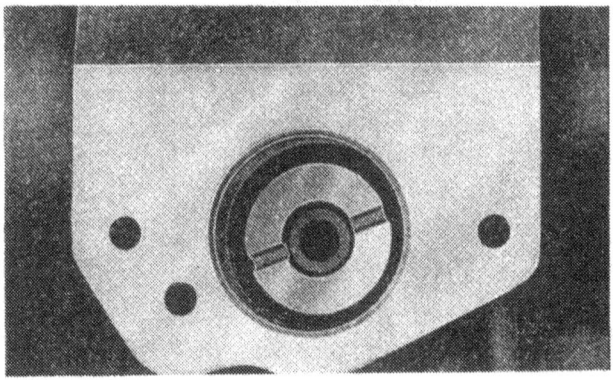

Distributor drive, showing the slot in the "Twenty-to-two" position.

5 — Replace the tachometer housing, rotating the external drive dog *until it* mates up with the slot in the distributor driving spindle. Ascertain that the smaller segment of the offset dog, situated within the tachometer housing is in the downward position.

Note: The internal dog should now be in the "twenty-to-two" position. Secure the tachometer housing to the block with its three setpins.

6 — Replace the distributor.

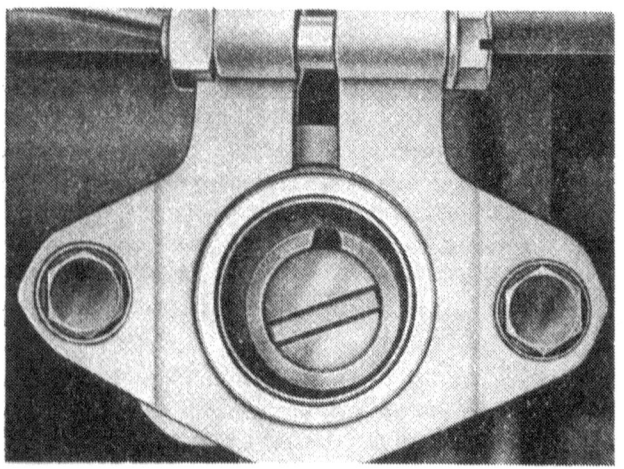

Tachometer spindle, showing the smaller segment of the offset dog in the downward position.

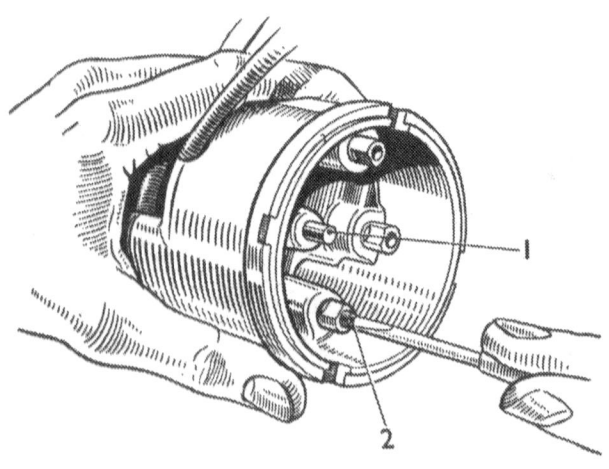

1. Carbon brush.   2. Screw securing cable.

HIGH-TENSION CABLES
To remove
1 — Pull the high-tension cable off the spark plug.
2 — Unscrew the moulded terminal to release the cable from the coil.
3 — Straighten out the bare strands of cable, remove the brass washer and withdraw the cable from the moulded terminal.
4 — Release the screw securing the cable in the distributor cover and withdraw the cable.

To Replace
1 — Thread the cable through the moulded terminal and brass washer and bend back the bare strands of the cable against the brass washer.
2 — Push the cable into the distributor cover and secure it with the pointed screw.
3 — Install the cables in the coil and distributor cover and onto the spark plugs in the correct order. The firing order is 1, 5, 3, 6, 2, 4, following round in an anti-clockwise direction.

SPARK PLUGS
The spark plug gap (for type of plug see 'General Data') should be maintained at .024 to .026 in. (.6096 to .660 mm.). If the gap is allowed to become too wide, misfiring at high speeds is liable to occur; and if too small, bad slow running and idling will be the result.

Plugs should be regularly inspected, cleaned and tested. This is of vital importance to ensure good engine performance, coupled with fuel economy.

When removing the plugs from the engine, use a spark plug wrench, this will avoid possible damage to the insulators. Always remove the copper washers. The plugs should then be placed in a suitable holder which has holes drilled to admit the upper end of the plugs and marked to identify each one with the cylinder from which it was removed.

The plugs should then be carefully examined.

Oil fouling will be indicated by a wet shiny black deposit on the insulator. This condition is usually caused by worn cylinders, pistons or gummed rings. Oil vapor is forced from the crankcase, during the suction stroke of the piston which fouls the plugs.

Fuel fouling will cause a dry, fluffy, black deposit to be apparent on the plugs. This is usually caused by faulty carburation, but a faulty coil or leaking and worn out ignition leads, may have the same effect.

Under the above conditions, if the plugs otherwise appear to be sound, they should be cleaned thoroughly, adjusted, and tested.

When preparing for cleaning, the plug washers should be removed and examined. The condition of these washers is important in that a large proportion of the heat from the plug insulator is dissipated to the cylinder head by them. The washer should therefore be reasonably compressed. A loose plug can be easily overheated, thus shortening plug life. On the other hand, do not over-tighten. All that is needed is a good seal between the cylinder head and the plug. Tightening too much will cause distortion of the washer with the possibility of blow-by which will again lead to overheating and resulting danger. If there is any question of defect, replace with new washers.

The plugs should now be thoroughly cleaned of all carbon deposit, resorting to scraping if necessary, removing as much as possible from the space between the insulator and shell. An oily plug should be washed out with solvent. If a plug cleaning machine is available, 5 to 10 seconds in this will remove all remaining signs of carbon. Remember to thoroughly "blow-out" the plug after treatment under these conditions, in order to remove all traces of abrasive. After cleaning, thoroughly examine the plug for cracked insulator or worn away insulator nose. Should either of these conditions be apparent a new plug should be installed.

Carbon deposit on the threads of the plugs, should be carefully removed by using a wire brush, or if available a wire buffing wheel. Take care not to damage the electrodes or insulator tip. Neglect of this cleaning operation will lead to tight threads and resultant loss of heat dissipation due to the carbon deposit, thereby causing overheating.

The condition of the electrodes should now be noted and any signs of corrosion removed, if it is felt that the plugs are worthy of further use. This can be carried out with the use of a small file to carefully dress the gap area. The gap should then be reset, to a clearance of .024 to .026 in. (.6096 to .660 mm.). When resetting bend the side electrode only.

It is advisable while the plugs are under pressure in the testing machine, to apply a spot of oil to the terminal end, to check for air leakage. Excessive leakage here will tend to cause compression loss, rapid deterioration of the electrode and overheating of the electrode tip. The top half of the insulator should also be carefully examined for any paint splashes or accumulation of grime and dust, which should be removed. Should there be any signs of cracks due to faulty use of the spanner, the plug should be renewed. When replacing the plug lead, make sure that it is securely attached.

It is recommended that plugs should be cleaned and tested every 3,000 miles (4800 km.), and renewed at 12,000 miles (19200 km.). Remember, plugs in good condition will ensure better fuel consumption and good engine performance.

N.5 SPARK PLUGS

Commencing at engine No. 6375, Champion N.5 plugs were fitted in lieu of Champion N.3 plugs. The N.3 plugs must however, be used for competition and high speed driving.

The circulation of the cooling water is effected by a centrifugal pump mounted in front of the cylinder block and driven by a belt from the crankshaft pulley. A thermostat is fitted in the water outlet pipe at the front end of the engine.

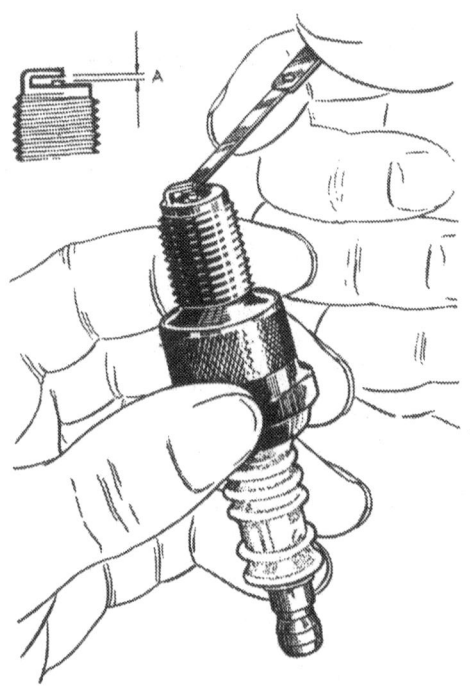

Checking sparking plug gap.

FAULT DIAGNOSIS

Symptom	No.	Possible Fault
	1	Battery discharged
	2	Distributor contact points dirty, pitted or out of adjustment
	3	Distributor cover "tracked" or cracked
(a) Engine Will Not Fire	4	Distributor carbon brush not in contact with cover
	5	Loose connection in low-tension circuit
	6	Distributor rotor arm cracked
	7	Coil faulty
	1	Distributor contact points dirty, pitted or out of adjustment
	2	Contact breaker spring weak
	3	Distributor cover "tracked" or cracked
	4	Coil faulty
(b) Engine Misfires	5	Loose connection in low-tension circuit
	6	High-tension cables cracked or perished
	7	Sparking plug loose
	8	Sparking plug insulation cracked
	9	Sparking plug gap incorrect
	10	Ignition timing too far advanced

FUEL SYSTEM

The fuel system of the Austin Healey consists of fuel tank, fuel pump and carburetors with attendant piping. The differences between the various models lie solely in the pumps and carburetors. The initial change was made on the later BN4 when H.D. carburetors were used in conjunction with the six port head. The adoption of Type LCS fuel pump was also carried out. All BN6 and later cars to engine No. 29/D/U/H2864 were fitted with the same units. Past this point an automatic choke (or Thermo-carburetor) type carburetor was used. Up to chassis No. BN5234 and BT5310 when the manual choke type H.D. was used. S.U. carburetors Type HS4 are fitted to the 3000, BN7 and BT7 Series and Type HS6 are used on the BJ7.

All of the carburetors are of the same basic construction and operating principle (i.e. variable venturi) but detail variations, needle sizes and linkage are of some significance. These will be dealt with in a discussion of each type.

Whether two carburetors or three are employed synchronization is of the most importance to smooth running, economy and performance. There are several aids to synchronizing and balancing of carburetors available to the owner-tuner or professional. One is, the **Unisyn,** a visual flowmeter. Another is the **S.U. Tool,** a non-mechanical device which permits synchronization without removing air cleaners and is of value in other carburetor adjustments such as setting float level, centering the jet, testing piston free movement and disassembling the carburetor. Both of these devices are available from Messrs. M. G. Mitten, Inc., 1631 E. Green St., Pasadena, California, U.S.A.

TO REMOVE THE FUEL TANK

1 — Remove the drain plug from the tank and drain.

2 — Within the luggage compartment release and remove the spare wheel by disconnecting its securing strap.

3 — Remove the carpet which covers the floor of the luggage compartment.

4 — Remove the tank feed pipe cover, situated in the top right-hand corner of the boot, by unscrewing the six securing Phillips screws. Disconnect the feed pipe from the tank.

5 — Disconnect the tank filler pipe at its union with the tank. The union is made by a rubber joint hose and two securing clips.

6 — Detach the insulated lead from the fuel gauge unit terminal.

7 — Release the tank securing straps by unscrewing the nut and locknut of each tank strap stud. These nuts are visible on the underside of the luggage compartment floor just in front of the rear body panel. Pull the straps through the compartment floor and hinge them back on their clevis pin anchorages.

8 — Lift out the tank.

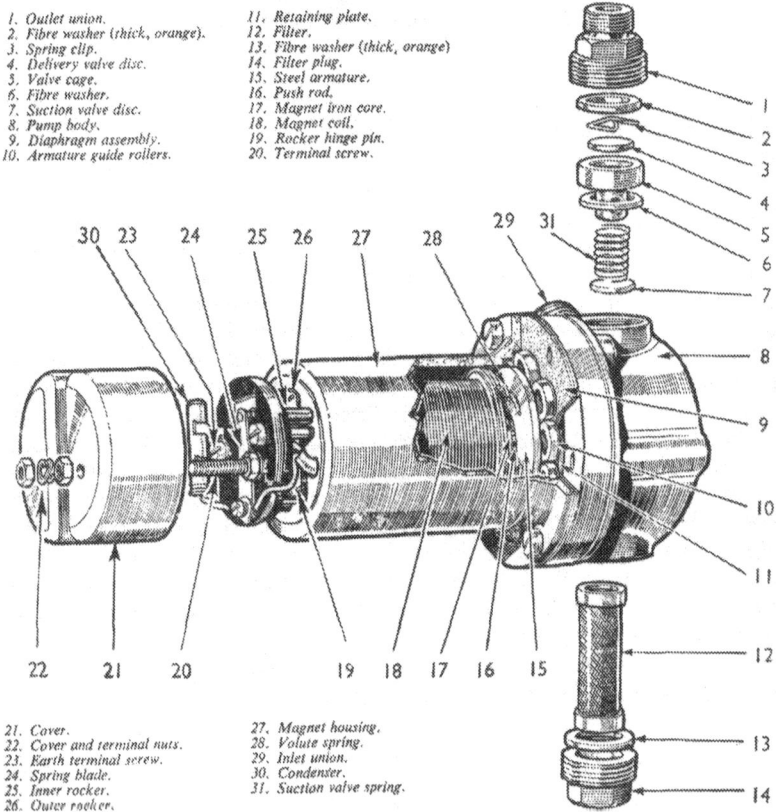

1. Outlet union.
2. Fibre washer (thick, orange).
3. Spring clip.
4. Delivery valve disc.
5. Valve cage.
6. Fibre washer.
7. Suction valve disc.
8. Pump body.
9. Diaphragm assembly.
10. Armature guide rollers.
11. Retaining plate.
12. Filter.
13. Fibre washer (thick, orange)
14. Filter plug.
15. Steel armature.
16. Push rod.
17. Magnet iron core.
18. Magnet coil.
19. Rocker hinge pin.
20. Terminal screw.
21. Cover.
22. Cover and terminal nuts.
23. Earth terminal screw.
24. Spring blade.
25. Inner rocker.
26. Outer rocker.
27. Magnet housing.
28. Volute spring.
29. Inlet union.
30. Condenser.
31. Suction valve spring.

S.U. FUEL PUMP TYPE H.P.

The pump consists of three main assemblies, the body, the magnet assembly and the contact breaker. Reference to the drawing will make the description clear.

The body is composed of a hollow alloy die-casting (8) in two parts, into the bottom of which the filter (12) is screwed. The pump inlet union (29) is screwed in at an angle on one side. The outlet union (1) is screwed into the top and tightens down on the delivery valve cage (5) which is clamped between the two fiber washers (2) and (6). In the top of the delivery cage is the delivery valve, a thin brass disc (4) held in position by a spring clip (3). Inserted in the bottom of the cage is the suction valve (7), being a similar disc to (4) and held lightly on a seating machined in the body of the spring. Holes connect the space between the valves and the pumping chamber, a shallow depression on the forward face of the body. This space is closed by a diaphragm assembly (9) clamped at its outside edge between the magnet housing (27) and the body (8) and at its center between the retaining plate and the steel armature (15). A bronze rod to which the diaphragm is attached (16) is screwed through the center of the armature, passes through the magnet core to the contact breaker, located at the other end. A volute spring (28) is interposed between the armature and the end plate of the coil to return the armature and diaphragm.

The magnet housing consists of a cast-iron pot containing an iron core (17), wound with a coil of copper wire to energize the magnet. Between the magnet housing and the armature are fitted eleven spherical-edged brass rollers (10). These locate the armature centrally within the magnet at all times, and allow absolute freedom of movement in a longitudinal direction. The contact breaker consists of a small bakelite molding carrying two rockers (25) and (26), which are both hinged to the molding at one end and are connected together at the top end by two small springs, arranged to give a "throw over" action. A trunnion is fitted into the center of the inner rocker, and the bronze push-rod (16) connected to the armature is screwed into this. The outer rocker (26) is fitted with a tungsten point, which makes contact with a further tungsten point on a spring blade (24). This spring blade is connected to one end of the coil, and the other end of the coil is connected to the terminal (20). A short length of flexible wire is connected to the outer rocker and to the other terminal (23) which also serves to hold the bakelite molding on the magnet housing.

The rocker mechanism is insulated by fiber bushes. Two fiber bushes are fitted to one of the spindles of the "throw over" mechanism in order to silence the operation of the contact breaker.

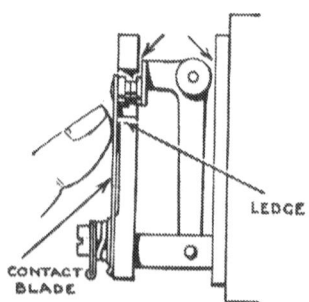

The correct armature setting.

Action of the Fuel Pump

When the pump is at rest, the outer rocker lies in the outer position and the tungsten points are in contact. The current passes from the terminal through the coil back to the blade, through the points and to the ground return, thus energizing the magnet and attracting the armature. This comes forward, bringing the diaphragm with it and sucking gasoline through the suction valve into the pumping chamber. When the armature has advanced nearly to the end of its stroke the "throw over" mechanism operates, and the outer rocker flies back, separating the points and breaking the circut. The spring (28) then pushes the armature and diaphragm back, forcing gasoline through the delivery valve at a rate determined by the requirements of the engine. As soon as the armature gets near the end of this stroke the "throw over" mechanism again operates, the points again make contact, and the cycle of operations is repeated.

SERVICING THE PUMP
The first thing to do is to determine, by the sense of smell, whether the parts in contact with the fuel have become coated with gum. The gum is a substance similar to varnish and can cause the eventual destruction of the diaphragm. Its presence can be detected by smelling the outlet union: if an unpleasant stale smell is noticed, gum is present. The ordinary smell of gasoline denotes that no gum has been formed.

To Dismantle the Pump

1 — Unscrew the filter plug and remove the plug, washer and filter. The latter may be found clogged with gum.

2 — Remove the inlet union and washer.

3 — Remove the outlet union and its washer.

4 — Extract the valve cage, valve cage washer, suction valve and spring. Remove the circlip retaining the delivery valve and withdraw the valve disc.

5 — Unscrew the six screws holding the two main components of the pump together. If the presence of gum has been detected, all parts (not aluminum) must be boiled in 20 percent caustic soda solution, dipped in nitric acid and then washed in boiling water. Aluminum parts must be cleaned by thoroughly soaking in denatured alcohol.

6 — If no evidence of gum formation has been found, separate the two parts of the pump and check the action of the valves. It should be possible to blow freely but not to suck air back through the inlet union, and to suck, but not blow, air through the delivery valve. If valve action is satisfactory there is no need to disturb their assembly.

7 — Clean the filter with a brush and swill out the body of the pump.

8 — Unscrew the diaphragm assembly from its trunnion in the contact breaker by rotating the whole assembly in an anti-clockwise direction. Take care not to lose the rollers fitted behind the diaphragm

9 — Remove the contact breaker cover and the nut on the terminal acting as a seating for the cover. Cut away the lead washer squeezed on the terminal threads below the nut, and push the terminal down a short way so that the tag on the coil end is free on the terminal.

10 — Unscrew the contact blade retaining screw and the two long pedestal screws; remove the blade and the pedestal. Do not damage the coil end in disengaging the tag from the terminal.

11 — Push out the rocker hinge pin.

Do not disturb the core of the magnet: special press tools are required for its correct location.

To Reassemble the Pump

1 — Make sure that all parts are clean.

2 — Fit each valve with its smooth side downwards and ensure the correct location of the circlip in its groove.

3 — Fit the red fiber washers as follows: the thin one below the valve cage, the next thickest above the cage, and the thickest on the inlet union. The washer on the filter plug is also a thick red fiber one.

4 — Assemble the contact breaker on its pedestal so that the rockers are free in their mountings without appreciable sideplay. Any excessive sideplay on the outer rocker allows the points to be out of line, while excessive tightness interferes with the action of the pump through sluggish contact breaker operation.

5 — In cases of tightness it may be necessary to square up the outer rocker with a pair of thin-nosed pliers.

6 — The hinge pin is case hardened and ordinary wire must never be used as a replacement.

7 — If the contact blade has been removed, replace it underneath the tag, bearing directly against the pedestal. When the points are separated, the blade should rest against the ledge of the pedestal and must not be so stiff as to prevent the outer rocker from coming right forward when the points are in contact. The points must make contact when the rocker is in the midway position. To check, hold the blade in contact with the pedestal without pressing on the overhanging portion, and test the gap between the white rollers and the body of the pump with a .030 in. (.76 mm.). If necessary, set the tip of the blade to give the correct clearance.

Note—Fit the spring washer on the ground connection screw between the tag and the pedestal as the spring washer is not a reliable conductor and the tag must bear directly against the head of the screw.

Solder the coil ends to their tags and the two terminals to the ground wire.

The assembly of components on the terminal screw holding the cover in position is as follows: spring washer, wiring tag, lead washer and recessed nut. In no circumstances omit the spring washer or shorten the assembly in any way or the pedestal may be broken when the cover retaining nut is tightened.

Fit the armature return spring with its larger diameter towards the coil and the smaller to the armature. Do not stretch the spring.

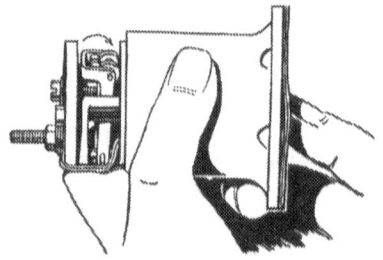

Checking the armature setting.

FUEL PUMP ADJUSTMENT

If the armature has been removed, reassemble and adjust as follows:

1 — Swing the contact blade on the pedestal to one side.
2 — Fit the impact washer to the armature recess.
3 — Screw the armature into position.
4 — Place the eleven guide rollers in position around the armature. Use no jointing compound on the diaphragm.
5 — Hold the magnet assembly in an approximately horizontal position and push in the armature firmly and steadily. If the contact breaker throws over, screw the armature farther in until it ceases to do so; unscrew the armature one-sixth of a turn at a time until a position is found where the rocker just throws over. It is important to press steadily and not to jerk the armature. When the correct position is found unscrew the armature a further two-thirds of a turn; **this is important.**

When a new diaphragm is fitted it is probable that considerable pressure will be needed to push the armature right home. If there is any doubt concerning the point at which the contact breaker throws over, turn it back one-sixth of a turn.

6 — Place the magnet housing in position on the main body with the drain hole at the bottom; make sure that the rollers are still in their correct position. If a roller drops it may get trapped between the two ports and cut a hole in the diaphragm.

Insert the coupling screws and the ground terminal screw. Do not screw up tightly before stretching the diaphragm to its outermost position. This is best accomplished by the use of a wedge as shown in the illustration Insert the wedge between the white rollers of the outer rocker and pressed under the tips of the inner rocker until it lifts the trunnion in the center of the inner rocker as far as it will go.

If no wedge is available, insert a matchstick under one of the white rollers and pass a current through the pump. This will excite the magnet, actuate the armature and stretch the diaphragm: the screws may then be tightened down fully while the diaphragm is held in this position. The spring blade rests against a small projection on the bakelite molding, and it must be set so that when the points are in contact it is deflected back from the molding. The width of the gap at the points is approximately .030 in. (.76 mm.).

Note—Three important points, which will seriously affect the working of the pump if overlooked, are the following:

1 — Keep the contact breaker blade out of contact while setting the diaphragm.
2 — Press firmly without jerking on the diaphragm.
3 — Stretch the diaphragm to its limit while tightening up the body screws.

TRACING THE TROUBLES

Should the pump cease to function: first disconnect the fuel delivery pipe from the pump. If the pump then works the most likely cause of the trouble is sticking needles in the float-chambers of the carburetors. Should the pump not work, disconnect the lead from the terminal and strike it against the body of the pump after switching on the ignition. If a spark occurs it indicates that the necessary current is available at the terminals, and that the trouble arises with the pump mechanism. If no spark can be detected, then it is an indication that the current supply has failed and that attention should be given to the wiring and battery. If current is present further investigation should be carried out by removing the bakelite cover which is retained by the terminal nut. Touch the terminal with the lead. If the pump does not operate and the contact points are in contact yet no spark can be struck off the terminal, it is very probable that the contact points are dirty and require cleaning. These may be cleaned by inserting a piece of card between them, pinching them together and sliding the card backwards and forwards.

If, when the wire is connected to the terminal and the tickler of the carburetor is depressed, the points fail to break, it is possible that there is either an obstruction in the suction pipe, which should be cleared by blowing it through with air, or some irregularity in the pump itself is preventing the correct movement. This may be due either to the diaphragm having stiffened, or to foreign matter in the roller assembly which supports the diaphragm, in which case the diaphragm should be removed and the whole assembly cleaned and reassembled.

On the other hand, if the points are not making contact, see that the tips of the inner rocker (25) are in contact with the magnet housing. If they are not, it is an indication that the armature has failed to return to the end of its normal travel.

To cure this, loosen the six screws which attach the magnet housing to the pump body, and make sure that the diaphragm is not sticking to the face of the magnet housing by carefully passing a penknife between the two. The hinge pin (19) should then be removed and the six retaining screws tightened up again. The tips of the inner rockers will probably now be found to be making contact with the face of the magnet housing, but if they are not, it will be necessary to remove and dismantle the whole magnet assembly in order to ascertain if an accumulation of foreign matter has caused a jam. Remember that whenever the magnet housing is removed, care should be taken to see that the guide rollers (10) do not drop out.

Pump Noisy

If the pump becomes noisy and works rapidly, it is usually an indication that there is an air leak on the suction side of the pump. Check the level of the fuel in the tank and see that it is not too low. The simplest way to test for air leakage is to disconnect the fuel pipe from the carburetor and place its end in a glass jar (approximately 1 pint or half a litre) and allow the pump to deliver fuel into it. If air bubbles appear when the end of the pipe has become submerged in the fuel, it is a clear indication of an air leak on the suction side of the pump in the fuel pipe between the tank and the pump, which should be found and cured. Check all the unions and joints, making sure that the filter union and inlet unions are quite air-tight.

Failure to Deliver Fuel

Should the pump continue beating without delivering fuel, it is probable that some dirt has become lodged under one of the valves, in which case they should be dismantled by unscrewing the top or delivery union and lifting out the valve cage, when they can be cleaned and reassembled. When replacing it, see that the thin hard red fiber washer is **below** the valve cage and the thick orange one above.

If the pump struggles to pump and becomes very hot, it is probable that the filter has become clogged or there is an obstruction on the suction side. The filter is readily removed for cleaning by unscrewing its retaining plug at the bottom of the pump.

FUEL PUMP MAINTENANCE

Apart from keeping the contacts clean and removing the filter at regular intervals for cleaning, there is no maintenance required on the fuel pump.

The filter can be removed by unscrewing the hexagon plug at the bottom of the pump, when it can be cleaned in fuel with a stiff brush. Never use rag to clean a filter.

Many of the troubles encountered with a pump are a result of the terminals not being tight, resulting in poor connections. Make sure that the ground wire terminal, in particular, is quite tight.

THE H TYPE CARBURETORS

The two S.U. carburetors are of the variable jet type, fitted with air cleaners.

A damper is provided in each carburetor, consisting of a plunger and non-return valve attached to the oil cap nut, and operates in the hollow piston rod which is partly filled with oil. Its function is to give a slightly enriched mixture on acceleration by controlling the rise of the piston and to prevent piston flutter.

MAINTENANCE

Remove the suction chamber cap and damper assembly and replenish the oil reservoir as necessary every 1,000 miles (1600 km.). It is first essential to run the engine until it has attained its normal running temperature before commencing any mixture or slow-running adjustments

The slow-running is governed by the setting of the jet adjusting screws and the throttle stop screws, all of which must be correctly set and synchronized if satisfactory results are to be obtained.

The two throttles are interconnected by a coupling shaft and spring coupling clips which enable them to be correctly synchronized when adjustments take place.

Before blaming the carburetor settings for bad slow-running, make sure that it is not due to badly set contact points, faulty plugs, bad valve clearance setting or faulty valves and valve springs.

Good slow-running cannot be obtained if the setting for the jets is incorrect. It is therefore advisable to commence any adjustments at this point.

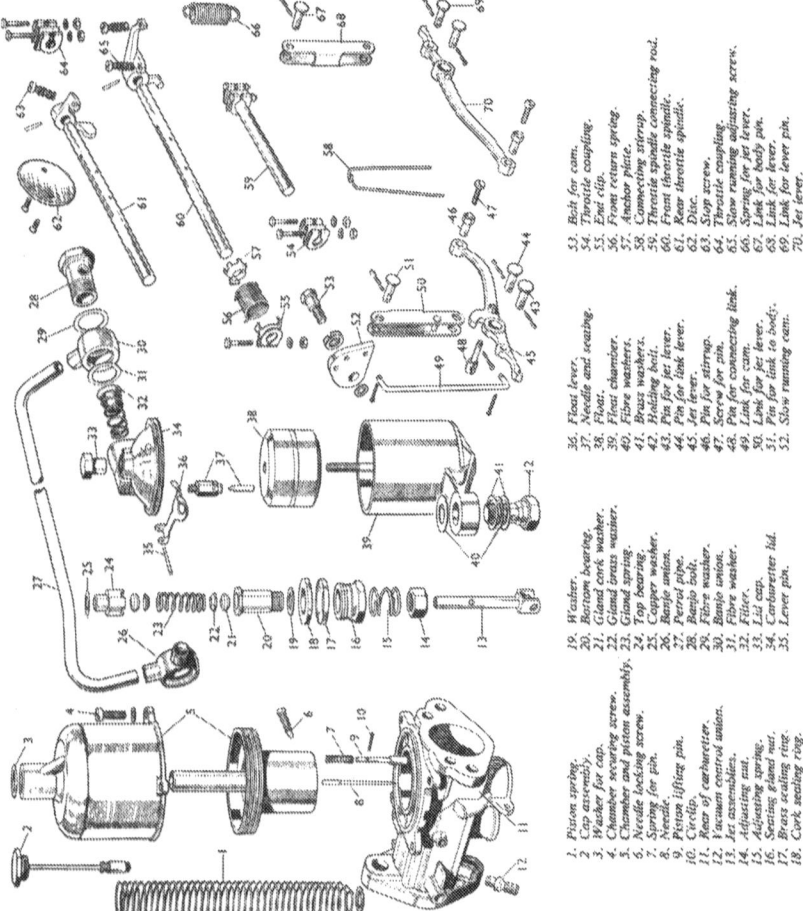

1. Piston spring.
2. Cap assembly.
3. Washer for cap.
4. Chamber securing screw.
5. Chamber and piston assembly.
6. Needle locking screw.
7. Spring for pin.
8. Needle.
9. Piston lifting pin.
10. Circlip.
11. Rear of carburetter.
12. Vacuum control union.
13. Jet assemblies.
14. Adjusting nut.
15. Adjusting spring.
16. Securing gland nut.
17. Brass sealing ring.
18. Cork sealing ring.
19. Washer.
20. Bottom bearing.
21. Gland cork washer.
22. Gland brass washer.
23. Gland spring.
24. Top bearing.
25. Copper washer.
26. Banjo union.
27. Petrol pipe.
28. Banjo bolt.
29. Fibre washer.
30. Banjo union.
31. Fibre washer.
32. Filter.
33. Lid cap.
34. Carburetter lid.
35. Lever pin.
36. Float lever.
37. Needle and seating.
38. Float.
39. Float chamber.
40. Fibre washers.
41. Brass washers.
42. Holding bolt.
43. Pin for jet lever.
44. Pin for link lever.
45. Jet lever.
46. Pin for stirrup.
47. Screw for pin.
48. Pin for connecting link.
49. Link for cam.
50. Link for jet lever.
51. Pin for link to body.
52. Slow running cam.
53. Bolt for cam.
54. Throttle coupling.
55. End clip.
56. Front return spring.
57. Anchor plate.
58. Connecting stirrup.
59. Throttle spindle connecting rod.
60. Front throttle spindle.
61. Rear throttle spindle.
62. Disc.
63. Stop screw.
64. Throttle coupling.
65. Slow running adjusting screw.
66. Spring for jet lever.
67. Link for body pin.
68. Link for lever.
69. Link for lever pin.
70. Jet lever.

In order to adjust the carburetors successfully it is necessary to remove the air cleaners and intake pipe assembly from the carburetors and engine valve cover and make sure the pistons work freely and the jets are properly centered unless the S.U. Tool mentioned earlier is used. If it is not available, follow this procedure:

Adjusting the Jets

1 — Slacken off the pinch-bolt of one of the spring coupling clips locating the inter-connecting shaft to the carburetor throttle spindles and also release the two screws securing the choke spring to the jet levers, so that each carburetor can be operated independently.

2 — Release the throttle lever adjusting screws until both throttles are completely closed.

3 — Turn the throttle lever adjusting screw for the rear carburetor clockwise until it is just touching the web on the carburetor body and then give it one full turn. This will set the rear carburetor for fast idling and leave the front one out of action. This can be ensured further by lifting the front carburetor piston a matter of ½ in. (13 mm.).

4 — With the engine running, set the jet adjusting screw for the rear carburetor so that a mixture strength is obtained which will give the best running speed for this throttle opening, taking care to see that the jet head is kept in firm contact with the adjusting nut the whole time.

5 — The correctness or otherwise of this setting can be checked by raising the suction piston with a small screwdriver, or similar instrument, to the extent of 1/32 in. (1 mm.). This should cause a very slight momentary increase in the engine speed without impairing the evenness of the running in any way.

If this operation has the effect of stopping the engine it is an indication that the mixture setting is too weak.

If an appreciable speed increase occurs and continues to occur when the piston is raised as much as ¼ in. (16 mm.) it is an indication that the mixture is too rich.

6 — When the rear carburetor mixture setting has been carried out correctly release its throttle adjusting screw so that it is clear of the stop and the throttle completely closed, and lift the piston ½ in. (13 mm.) to render it inoperative. Then repeat the jet-adjusting operation on the front carburetor.

7 — When both carburetors are correctly adjusted individually for mixture strength the throttles of each should be set so as to give the required slow-running and synchronization.

Slow-running and Synchronization

Screw each throttle lever adjusting screw so that its end is only just making contact with the web on the carburetor body, then give each screw one full turn exactly.

Start the engine, which will now idle on the fast side.

Unscrew each throttle lever adjusting screw an equal amount, a fraction of a turn at a time, until the desired slow-running speed is achieved.

Correct synchronization can be checked by listening at each carburetor air intake through a length of rubber tube and noticing if the noise produced by the incoming air is the same at both. Any variation in the intensity of the sound indicates that one throttle is set more widely open than the other—the louder sound indicating the throttle with the greater opening.

When the same intensity of sound is given by both carburetors the intercoupling shaft clip should be tightened up firmly to ensure that the throttles work in unison.

If a Unisyn is available it should be used to give a visual indication of incoming air.

Since the delivery characteristics, when both carburetors are operating together, vary somewhat from those existing when each is working separately, it will be found necessary to check them again for correctness of mixture strength by lifting the pistons in turn as described in **"Adjusting the Jets,"** making such adjustments of the jet adjusting screws as are required to balance the mixture.

Fitting New Needles

If the road performance is not satisfactory after the above adjustments have been made, larger or smaller needles may be necessary. To change the needles, remove the screws and lift off the suction chambers, having marked them to ensure their refitting to their respective carburetors. Remove the pistons and return springs.

Unscrew the screw at the side of each piston tube and withdraw the needles.

Fit the new needles: a needle should be fitted with its shoulder flush with the face of the piston as shown in the drawing.

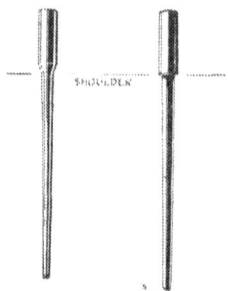

The Float-chamber

The position of the forked lever in the float-chamber must be such that the level of the float (and therfore the height of the fuel at the jet) is correct.

This is checked by inserting a 7/16 in. (11.11 mm.) round bar between the forked lever and the machined lip of the float-chamber lid. The prongs of the lever should just rest on the bar when the needle is on its setting. If this is not so, the lever should be reset at the point where the prongs meet the shank. Care must be taken not to bend the shank, which must be perfectly flat and at right angles to the needle when it is on its seating.

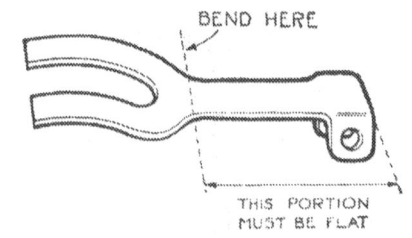

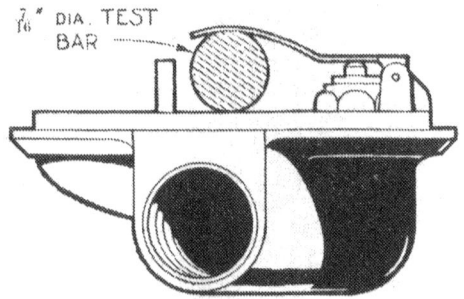

The correct setting of the float lever.

Centering a Jet

First remove the clevis pin at the base of the jet which attaches the jet head to the jet operating lever; withdraw the jet completely, and remove the adjusting nut and the adjusting nut spring. Replace the adjusting nut without its spring and screw it up to the highest position. Slide the jet into position until the jet head is against the base of the adjusting nut. When this has been done, feel if the piston is perfectly free by lifting it up with the finger with the dashpot piston removed. If it is not, slacken the jet holding screw and manipulate the lower part of the assembly, including the projecting part of the bottom half jet bearing, adjusting nut and jet head. Make sure that this assembly is now slightly loose. The piston should then rise and fall quite freely as the needle is now able to move the jet into the required central position. The jet holding screw should now be tightened and a check made to determine that the piston is still quite free. If it is not found to be so, the jet holding screw should be slackened again and the operation repeated. When complete freedom of the piston is achieved the jet adjusting nut should be removed, together with the jet, and the spring replaced. The adjusting nut should now be screwed back to its original position.

Experience shows that a large percentage of carburetors have had jets removed and incorrectly centered on replacement.

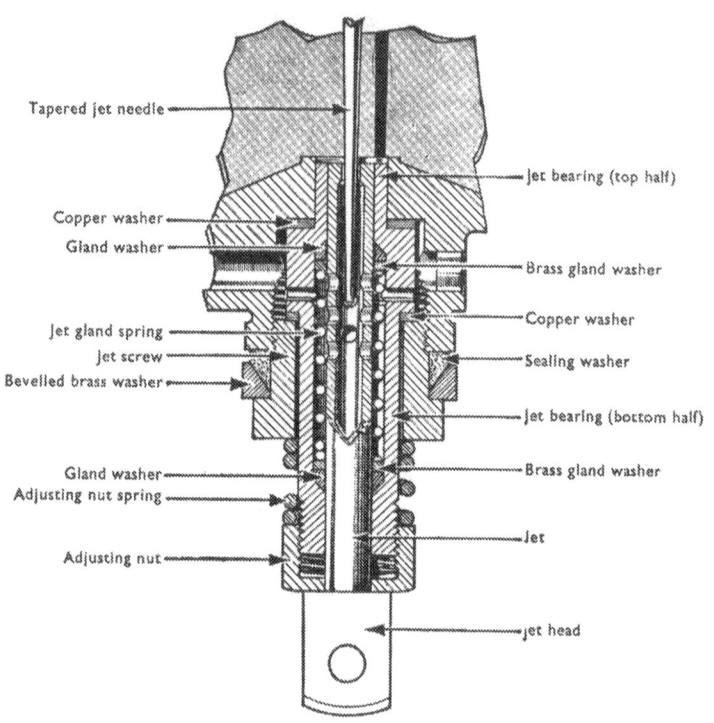

The jet assembly.

SOURCES OF CARBURETOR TROUBLE
Piston Sticking
The piston assembly comprises the suction disc and the piston forming the choke, into which is inserted the hardened and ground piston rod which engages in a bearing in the center of the suction chamber and in which is, in turn, inserted the jet needle. The piston rod running in the bearing is the only part which is in actual contact with any other part, the suction disc, piston, and needle all having suitable clearances to prevent sticking. If sticking does occur the whole assembly should be cleaned carefully and the piston rod lubricated with a spot of thin oil. No oil must be applied to any other part except the piston rod. A sticking piston can be ascertained by removing the dashpot piston damper, inserting a finger in the air intake and lifting the piston, which should come up quite freely and fall back smartly onto its seating when released.

Water or dirt in the Carburetor
When this is suspected, lift the piston; the jet can then be seen. Flood the carburetor and watch the jet; if the fuel does not flow through freely there is a blockage. To remedy this, start the engine, open the throttle, and block up the air inlet momentarily without shutting the throttle, keeping the throttle open until the engine

starts to race. This trouble seldom arises with the S.U. carburetor owing to the size of the jet and fuel ways. When it does happen the above method will nearly always clear it. Should it not do so, the only alternative is to remove the jet.

Float-chamber Flooding
This can be seen by the fuel flowing over the float-chamber and dripping from the air inlet, and is generally caused by grit between the float-chamber needle and its guide. This can usually be cured by depressing the float plunger to allow the incoming flow of fuel to wash the grit through the guide and into the float-chamber.

Float Needle Sticking
If the engine stops, apparently through lack of fuel, when there is plenty in the tank and the pump is working properly, the probable cause is a sticking float needle. An easy test for this is to disconnect the pipe from the electric pump to the carburetor, switch on the ignition to check if fuel is delivered; if it is, starvation has almost certainly been caused by the float needle sticking to its seating, and the float-chamber lid should therefore be removed, the needle and seating cleaned, and refitted. At the same time it will be advisable to clean out the entire fuel feed system, as this trouble is caused by foreign matter in the fuel, and unless this is removed it is likely to recur. It is of no use whatever renewing any of the component parts of the carburetor, and the only cure is to make sure that the fuel tank and pipe lines are entirely free from any kind of foreign matter or sticky substance capable of causing this trouble.

THE AIR CLEANERS
Remove the units and wash the gauze in gasoline every 6,000 miles (9600 km.) or every 3,000 miles (4800 km.) in exceptionallly dusty conditions. When the gauze is clean and dry, re-oil it with engine oil

THE H.D. TYPE CARBURETORS
The S.U. H.D. carburetors are fitted to 6 port cylinder head engines. They differ from the more familiar S.U. type in so far that the jet glands are replaced by a flexible diaphragm, and the idling mixture is conducted along a passage-way, in which is located a metering screw, instead of being controlled by the throttle disc; the throttle and jet interconnection mechanism is also re-designed.

The jet (1) which is fed through its lower end is attached to a synthetic rubber diaphragm (5) by means of the jet cup (4) and jet return spring cup (7), the center of the diaphragm being depressed between these two parts; at its outer edge it is held between the diaphragm casing (9) and the float-chamber arm. The jet (1) is controlled by the jet return spring (8) and the jet actuating lever (10), the latter having an adjusting screw (18) which limits the upward travel of the jet (1) and thus constitutes the idler adjustment; screwing it in (clockwise) enriches the mixture, and unscrewing it weakens the mixture.

FUEL SYSTEM

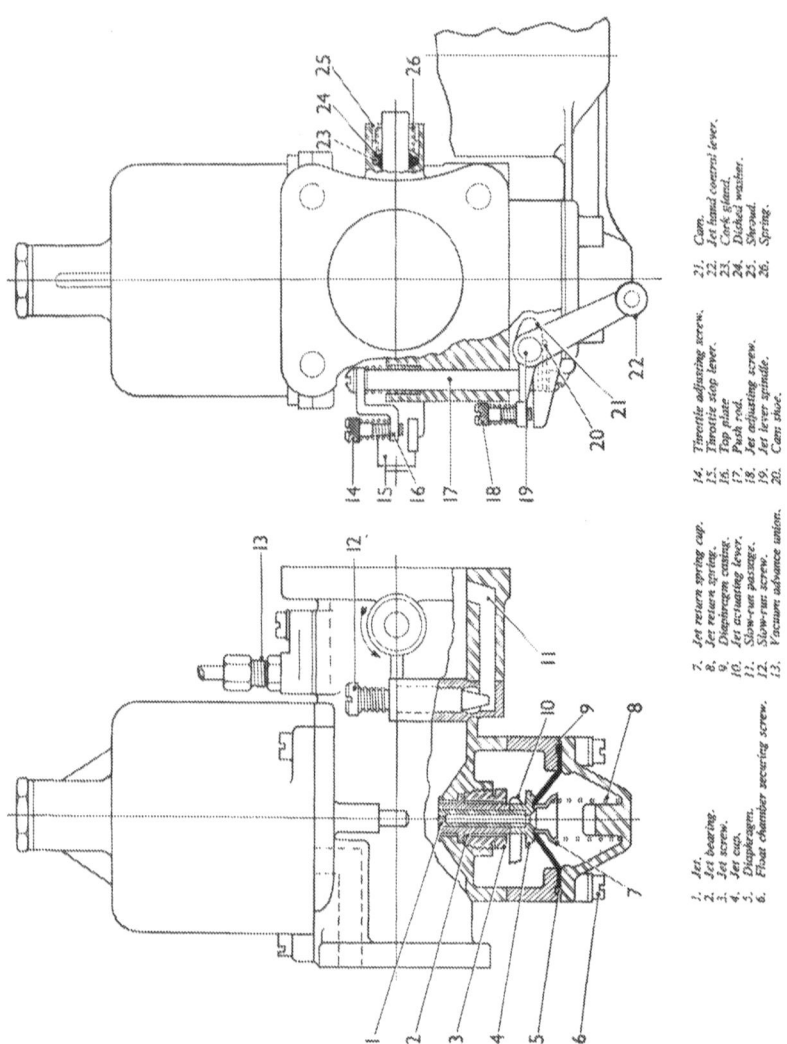

1. Jet.
2. Jet bearing.
3. Jet screw.
4. Jet cups.
5. Diaphragm.
6. Float chamber securing screw.
7. Jet return spring cup.
8. Jet return spring.
9. Diaphragm casing.
10. Jet actuating lever.
11. Slow-run passage.
12. Slow-run screw.
13. Vacuum advance union.
14. Throttle adjusting screw.
15. Throttle stop lever.
16. Top plate.
17. Push rod.
18. Jet actuating screw.
19. Jet lever spindle.
20. Cam shoe.
21. Cam.
22. Jet hand control lever.
23. Cork gland.
24. Dished washer.
25. Shroud.
26. Spring.

Throttle and Jet Interconnection

The throttle and jet interconnection mechanism is operated by a cam (21) mounted on the jet lever spindle (19), the whole being housed in the diaphragm casing (9). The cam (2) on being rotated by means of the jet hand control lever (22) actuates the cam shoe (20), thereby causing vertical movement of the push-rod (17). To the top of this push-rod is attached the top plate (16), which is fitted with an adjusting screw making contact with the throttle stop lever (15).

It will be seen that angular movement of the jet hand control lever (22) will turn the jet lever spindle (19) and, therefore, the jet actuating lever (10) controls the jet cup (4) and the jet (1). The cam controls the cam shoe (20), push-rod (17), top plate (16) and the throttle. Suitable setting of the two adjustments screws (14) and (18) will give any desired combination of mixture enrichment and throttle opening.

Vacuum Controlled Ignition and Economizer Ports
The connection to the vacuum ignition control is made at the top of the carburetor instead of underneath or at the side, as with the older type.

Throttle Spindle Glands
Provision is made for the use of throttle spindle glands consisting of the cork gland itself (23), a dished retaining washer (24), a spring (26) and a shroud (25). This assembly should not require servicing and can only be removed by dismantling the throttle spindle and disc.

Idling
The H.D. carburetor idles on the main jet, the mixture, passing under the throttle disc, is conducted along the passage-way (11) connecting the choke space to the other side of the throttle disc. The quantity of mixture passing through the passage-way (11) and, therefore, the idling speed of the engine, is controlled by the "slow-run" valve (12), the quality, or relative richness of the mixture, being determined by the jet adjusting screw (18). It follows that when idling, once the engine has reached its running temperature, the throttle remains completely closed against the bore of the carburetor; for fast idle, when the engine is cold, it continues to be partially open, the mixture passing under the throttle disc as well as along the passage-way (11).

Centering the Jet
This is carried out in much the same way as on the standard type carburetor, except that the float-chamber must be removed and the jet held in the uppermost position by hand, the jet adjusting screw (18) having first been undone sufficiently to allow the jet cup (4) to make contact with the jet bearing (2), with a distinct clearance between the jet adjusting screw (18) and its abutment. It is important to keep the diaphragm and therefore the jet in the same radial position, in relation to the carburetor body and jet casing throughout this operation, as the jet orifice is not necessarily concentric with its outside diameter, and turning might cause decentralization. The simplest way to do this is to mark one of the diaphragm and corresponding jet screw casing holes with a soft pencil.

Adjustment
The adjustment of the H.D. carburetor is extremely simple. Whereas with the older type the jet was controlled by a nut, it is now set by a screw (18), and whereas the engine speed was determined by adjustment of the throttle, it is now controlled by the "slow-run"

valve (12). To enrich the mixture the screw (18) should be screwed in, and to increase the idling speed the "slow-run" valve (12) should be unscrewed.

The adjustment procedure is as follows:

1 — Run the engine until its normal operating temperature is reached.

2 — Disconnect the interconnecting rod between the jet actuating levers.

3 — The throttle stop screws on each carburetor must be undone so that they are clear of the stops. This ensures that the throttles are fully closed.

4 — Screw the slow running valve screw right down on each instrument and then unscrew them 2¼ turns.

5 — If the engine runs too fast when this has been done, screw in both slow running screws a little at a time until even idling is achieved.

6 — Set the mixture strength by means of the jet lever adjusting screws.

7 — The correctness of this setting can be checked by raising the suction piston with a small screwdriver, or the piston lifting pin, to the extent of 1/32 inch (1 mm.). This should cause a very slight momentary increase in the engine speed without impairing the evenness of the running in any way. If this operation has the effect of stopping the engine it is an indication that the mixture setting is too weak.

If an appreciable speed increase occurs and continues to occur when the piston is raised as much as ¼ inch (6 mm.) it is an indication that the mixture is too rich.

8 — The interconnecting rod should now be refitted taking care not to alter the positions of the jet actuating levers. It may be necessary to adjust its length.

9 — With the foregoing adjustments complete, it is only necessary to reset the amount of automatic throttle opening which should occur when the choke is operated. Do this by screwing down the throttle stop screw on each carburetor an equal amount until a fast idle is obtained with approximately half choke. This will give the necessary cold start throttle opening. After this is done, ensure that when the choke is fully released the throttles are closed.

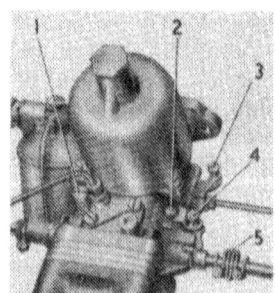

1. Slow-run valve. 2. Top plate securing screw. 3. Jet adjusting screw. 4. Throttle stop lever screw. 5. Throttle shaft interconnection clip.

Defects in Operation

Since the jet of the H.D. carburetor is fed through its center and has no glands, leakage can only be caused by an insecure fit of the jet cup, an imperfect seal of the diaphragm, either at its outer edge, where it is compressed between the float-chamber and the diaphragm casing, or at its inner edge, where it is fitted to the jet, or by fracture of the diaphragm. Leakage at the outer edge may be cured by tightening the float-chamber securing screws (6) but fracture, or leaking at the inner edge will probably call for a new jet assembly.

The jet may also stick, either up or down, due to dirt between it and its bearing (2), or due to corrosion. The cure is to remove the parts by undoing the jet screw (3), clean and refit.

CARBURETOR REMOVAL

To remove the carburetors from the inlet manifold proceed as follows:

1 — Disconnect the fuel feed pipe from the union on the forward carburetor.

2 — Remove the air cleaners from the flanges.

3 — The float chamber overflow pipes must be removed.

4 — Release the choke wire from the jet hand control lever on the rear carburetor, and from the clamping bracket.

5 — Disconnect the throttle valve rod from the lever on the carburetor throttle shaft.

6 — Disconnect the acelerator link rod from the carburetor throttle shaft.

7 — Release the vacuum advance pipe from its union on the rear carburetor.

8 — Remove the four nuts from each carburetor flange and pull the units off the studs together, after taking the bracket, which locates the rear extension of the throttle shaft, off the car bulkhead. If only one carburetor is to be removed the interconnecting fuel feed pipe must be released. In this case it is also necessary to split the throttle shaft at the center connecting clip. The connecting rod for the jet hand control levers must also be released by taking out the clevis pins from the yokes.

S.U. FUEL PUMP TYPE LCS

The type LCS fuel pump as fitted to later series cars consists of three main assemblies, body, magnet assembly (coil housing assembly., and the contact breaker. This pump is consistent in description with the type HP pump given above, with the exception of the body which is an aluminum die-casting with two identical cover plates each secured by 6, 2 BA screws. Removal of the lower cover plate gives access to the fuel filter and the top cover plate access to the valve cage and with this exception the servicing, tracing pump troubles and maintenance are the same as those given for the HP pump.

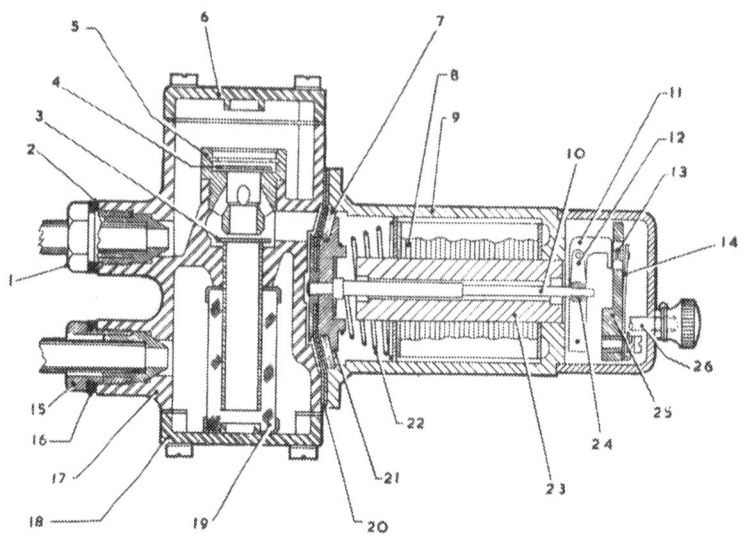

The type LCS fuel pump with the inlet and outlet connections shown 90° out of position for clarity.

1. Outlet union.
2. Rubber ring.
3. Inlet valve.
4. Outlet valve.
5. Outlet valve cage.
6. Top cover plate.
7. Spherical rollers.
8. Magnet coil.
9. Iron coil housing.
10. Bronze rod.
11. Outer rocker.
12. Inner rocker.
13. Tungsten points.
14. Spring blade.
15. Inlet union.
16. Rubber ring.
17. Body.
18. Lower cover plate.
19. Filter.
20. Diaphragm.
21. Armature.
22. Armature spring.
23. Magnet core.
24. Trunnion.
25. Bakelite moulding.
26. Terminal screw.

THERMO-CARBURETOR
(Fitted from Engine No. 29D/U/H2864)

The enrichment apparatus to assist cold starting is, in effect, an auxiliary carburation system. The main body casting (36) containing a solenoid-operated valve and fuel metering system is attached by means of a ducted mounting arm to the base of the main carburetor fuel inlet.

The auxiliary carburetor forms, therefore, a separate unit additional to the normal float-chamber, but drawing its fuel supply directly from it. Fuel is supplied to the base of the jet (29) which is obstructed to a greater or lesser degree by the tapered slidable needle (25).

When the device is in action air is drawn from the atmosphere through the air intake (26) and thence through the passage (28), being mixed with fuel as it passes the jet (29). The mixture is thence carried upwards past the shank of the needle (25) through the passage (37) and so past the aperture provided between the valve (33) and its seating (35). From here it passes directly to the induction manifold through the external feed pipe shown.

The device is brought into action by energizing the winding of the solenoid (31) from the terminal screws (30). The centrally located iron core (32) is thus raised magnetically, carrying with it the ball-jointed disc valve (33) against the load of the small conical spring (34) and thus uncovering the aperture provided by the seating (35).

FUEL SYSTEM

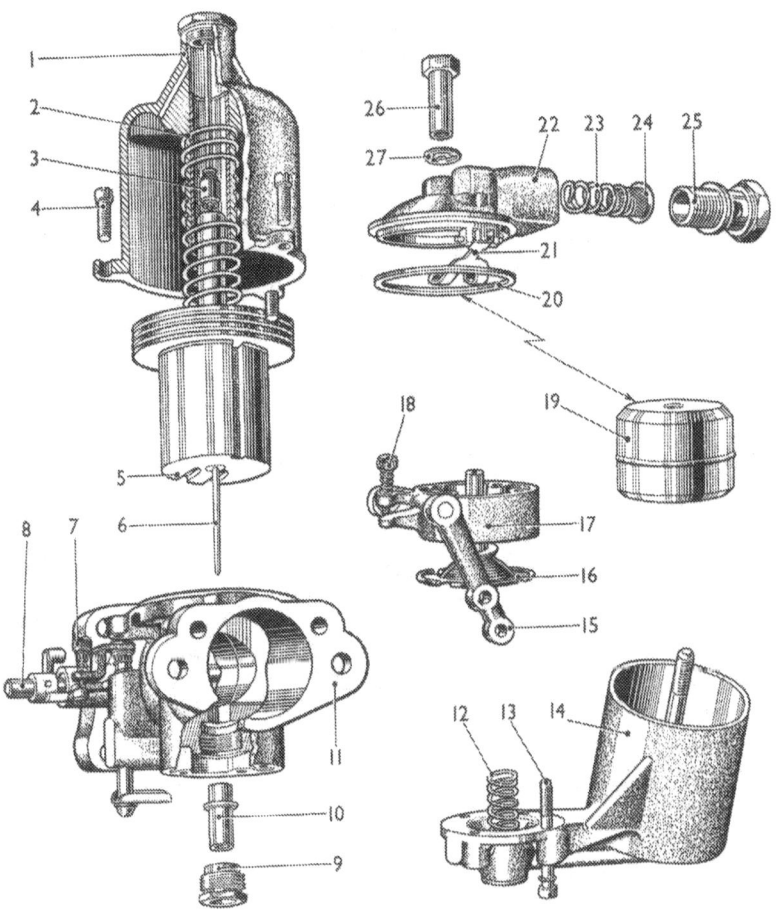

1. Suction chamber.
2. Piston spring.
3. Hydraulic damper.
4. Suction chamber screw.
5. Piston.
6. Needle.
7. Throttle stop lever adjusting screw.
8. Throttle spindle.
9. Jet screw.
10. Jet bearing.
11. Carburetter body.
12. Jet return spring.
13. Float chamber securing screw.
14. Float chamber.
15. Jet hand control lever.
16. Jet and diaphragm.
17. Diaphragm casing.
18. Jet adjusting screw.
19. Float.
20. Cover joint washer.
21. Float lever.
22. Float chamber cover.
23. Filter spring.
24. Filter.
25. Inlet union.
26. Float chamber cover screw.
27. Fibre washer.

In this installation item 15 is at the rear of the carburetter.

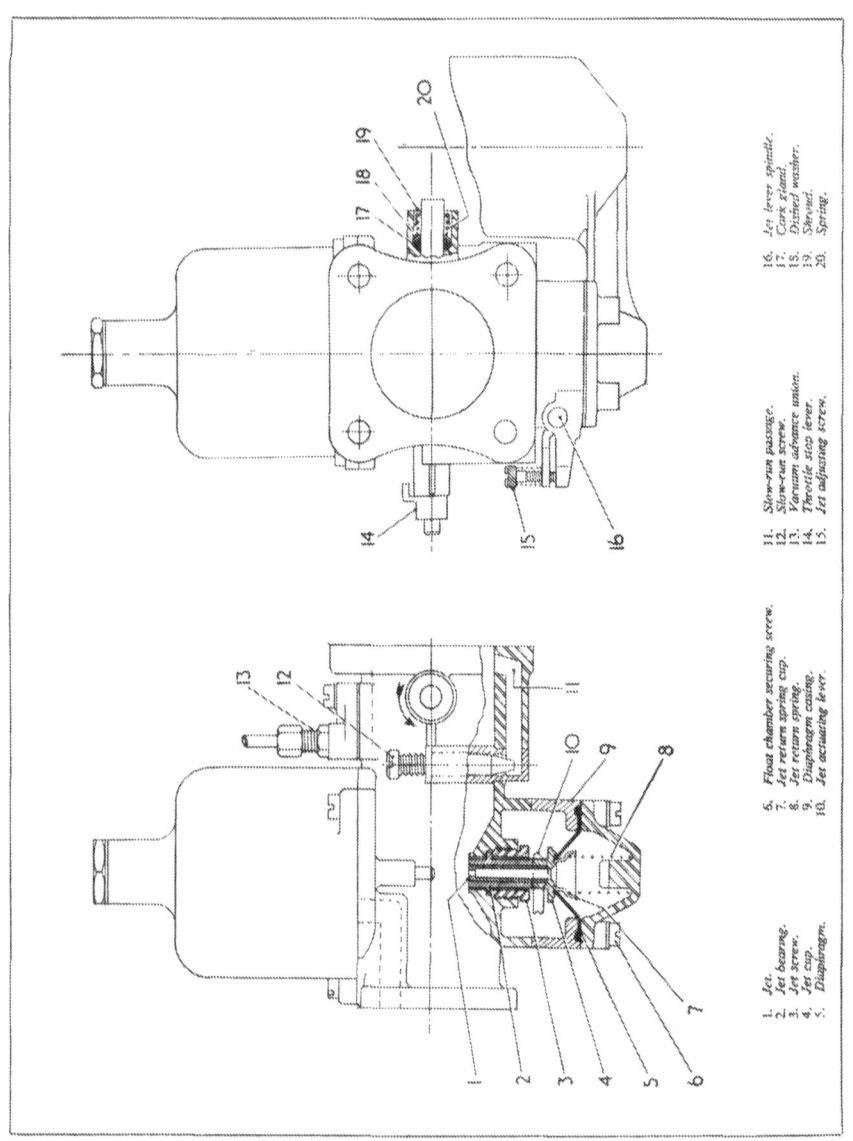

Considering the function of the slidable needle (25), it will be seen that this is loaded upwards in its open position by means of the slight compression spring (24) which abuts against a disc (23), attached to the shank of the needle. The needle continues upwards through the vertically adjustable stop (22) in which it is slidably mounted and it finally terminates in an enlarged head.

Depression within the space surrounding the spring (24) is directly derived from that prevailing in the induction tract, and this exerts a downward force upon the disc (23), which is provided with an adequate clearance with its surrounding bore. This tends to overcome the load of the spring (24) and to move the needle downwards, thus increasing the obstruction afforded by the tapered section which enters the jet (29).

The purpose of this device is to provide two widely different degrees of enrichment, the one corresponding to idling or light cruising conditions and the other to conditions of open throttle or full-power operation. In effect, under the former conditions the high induction depression prevailing will cause the disc (23) to be drawn downwards, drawing the tapered needle into the jet (29), while under the latter, the lower depression existing in the induction tract will permit the collar to maintain its upward position with the needle withdrawn from the jet. The only adjustment provided is the needle stop screw (22) which limits the degree of movement provided for the needle assembly.

The size and degree of taper of the lower end of the needle (25), the diameter of the disc (23), and the load provided by the spring (24) are not adjustable.

The solenoid (31) is energized by means of a thermostatically operated switch housed within the cylinder head water jacket. This is arranged to bring the apparatus into action at temperatures below 86-95°F. (30-35°C.).

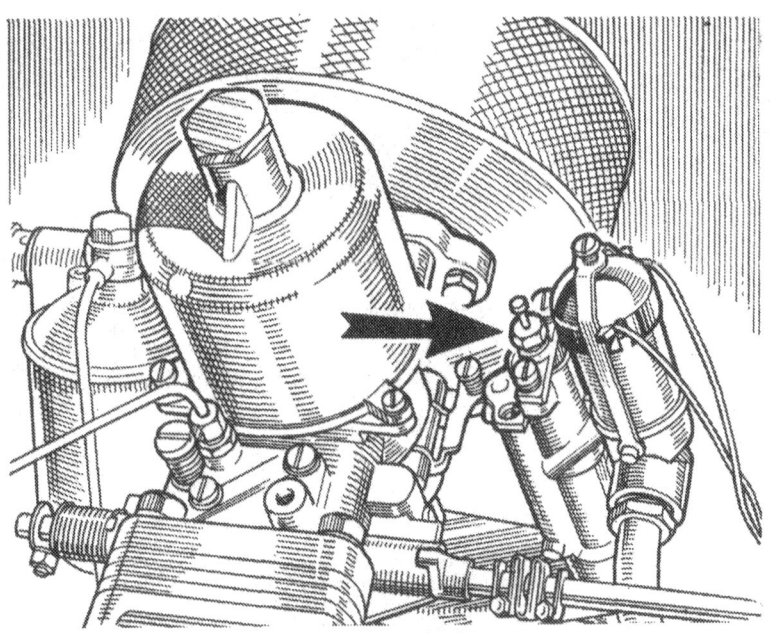

The needle stop screw indicated by the arrow adjusts the mixture strength of the thermo-carburetter.

Centering the Jet

Adjustment of the auxiliary carburetor is confined to the stop screw which limits the downwards movement of the needle. Anti-clockwise rotation of the stop screw will raise the needle and increase the mixture strength, while rotation in the opposite direction will have the opposite effect.

FUEL SYSTEM

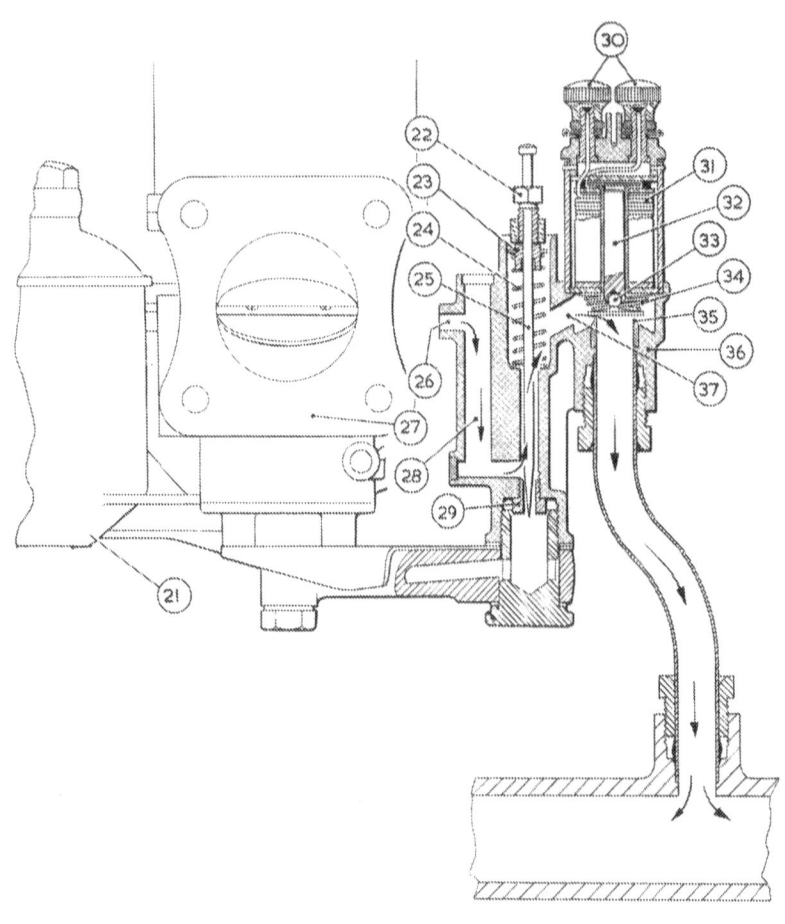

21. *Float chamber.*
22. *Stop screw.*
23. *Disc.*
24. *Spring.*
25. *Needle.*
26. *Air intake.*
27. *Carburetter body.*
28. *Air passage.*
29. *Jet.*
30. *Terminals.*
31. *Solenoid.*
32. *Core.*
33. *Valve.*
34. *Conical spring.*
35. *Valve seating.*
36. *Body casting.*
37. *Passage.*

An approximate guide to its correct adjustment is provided by energizing the solenoid when the engine has already attained its normal running temperature. The stop screw should then be so adjusted that the mixture is distinctly although not excessively rich, that is to say, until the exhaust gases are seen to be discernibly black in color, but just short of the point where the engine commences to run with noticeable irregularity.

In order to energize the solenoid under conditions when the thermostatic switch will normally have broken the circuit, it is merely necessary to short-circuit the terminal of the thermostatic switch directly to ground or, by means of a separate wire, ground the solenoid terminal which is connected to the switch (Blue—White Wire).

NOTE—**Should difficulty be experienced when starting from cold on the next occasion, unscrew the stop screw (22) one or two flats only.**

MODIFIED STARTING JET NEEDLE SPRING

To improve starting characteristics, the green spring (24), fitted to the starting jet needle has been changed to a blue spring (Part No. AUC1041) commencing at engine No. 3664. It is recommended that all engines between 2864 and 3664 be checked and that the blue spring be fitted if it is not already incorporated.

CLUTCH

The clutch is a Borg & Beck single dry-plate-type operated hydraulically. A steel cover bolted to the flywheel encloses the driven plate, the pressure plate, the pressure springs, and the release levers. The driven plate, to which the friction linings are riveted, incorporates springs assembled around the hub to absorb power shocks and torsional vibration. The pressure springs force the pressure plate against the friction linings, gripping the driven plate between the pressure plate and the engine flywheel. When the clutch pedal is depressed, the release bearing is moved forward against the release plate which bears against the three levers. Each release lever is pivoted on a floating pin, which remains stationary in the lever and rolls across a short, flat portion of the enlarged hole in the eyebolt. The outer ends of the eyebolts extend through holes in the clutch cover and are fitted with adjusting nuts, by means of which each lever is located and locked in position. The outer or shorter ends of the release levers engage the pressure plate lugs by means of struts which provide knife-edge contact between the outer ends of the levers and the pressure plate lugs, so eliminating friction at this point. Pressure applied by the release bearing causes the pressure plate to be pulled away from the driven plate, compressing the pressure springs which are assembled between the pressure plate and the clutch cover. As the friction linings wear, the pressure plate moves closer to the flywheel face and the outer or shorter ends of the release levers follow. This causes the inner or longer ends of the levers to travel farther towards the gearbox and decreases the cleanrance between the release lever plate and the release bearing. This is automatically compensated unless the master cylinder has been disturbed.

When the clutch pedal is depressed, fluid pressure is transmitted through the master cylinder to the slave cylinder, which is mounted on the clutch housing, moving the slave cylinder piston, and push rod. As the push-rod is connected to the lower arm of the clutch withdrawal lever, thereby the clutch is released. The push rod is non-adjustable.

Owing to the hydraulic design of the clutch controls no adjustment is necessary to the clutch pedal.

CLUTCH ASSEMBLY
To Remove
1 — Remove the gearbox.

2 — Slacken the clutch cover screws a turn at a time by diagonal selection until the spring pressure is relieved, when the screws can be taken out and the clutch removed.

To Replace
Before installing the clutch assembly the engine flywheel should be checked for misalignment. To install the clutch proceed as follows:

1 — Hold the clutch cover assembly and driven plate on the fly-

CLUTCH

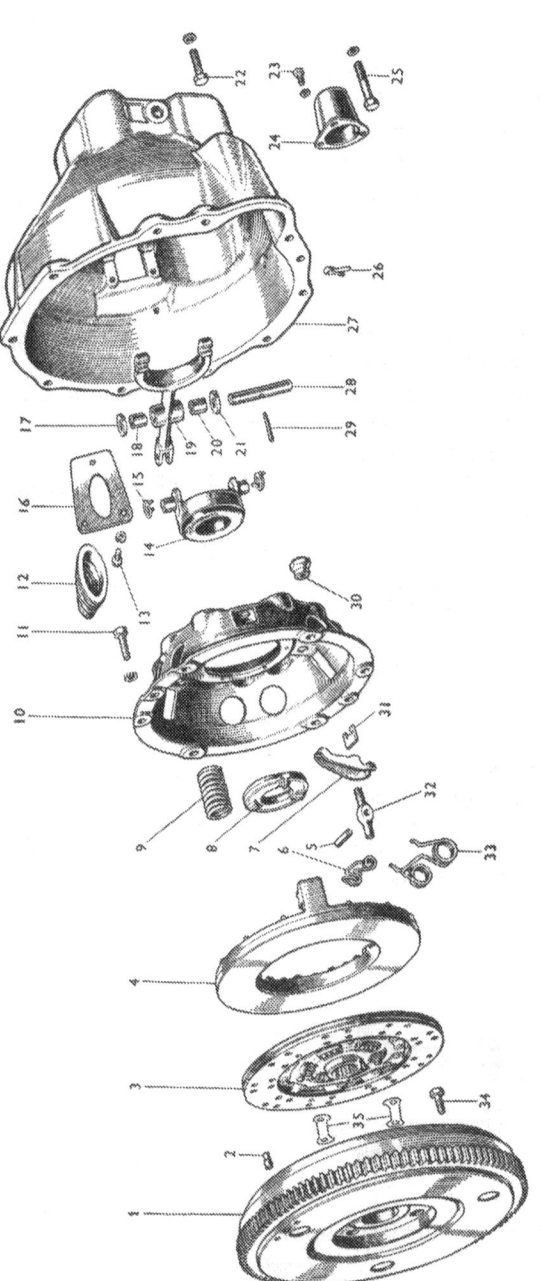

The clutch exploded.

1. Flywheel.
2. Locating peg.
3. Clutch plate with lining.
4. Pressure plate.
5. Release lever pin.
6. Release lever retainer.
7. Release lever.
8. Release lever plate.
9. Pressure plate spring.
10. Clutch cover.
11. Cover setpin.
12. Fork and lever seal.
13. Retaining plate screw.
14. Release bearing.
15. Release bearing retainer spring.
16. Seal retaining plate.
17. Fork and lever thrust washer.
18. Fork and lever shaft bush.
19. Clutch fork and lever.
20. Fork and lever shaft bush.
21. Fork and lever thrust washer.
22. Clutch to gearbox setpin.
23. Starter cover screw.
24. Cover.
25. Clutch to gearbox setpin.
26. Split pin for drain hole.
27. Clutch housing.
28. Fork and lever shaft.
29. Taper pin.
30. Eye bolt nut.
31. Release lever strut.
32. Eye bolt.
33. Anti-rattle spring.
34. Flywheel to crankshaft bolt.
35. Lockwashers.

wheel and screw in the cover securing bolts finger-tight. Note that the splines in the hub of the driven plate are chamfered at one end to permit ready entry of the first motion shaft splines. The longer side of the driven plate hub, with the chamfered splines, should be toward the rear.

2 — Insert a pilot shaft or an aligning arbor (No. 18G 79), through the clutch cover and driven plate hub so that the pilot enters the spigot bearing in the rear end of the engine crankshaft. This will centralize the driven plate.

3 — Tighten the clutch cover securing bolts a turn at a time in diagonal sequence to avoid distorting the cover.

4 — Remove the pilot shaft or aligning arbor.

5 — Install the gearbox.

CLUTCH PEDAL
To Remove

1 — The clutch and brake pedal linkages are mounted in a common bracket and thus have to be released as a unit.

2 — Inside the car disconnect the clutch and brake cylinder levers from their master cylinder push rods by removing the clevis pins.

3 — Working under the bonnet unscrew the six securing setpins sufficiently to allow the clutch and brake pedal linkage bracket to be withdrawn from inside the car.

4 — Release the clutch and brake pedal return springs.

5 — Unscrew the nut securing the clutch and brake pedal shaft and withdraw the shaft to release the clutch and brake pedal levers together with their spacer.

6 — Inspect the lever bushes for wear and renew if necessary. Replacement is the reverse of the procedure.

MASTER CYLINDER

The master cylinder consists of an alloy body with a polished finish bore, and reservoir with cap. The innner assembly is made up of the push rod, dished washer, circlip, plunger, plunger seal, spring thimble, plunger return spring, valve spacer, spring washer, valve stem and valve seal. The open end of the cylinder is protected by a rubber dust cover.

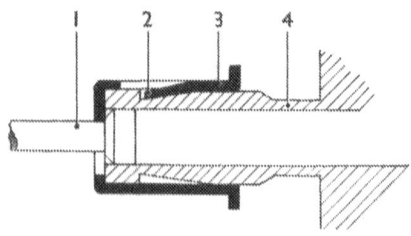

Diagrammatic section of master cylinder.

1. Valve stem.
2. Thimble leaf.
3. Thimble.
4. Plunger.

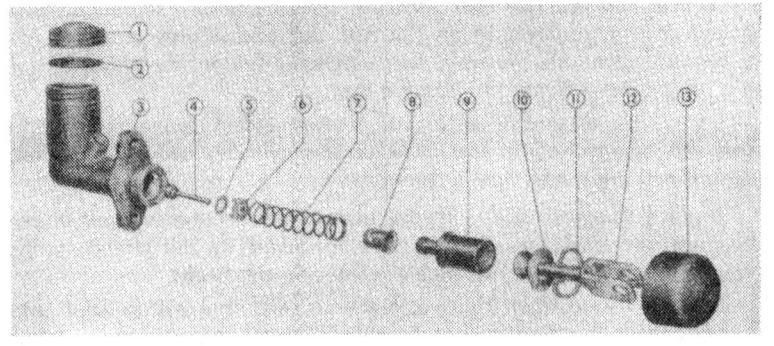

Components of master cylinder and reservoir.

1. Filler cap.
2. Washer.
3. Master cylinder.
4. Valve stem.
5. Spring washer.
6. Valve spacer.
7. Return spring.
8. Thimble.
9. Plunger.
10. Dished washer.
11. Circlip.
12. Fork.
13. Dust cover.

Dismantling the Clutch Master Cylinder

1 — Release the master cylinder push rod from the clutch pedal.

2 — Disconnect the pressure pipe union from the cylinder and remove the securing bolts, then the master cylinder and fluid reservoir may be withdrawn complete from the car.

3 — Remove the filler cap and drain out the fluid. Pull back the rubber dust cover and remove the circlip with a pair of long nosed pliers. The push rod and dished washer can then be removed.

4 — When the push rod has been removed the plunger with seal attached will be exposed; remove the plunger assembly complete. The assembly can be separated by lifting the thimble leaf over the shouldered end of the plunger.

5 — Depress the plunger return spring allowing the valve stem to slide through the elongated hole of the thimble thus releasing the tension on the spring.

6 — Remove the thimble, spring and valve complete.

7 — Detach the valve spacer, taking care not to lose the spacer spring washer which is located under the valve head. Remove the seal.

8 — Examine all parts, especially the seals, for wear or distortion and replace with new parts where necessary.

Assembling the Clutch Master Cylinder

1 — Replace the valve seal so that the flat side is correctly seated on the valve head.

2 — The spring washer should then be located with the dome side against the underside of the valve head, and held in position by the valve spacer, the legs of which face towards the valve seal.

3 — Replace the plunger return spring centrally on the spacer, insert the thimble into the spring and depress until the valve stem engages through the elongated hole of the thimble, making sure the stem is correctly located in the center of the thimble. Check that the spring is still central on the spacer.

4 — Refit a new plunger seal with the flat of the seal seated against the face of the plunger. Insert the reduced end of the plunger into the thimble until the thimble leaf engages under the shoulder of the plunger. Press home the thimble leaf.

5 — Smear the assembly with the recommended brake fluid, and insert the assembly into the bore of the cylinder valve, end first, easing the plunger seal lips in the bore.

6 — Replace the push rod with the dished side of the washer under the spherical head, into the cylinder followed by the circlip which engages into the groove machined in the cylinder body.

7 — Replace the rubber dust cover and refit the whole unit into its aperture in the scuttle, not forgetting to fit the packing washer first. Secure the unit by means of the two bolts on the flange and refit the pressure pipe union into the cylinder.

8 — Reconnect the push rod fork with its corresponding hole in the clutch pedal lever, securing it with the circlip.

9 — Bleed the hydraulic system.

SLAVE CYLINDER

The cylinder is bolted to the clutch housing and comprises a piston, rubber cap, cup filler, spring, push-rod and bleeder screw. Fluid from the master cylinder is delivered through a flexible hose leading from a union in a bracket on the longitudinal member.

To Remove

1 — Place a receptacle to catch the fluid and remove the flexible hose from the slave cylinder. Note that the thicker washer on the hose connection is nearest the cylinder.

2 — Remove the split pin and clevis pin from the clutch withdrawal lever jaw end, thus freeing the slave cylinder push rod.

3 — Remove the two bolts and spring washers securing the cylinder to the clutch housing.

To Dismantle

1 — Remove all dirt from the outside of the cylinder.

2 — Remove the rubber dust cap from the bleed nipple, attach a bleed tube, open the bleed screw three-quarters of a turn and pump the clutch pedal until all the fluid has been drained into a clean container.

3 — Unscrew the pressure pipe union at the cylinder and remove the setpins from the flange. The slave cylinder can now be removed.

4 — Remove the rubber cover and if an air line is available, blow out the piston and seal. The spring can also be removed.

5 — Clean the slave cylinder components, **using only hydraulic fluid or alcohol**. The main casting may be cleaned with any of the normal cleaning fluids, but all traces of the cleaning fluid must be dried out.

6 — Dry off and examine all rubber components and renew them if they are swollen, distorted or split. If there is any doubt at all as to their condition they must be renewed.

FAULT DIAGNOSIS

Symptom	No.	Possible Fault
(a) Drag or Spin	1 2 3 4 5 6 7 8 9 10	Oil or grease on driven plate linings Bent engine backplate Misalignment between engine and first motion shaft Leaking operating cylinder, pipe line or air in system Driven plate hub binding on first motion shaft splines First motion shaft binding on its spigot bush Distorted clutch plate Warped or damaged pressure plate or clutch cover Broken clutch plate linings Dirt or foreign matter in clutch
(b) Fierceness or Snatch	1 2	Check 1, 2 and 3 in (a) Check 4 in (a) Worn clutch linings
(c) Slip	1 2	Check 1, 2 and 3 in (a) Check 1 in (b) Weak thrust springs Weak anti-rattle springs
(d) Judder	1 2 3 4 5 6 7 8 9	Check 1, 2 and 3 in (a) Pressure plate out of parallel with flywheel face Friction facing contact area not evenly distributed Bent first motion shaft Buckled driven plate Faulty engine or gearbox rubber mountings Worn shackles Weak rear springs Propeller shaft bolts loose Loose rear spring clips
(e) Rattle	1 2 3 4 5	Check 3 in (d) Damaged driven plate, i.e. broken springs, etc. Worn parts of release mechanism Excessive transmission backlash Wear in transmission bearings Release bearing loose on fork
(f) Tick or Knock	1 2 3 4 5	Worn first motion shaft bush Badly worn centre plate hub splines Out of line thrust plate Faulty bendix drive on starter Loose flywheel
(g) Driven Plate Fracture	1	Check 2 and 3 in (a) Drag and metal fatigue due to hanging gearbox in driven plate

7 — Inspect the piston and cylinder bore for wear and scores, and renew them as necessary.

Assembling the Slave Cylinder

1 — Place the seal into the stem of the piston, with the back of the seal against the piston.

2 — Replace the springs with the small end on the stem, smear well with the recommended fluid and insert into the cylinder.

3 — Replace the rubber dust cover and mount the cylinder in position, making sure the push rod enters the hole in the rubber boot.

To Replace

1 — Secure the cylinder to the clutch housing, and screw in the pipe union.

2 — Bleed the clutch hydraulic system.

BLEEDING THE CLUTCH SYSTEM

1 — Remove the bleed screw dust cap at the slave cylinder, open the bleed screw approximately three-quarters of a turn and attach a tube immersing the open end into a clean receptacle containing a small amount of brake fluid.

2 — Fill the master cylinder reservoir with the recommended fluid and by using slow, full strokes, pump the clutch pedal until the fluid entering the container is free from air bubbles.

3 — On a down stroke of the pedal, screw up the bleed screw, remove the bleed tube and replace the dust cap.

GEARBOX

The gearbox has four forward speeds and one reverse, and synchromesh is incorporated on second, third and top gears.

Top gear is a direct drive; third and second are in constant mesh; first and reverse are obtained by sliding spur pinions.

The gearbox oil level should be checked by the dipstick every 1,000 miles (1500 km.) and topped up if necessary.

The filler plug, which incorporates the dipstick, is located beneath a rubber cover, and is accessible when the floor mat and rubber cover have been raised.

After the first 500 miles (800 km.) the gearbox, and overdrive if fitted, should be drained and refilled with fresh oil. This procedure should be repeated afterwards every 6,000 miles (96000 km.).

Drain plugs are provided in the base of the gearbox and overdrive. Ensure that the hollow center of the gearbox drain plug is kept clean. Do not forget to replace the plugs after draining.

The capacity of the gearbox is given in **"General Data"**.

REMOVAL AND REPLACEMENT

1 — Turn the battery master switch, which is situated inside the luggage compartment, to the "off" position.

2 — Inside the car remove the seat cushions and release the clips securing the padded arm rest to the central tunnel.

3 — Unclip and roll back the carpet over the short gearbox tunnel to expose the twelve screws securing the tunnel to the body of the car. Unscrew the setscrews and remove the tunnel and its carpeting.

4 — Unscrew the six setscrews, three on either side, which secure the carpet covered bulkhead and remove the bulkhead.

5 — Using a suitable tool tap back the locking washer on the propeller shaft flange bolts and remove the bolts.

6 — Unscrew the four setpins from the gearbox mounting brackets, also unscrew the speedometer cable at its connection to the gearbox.

Components of the Gearbox.

1. Synchromesh sleeve.
2. Baulking ring.
3. Synchronizer spring.
4. Synchronizer ball.
5. 3rd and 4th speed synchronizer.
6. Baulking ring.
7. Locking plate.
8. Needle rollers.
9. Third speed gear.
10. Second speed gear.
11. Needle rollers.
12. Gear washer.
13. Locking plate.
14. Baulking ring.
15. 2nd speed synchronizer.
16. First speed gear.
17. Plunger spring.
18. Gear plunger.
19. Main shaft.
20. Thrust plate.
21. Thrust washer.
22. Needle rollers.
23. Washer, roller.
24. Spacer, roller.
25. Laygear.
26. Washer.
27. Thrust plate.
28. Layshaft.
29. Interlocking balls.
30. Selector ball and spring.
31. Bearing nut.
32. Bearing nut lockwasher.
33. Bearing spring plate.
34. Bearing plate.
35. Bearing circlip.
36. First motion shaft bearing.
37. First motion shaft.
38. Needle rollers.
39. Joint washer.
40. Side cover dowel.
41. Drain plug.
42. Gearbox casing.
43. Bearing housing.
44. Locating peg.
45. Joint washer.
46. Gear lever.
47. Nut and washer.
48. Cup.
49. Rubber washer (thick).
50. Steel washer.
51. Rubber washer (thin).
52. Distance piece.
53. Side cover.
54. Washer.
55. Gear lever locating screw.
56. Rubber dust covers.
57. 1st and 2nd speed fork.
58. Screw for fork.
59. 3rd and 4th speed fork rod.
60. 1st and 2nd speed fork rod.
61. Interlocking pin and rivet.
62. Reverse fork rod.
63. 3rd and 4th speed fork.
64. Reverse shaft.
65. Bush.
66. Reverse gear.
67. Locking screw.
68. Selector plunger.
69. Selector plunger spring.
70. Detent plunger.
71. Detent plunger spring.
72. Reverse fork.
73. Control shaft locating screw.
74. Locking washer.
75. Control shaft.
76. Control lever.

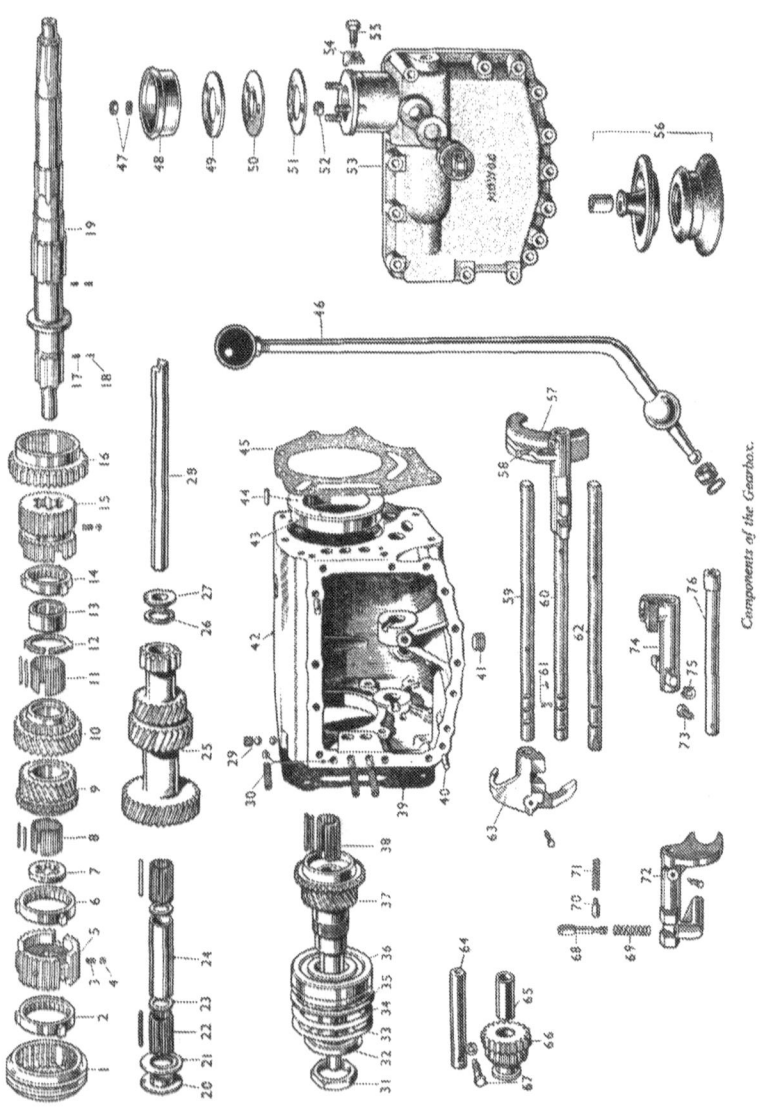

Note—When an overdrive gearbox is fitted it will also be necessary to unclip the cable to the gearbox switch and release it at its terminal on the switch.

7 — Working beneath the vehicle remove setpins (1) and unscrew the nuts (2) and (3) to release the stabilizer bar.

8 — Detach the clutch slave cylinder from the gearbox bell housing by removing the two securing setpins. The slave cylinder push rod is released from the clutch operating lever by the removal of the securing clevis pin.

9 — Remove the starter motor.

10 — Place suitable supports underneath the gearbox bell housing and engine sump, and unscrew the nuts, bolts and setpins securing the bell housing to the engine backplate.

11 — Withdraw the gearbox first motion shaft from the flywheel bearing and clutch by gently easing the gearbox rearwards.

If the unit does not detach itself readily it will be necessary to raise the rear of the engine.

2 — The replacement of the gearbox is a reversal of the removal procedure.

DISMANTLING

1 — Remove the dipstick. Unscrew the breather from the overdrive unit, if fitted. Drain the oil from the gearbox and overdrive by removing the drain plug beneath each unit.

2 — Unscrew the speedometer drive from the right-hand side of the rear extension.

3 — Unscrew the seven short and one long bolt and remove the clutch housing.

4 — Remove the three nuts threaded on studs mounted on the gear lever cup. With the removal of these nuts the cup may be withdrawn together with the three washers and three distance pieces located on the studs.

5 — Withdraw the gear lever from the gearbox.

6 — Unscrew the thirteen bolts securing the side cover to the gearbox housing and remove the cover; there are two dowels locating the cover. Take care not to lose the three selector balls and springs which will be released as the cover is withdrawn.

7 — Unscrew the eight bolts and remove the rear extension.

Note—For models fitted with overdrive.
Once the overdrive unit has been separated from the gearbox, the removal of the adaptor plate is accomplished by unscrewing the eight setpins mounted in the recess in the adapter plate.

The overdrive pump cam should slide freely along the third motion shaft thus giving access to the circlip holding the distance piece to the rear adapter plate. Remove the circlip and slide the distance piece off the shaft. The adapter plate should now pull away from the gearbox, together with the rear main bearing. It may be necessary for one operator to hold the gearbox vertically by the adapter plate while a second operator taps the third motion shaft until the ball race in the adapter plate is free of the shaft.

8 — Cut the locking wires and unscrew the fork retaining screws. Remove the shifter shafts and forks in the following order:
(a) The reverse shaft and fork together with its selector and detent plungers and springs.
(b) Top gear shifter shaft only.
(c) First and second shaft and fork.
(d) Top gear fork.

Take care not to lose the two interlock balls, normally located one at each side of the center shifter shaft, which will be released when the shaft is removed.

9 — Unscrew the reverse shaft locating screw and push out the shaft; lift the gear from the box.

10 — Tap out the layshaft and allow the gear to rest in the bottom of the box.

11 — Withdraw the first motion shaft assembly; note that there are 16 spigot rollers.

12 — Withdraw the mainshaft rearwards.

13 — Lift out the layshaft gear and thrust washers.

DISMANTLING THE MAINSHAFT

1 — Slide the top and third gear hub and interceptors from the forward end.

2 — Depress the plunger locating the third gear locking plate, rotate the plate to line up the splines and slide it from the shaft. Extract the plunger and spring, and slide off the third speed gear and its 32 rollers.

3 — Unscrew the main shaft nut; remove the nut, locking washer, speedometer drive gear, bearing with housing and distance collar.

4 — Slide the first and second speed hub, second speed interceptor and first speed gear rearwards from the shaft; taking care to retain the balls and springs located in holes in the hub, disassemble hub with caution.

5 — Depress the second gear locking collar plunger and rotate the collar to line up the splines; slide the collar from the shaft and extract the two halves of the second gear washer, retaining the spring and plunger.

6 — Withdraw the second speed gear and its 33 rollers from the shaft.

7 — To dismantle the first motion shaft assembly, tap up the locking tab, unscrew the nut and remove the bearing.

NOTE—The method of dismantling and reassembling the overdrive gearbox is the same as that described for the standard gearbox, with the exception that no speedometer drive gear or locking washer and nut is fitted.

REASSEMBLY
Mainshaft

1 — Smear the shaft with grease and assemble the 33 second speed gear rollers; slide the second gear into position.

2 — Replace the plunger and spring. Fit the two halves of the second gear washer and slide the collar on to the splines. Depress the plunger and push the collar into position, locating the lugs of the washer in the cut-out of the collar; rotate the collar to bring the splines out of line.

3 — Replace the balls and springs in the second and first speed hub; depress the balls and slide the first speed gear on to the hub; refit the assembly to the shaft.

4 — Refit the bearing distance collar, the bearing and housing, the speedometer drive gear key and gear, locking washer and nut. Tighten the nut and tap over the locking washer.

5 — Fit the third gear and its 32 rollers to the shaft; replace the plunger and spring and the third speed locking plate; rotate the plate to bring the splines out of line.

6 — Fit the balls and springs to the top and third speed hub and slide the striking dog into position on the hub.

7 — Replace the hub, striking dog and interceptors on the shaft.

Assembling gear and synchronizer.
1. Gear.   2. Baulking ring.   3. Synchronizer.

Layshaft

1 — Fit the distance tube to the layshaft gear with a washer at each end of the tube.

2 — Smear the rollers with grease and position them in the gear. Place the thrust washers and plates in position at each end of the gear.

3 — To retain the rollers in position, a length of round bar of layshaft diameter and just long enough to hold the thrust washers and plates, should be inserted in the gear assembly.

4 — Place the gear in the box and allow it to rest at the bottom.

Gearbox

1 — Insert the mainshaft assembly from the rear of the box.

2 — Position the first motion shaft rollers and the first motion shaft assembly in the box.

3 — Lift the layshaft gear into position, locating the thrust washer tags in the grooves provided. Push the layshaft through the housing and gear, and withdraw the retaining bar as the shaft pushes it out of the gear. The cut-away portion of the shaft must be aligned to fit the groove in the bell housing provided to prevent the layshaft from turning.

4 — Refit the reverse gear and shaft and tighten the setscrew. Place the top gear shifter fork in the box. Replace the first and second gear shifter fork and shaft.

5 — Replace one interlock ball above the first and second shifter shaft and insert the top gear shifter shaft.

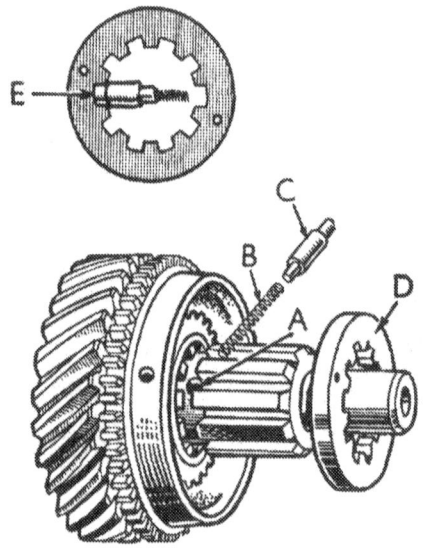

Securing the third motion shaft gears.
A. Hole for spring
B. Spring.
C. Location peg.
D. Locking washer.
E. Peg located in washer.

6 — Position the remaining interlock ball, holding it with grease and refit the reverse fork and shaft together with its selector and detent plungers and springs.

7 — Screw in the fork setscrews, tighten up and wire.

8 — Bolt the rear extension into position, using a new gasket if necessary. Note that the plain bearing plate is fitted against the bearing.

Note—For models fitted with overdrive:
Slide the the adapter plate, together with its bearing and paper joint washer, along the third motion shaft. Fit and tighten down the eight setpins securing the adapter plate to the gearbox.
Fit the distance piece which covers the space between the rear main bearing and the groove allocated for the circlip, and fix on the latter.
9 — Refit the selector balls to the holes in the gearbox housing and the springs in the holes in the side cover.
10 — The gear lever together with its cup, washers and distance pieces may now be attached to the side cover. Ensure that the ball of the lever makes a good fit with its mating socket.
11 — Refit the cover, fitting a new gasket as required. Observe that the top right-hand setpin is longer than the other twelve.
12 — Refit the clutch housing with plain bearing plate against the bearing.
Refit the speedometer drive, breather and dipstick.

MODIFIED GEARS

Commencing at engine number 11342, the gears were modified to increase their rigidity. In earlier versions of this modification the laygear was fitted with plain bushes, but this was later replaced by a layshaft assembly with needle roller bearings.
The modified gears are only interchangeable with earlier types in complete sets.

FAULT DIAGNOSIS

Symptom	No.	Possible Fault
(a) Jumping out of Gear	1	Broken change speed fork rod spring
	2	Excessively worn fork rod groove
	3	Worn coupling dogs
	4	Fork rod securing screw loose
(b) Noisy Gearbox	1	Insufficient oil in gearbox
	2	Excessive end play in laygear
	3	Damaged or worn bearings
	4	Damaged or worn teeth
(c) Difficulty in Engaging Gear	1	Incorrect clutch operation
(d) Oil Leaks	1	Damaged joint washers
	2	Damaged or worn oil seals
	3	Front, rear or side covers loose or damaged

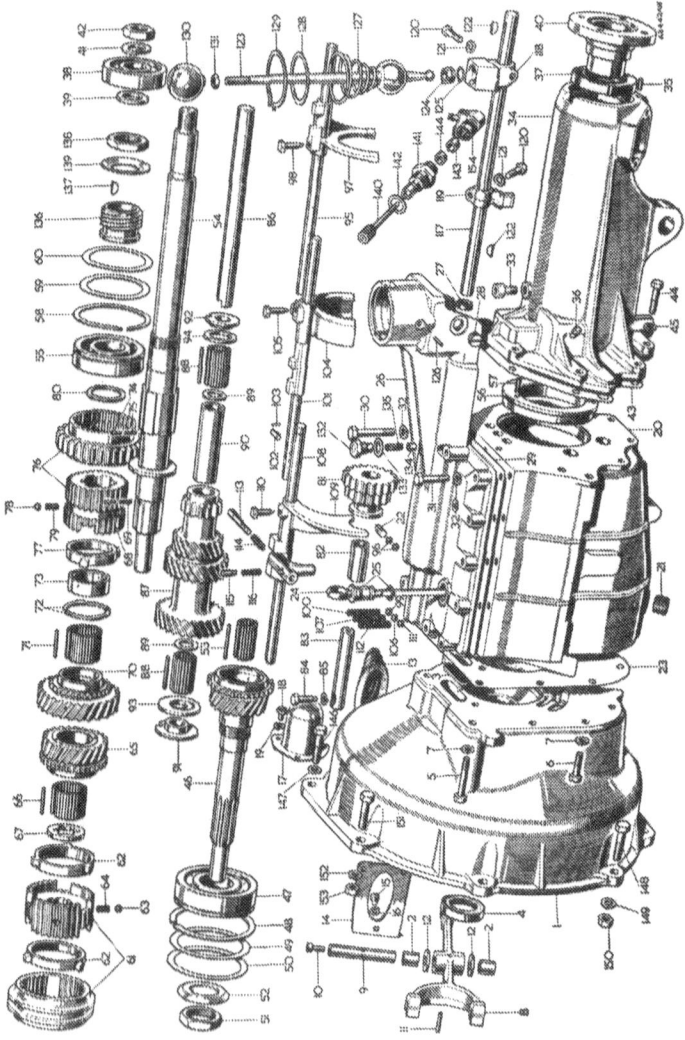

KEY TO THE GEARBOX COMPONENTS
(Gearbox without overdrive)

No.	Description
1.	Clutch housing.
2.	Fork and lever shaft bush.
3.	Buffer pad.
4.	Oil seal.
5.	Bolt—long.
6.	Bolt—short.
7.	Spring washer.
8.	Clutch fork and lever.
9.	Fork and lever shaft.
10.	Clutch withdrawal fork screw.
11.	Taper pin.
12.	Thrust washer for fork and lever.
13.	Fork and lever seal.
14.	Seat retaining plate.
15.	Retaining plate screw.
16.	Spring washer.
17.	Starter end cover.
18.	End cover screw.
19.	Spring washer.
20.	Gearbox case.
21.	Oil drain plug.
22.	Interlock ball hole plug.
23.	Case to clutch housing joint.
24.	Oil level indicator.
25.	Rubber grommet.
26.	Gearbox top cover.
27.	Cover oil seal.
28.	Cover plug.
29.	Cover to gearbox joint.
30.	Bolt—long.
31.	Bolt—short.
32.	Spring washer.
33.	Gearbox breather.
34.	Gearbox extension casting.
35.	Casing taper plug.
36.	Speedometer pinion thrust button.
37.	Oil seal.
38.	Bearing.
39.	Bearing washer.
40.	Coupling flange.
41.	Spring washer.
42.	Flange nut.
43.	Casing to gearbox joint.
44.	Bolt—casing to gearbox.
45.	Spring washer.
46.	Drive gear.
47.	Bearing for drive gear.
48.	Bearing circlip.
49.	Bearing plate.
50.	Bearing plate (spring).
51.	Bearing nut.
52.	Lock washer.
53.	Roller for drive gear.
54.	Mainshaft.
55.	Mainshaft bearing.
56.	Bearing housing.
57.	Locating peg.
58.	Bearing circlip.
59.	Bearing plate.
60.	Bearing plate (spring).
61.	Top and third sliding hub with striking dog.
62.	Sliding clutch interceptor.
63.	Sliding hub ball.
64.	Ball spring.
65.	Third speed gear.
66.	Gear roller.
67.	Locking plate.
68.	Gear plunger.
69.	Plunger spring.
70.	Second speed gear.
71.	Gear washer.
72.	Locking plate.
73.	Gear plunger.
74.	Plunger spring.
75.	First speed gear with first and second sliding hub.
76.	Sliding hub interceptor.
77.	Sliding hub ball.
78.	

No.	Description
79.	Ball spring.
80.	Mainshaft distance collar.
81.	Reverse gear.
82.	Gear bush.
83.	Gear shaft.
84.	Shaft retaining screw.
85.	Spring washer.
86.	Layshaft.
87.	Layshaft gear unit.
88.	Gear unit roller.
89.	Roller washer.
90.	Roller spacer.
91.	Gear unit thrust plate—front.
92.	Gear unit thrust plate—rear.
93.	Gear unit thrust washer—front.
94.	Gear unit thrust washer—rear.
95.	Top and third shifter shaft.
96.	Shaft interlocking ball.
97.	Top and third striking fork.
98.	Screw for striking fork.
99.	Shifter shaft ball.
100.	Ball spring.
101.	First and second shifter shaft.
102.	Shaft interlocking pin.
103.	Interlocking pin rivet.
104.	First and second striking fork.
105.	Screw for striking fork.
106.	Shifter shaft ball.
107.	Ball spring.
108.	Reverse shifter shaft.
109.	Reverse striking fork.
110.	Screw for striking fork.
111.	Shifter shaft ball.
112.	Ball spring.
113.	Reverse selector plunger.
114.	Plunger spring.
115.	Detent plunger.
116.	Detent plunger spring.
117.	Remote control shaft.
118.	Change speed lever shaft.

No.	Description
119.	Selector lever.
120.	Selector lever and change speed lever socket screw.
121.	Spring washer.
122.	Selector lever and change speed lever socket key.
123.	Change speed lever.
124.	Lever bush.
125.	Circlip for bush.
126.	Rollpin.
127.	Ball end retaining spring.
128.	Spring washer.
129.	Circlip.
130.	Change speed lever knob.
131.	Locknut for knob.
132.	Plunger retaining plug.
133.	Plug washer.
134.	Plunger.
135.	Plunger spring.
136.	Speedometer gear.
137.	Key for gear.
138.	Locknut for gear.
139.	Lockwasher for gear.
140.	Speedometer pinion.
141.	Pinion bearing.
142.	Washer for bearing.
143.	Pinion distance collar.
144.	Pinion oil seal.
145.	Reverse switch hole plug.
146.	Clutch housing bolt—long.
147.	Spring washer.
148.	Clutch housing bolt—short.
149.	Spring washer.
150.	Nut.
151.	Clutch housing dowel bolt.
152.	Spring washer for dowel bolt.
153.	Nut for dowel bolt.
154.	Speedometer drive adaptor box.

THE GEARBOX COMPONENTS
(Gearbox with overdrive)

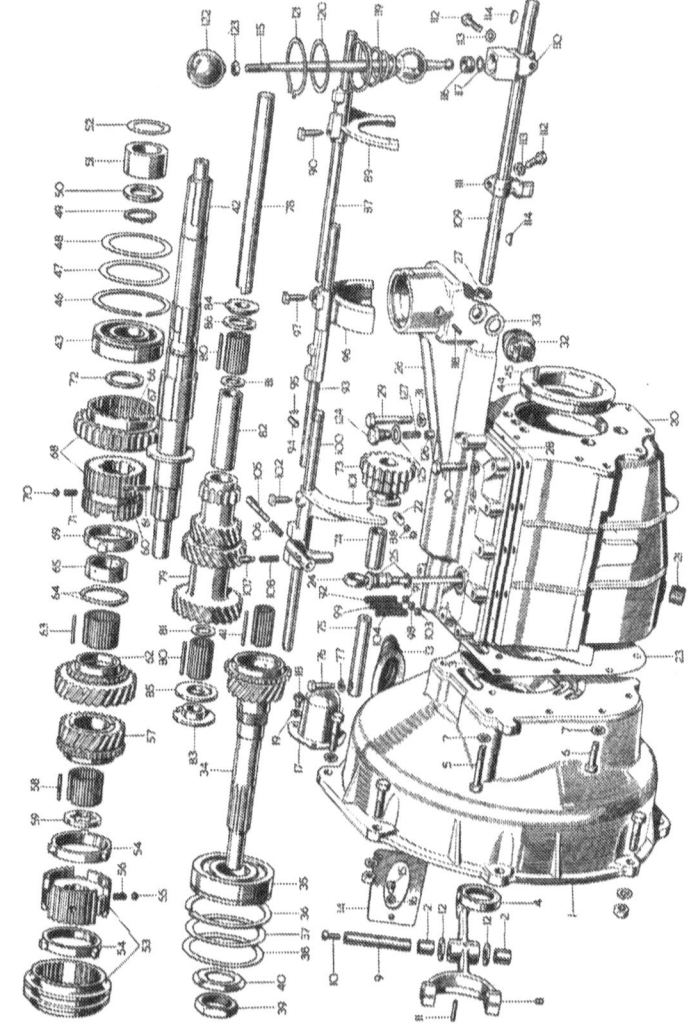

KEY TO THE GEARBOX COMPONENTS
(Gearbox with overdrive)

No.	Description
1.	Clutch housing.
2.	Fork and lever shaft bush.
3.	Buffer pad.
4.	Oil seal.
5.	Bolt—long.
6.	Bolt—short.
7.	Spring washer.
8.	Clutch fork and lever.
9.	Fork and lever shaft.
10.	Clutch withdrawal fork, screw.
11.	Taper pin.
12.	Thrust washer for fork and lever.
13.	Fork and lever seal.
14.	Seal retaining plate.
15.	Retaining plate screw.
16.	Spring washer.
17.	Starter end cover.
18.	End cover screw.
19.	Spring washer.
20.	Gearbox case.
21.	Oil drain plug.
22.	Interlock ball hole plug.
23.	Case to clutch housing joint.
24.	Oil level indicator.
25.	Rubber grommet.
26.	Gearbox top cover.
27.	Cover oil seal.
28.	Cover to gearbox joint.
29.	Bolt—long.
30.	Bolt—short.
31.	Spring washer.
32.	Overdrive switch.
33.	Joint for switch.
34.	Drive gear.
35.	Bearing for drive gear.
36.	Circlip for bearing.
37.	Plate for bearing.
38.	Plate for bearing (spring).
39.	Nut for bearing.
40.	Lock washer.
41.	Drive gear roller.
42.	Mainshaft.
43.	Mainshaft bearing.
44.	Bearing housing.
45.	Locating peg.
46.	Bearing circlip.
47.	Plate for bearing.
48.	Plate for bearing (spring).
49.	Mainshaft circlip.
50.	Bearing abutment collar.
51.	Abutment collar retaining ring.
52.	Shim.
53.	Top and third sliding hub with striking dog.
54.	Sliding hub interceptor.
55.	Sliding hub ball.
56.	Ball spring.
57.	Third speed gear.
58.	Roller for gear.
59.	Locking plate.
60.	Gear plunger.
61.	Plunger spring.
62.	Second speed gear.
63.	Roller for gear.
64.	Gear washer.
65.	Locking plate.

No.	Description
66.	Gear plunger.
67.	Plunger spring.
68.	First speed gear with first and second sliding hub.
69.	Sliding hub interceptor.
70.	Sliding hub ball.
71.	Ball spring.
72.	Mainshaft distance collar.
73.	Reverse gear.
74.	Gear bush.
75.	Gear shaft.
76.	Shaft retaining screw.
77.	Spring washer.
78.	Layshaft.
79.	Layshaft gear unit.
80.	Gear unit roller.
81.	Roller spacer.
82.	Roller spacer.
83.	Gear unit thrust plate—front.
84.	Gear unit thrust plate—rear.
85.	Gear unit thrust washer—front.
86.	Gear unit thrust washer—rear.
87.	Top and third shifter shaft.
88.	Shaft interlocking ball.
89.	Top and third striking fork.
90.	Screw for striking fork.
91.	Shifter shaft ball.
92.	Ball spring.
93.	First and second shifter shaft.
94.	Shaft interlocking pin.
95.	Interlocking pin rivet.
96.	First and second striking fork.
97.	Screw for striking fork.
98.	Shifter shaft ball.
99.	Ball spring.
100.	Reverse shifter shaft.
101.	Reverse striking fork.
102.	Screw for striking fork.
103.	Shifter shaft ball.
104.	Ball spring.
105.	Reverse selector plunger.
106.	Plunger spring.
107.	Detent plunger.
108.	Detent plunger spring.
109.	Remote control shaft.
110.	Change speed lever rocket.
111.	Selector lever.
112.	Selector lever and change speed lever socket screw.
113.	Spring washer.
114.	Selector lever and change speed lever socket key.
115.	Change speed lever.
116.	Lever bush.
117.	Circlip for bush.
118.	Rollpin.
119.	Ball end retaining spring.
120.	Washer for spring.
121.	Circlip.
122.	Change speed lever knob.
123.	Locknut for knob.
124.	Plunger retaining plug.
125.	Plug washer.
126.	Plunger.
127.	Plunger spring.

OVERDRIVE

LUBRICATION

The lubricating oil in the overdrive unit is common with that in the gearbox and the level should be checked with the gearbox dipstick. It is essential that an approved lubricant be used when refilling. Trouble may be experienced if some types of extreme pressure lubricants are used because the planet gears act as a centrifuge to separate the additives from the oil.

Recommended lubricants are given on page 229. It should be emphasized that any hydraulically controlled transmission must have clean oil at all times and great care must be taken to avoid the entry of dirt whenever any part of the casing is opened.

Every 1,000 miles (1600 kilometers) check the oil level of the gearbox and overdrive and top up if necessary through the dipstick hole.

Every 6,000 miles (9600 kilometers) drain and refill the gearbox and overdrive unit. In addition to the normal drain plug fitted to the gearbox the overdrive unit incorporates a plug at its base which gives access to a filter. This plug should also be withdrawn to ensure that all used oil is drained away from the system.

Every 6,000 miles (9600 kilometers) after draining the oil, remove the overdrive oil pump filter and clean the filter gauze by washing in gasoline. The filter is accessible through the drain plug hole and is secured by a central set bolt.

Refilling of the complete system (gearbox and overdrive) is accomplished through the gearbox filler plug. The capacity of the combined gearbox and overdrive unit is 6¼ pints (7.5 U.S. pints; 3.55 litres).

After draining, ¼ pint of oil will remain in the overdrive hydraulic system, so that only 6 pints will be needed for refilling. If the overdrive has been dismantled the total of 6¼ pints will be required. After refilling the gearbox and overdrive with oil, recheck the level after the car has been run, as a certain amount of oil will be retained in the hydraulic system of the overdrive unit.

WORKING DESCRIPTION

The overdrive unit comprises a hydraulically controlled epicyclic gear housed in a casing which is directly attached to an extension at the rear of the gearbox.

The synchromesh gearbox third motion shaft is extended and carries at its end the inner member of an uni-directional clutch. The outer member of this clutch is carried in the combined annulus and output shaft.

Also mounted on the third motion shaft are the planet carrier G and a freely rotatable sun wheel. Splined to a forward extension E of the sun wheel and sliding thereon is a cone clutch member D, the inner lining of which engages the outside of the annulus F while the outer lining engages a cast-iron brake ring sandwiched between the front and rear parts of the unit housing.

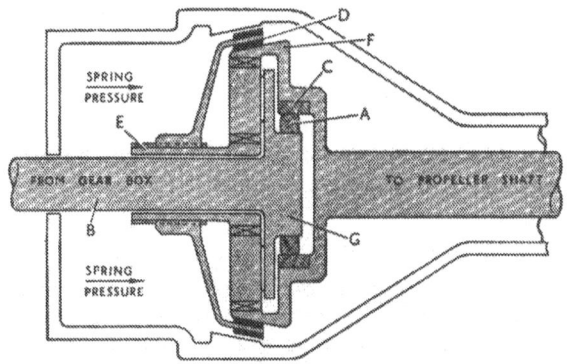

Overdrive disengaged.

A number of compression springs are used to hold the cone clutch in contact with the annulus, locking the sun wheel to the latter so that the entire gear train rotates as a solid unit, giving direct drive. In this condition the drive is taken through the uni-directional clutch, the cone clutch taking over-run and reverse torque, as without it there would be a free-wheel condition.

The spring pressure can be overcome through the medium of two pistons, working in cylinders formed in the unit housing, supplied with oil under pressure from a hydraulic accumulator. This hydraulic pressure causes the cone clutch to engage the stationary brake ring and bring the sun wheel to rest, allowing the annulus to over-run the uni-directional clutch and give an increased speed to the output shaft, i.e. "overdrive".

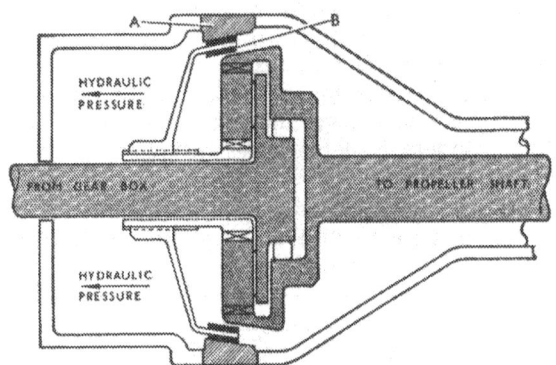

Overdrive engaged.

When changing from overdrive to direct gear, if the accelerator pedal is released (as in a change down for engine braking) the cone clutch, being oil immersed, takes up smoothly. If the accelerator pedal is not released, when contact between the cone clutch and brake ring is broken, the unit still operates momentarily in its overdrive ratio as engine speed and road speed remain unchanged.

But the load on the engine is released and it begins to accelerate, speeding up the sun wheel from rest until, just at the instant when its speed synchronizes with the speed of the annulus, the whole unit revolves solidly and the uni-directional clutch takes up the drive once more. The movement of the cone clutch is deliberately slowed down so that the uni-directional clutch is driving before the cone clutch contacts, ensuring a perfectly self-synchronized change.

CONSTRUCTION

The third motion shift of the synchromesh gearbox is extended to carry first a cam operating the oil pump and then a steady bearing with two opposed plain bushes carried in the front housing. Next is the sun wheel of the epicyclic gear carried on a Clevite bush, and beyond this the shaft is splined to take the planet carrier and uni-directional clutch. The end of the shaft is reduced and carried in a plain bush in the output shaft. The latter is supported in the rear housing by two ball bearings. The clutch member slides on the splines of the sun wheel extension to contact either the annulus or a cast iron brake ring forming part of the unit housing.

To the hub of the cone clutch member is secured a ball bearing housed in a flanged ring. This ring carries on its forward face a number of pegs acting as guides to compression springs by which the ring, and with it the clutch member, is held against the annulus. The springs prevent free-wheeling on over-run and are of sufficient strength to handle reverse torque. Also secured to the ring are four studs picking up two bridge pieces against which bear two pistons operating in cylinders formed in the unit housing. The cylinders are connected through a valve to an accumulator in which pressure is maintained by the oil pump. The operating pistons are fitted with special three-piece cast-iron rings, as also is the accumulator piston.

When the valve is open, oil under pressure is admitted to the cylinders and pushes the pistons forward to engage the overdrive clutch. Closing the valve cuts off the supply of oil to the cylinders and allows it to escape. Under the influence of the springs the clutch member moves back to engage direct drive position. The escape of oil from the cylinders is deliberately restricted so that the clutch takes about half a second to move over.

The sun wheel and pinions are cyanide case-hardened and the annulus heat-treated. Gear teeth are helical. The pinions have Clevite bushes and run on case-hardened pins.

Components of overdrive front casing.

1. Joint washer.	19. Valve push rod.	37. Ball valve.	55. Spring washer.
2. Adapter plate.	20. Ball valve.	38. Pump filter.	56. Setpin.
3. Joint washer.	21. Ball valve plunger.	39. Distance piece.	57. Plain washer.
4. Locating stud.	22. Valve spring.	40. Filter bolt.	58. Spring washer.
5. Nut.	23. Valve plug.	41. Plain washer.	59. Solenoid shield.
6. Spring washer.	24. Copper washer.	42. Spring washer.	60. Thrust washer.
7. Main casing.	25. Third motion shaft.	43. Accumulator spring.	61. Spacing washer.
8. Stud.	26. Pump plunger.	44. Distance tube.	62. Rubber stop.
9. Stud.	27. Plunger spring.	45. Piston assembly.	63. Drain plug.
10. Welch plug.	28. Guide peg.	46. Piston rings.	64. Drain plug washer.
11. Valve operating shaft.	29. Pump body.	47. Rubber rings.	65. Breather.
12. Setting lever.	30. Pump body plug.	48. Solenoid unit.	66. Piston.
13. Collar.	31. Body screw.	49. Unit screw.	67. Piston rings.
14. Shaft cam.	32. Spring washer.	50. Spring washer.	68. Nut.
15. Solenoid lever.	33. Valve plug.	51. Solenoid lever housing.	69. Spring washer.
16. Adjusting screw.	34. Plug washer.	52. Joint washer.	70. Cotter pin.
17. Nut.	35. Valve spring.	53. Stud.	71. Oil seal.
18. Washer.	36. Ball valve plunger.	54. Nut.	72. Peg.

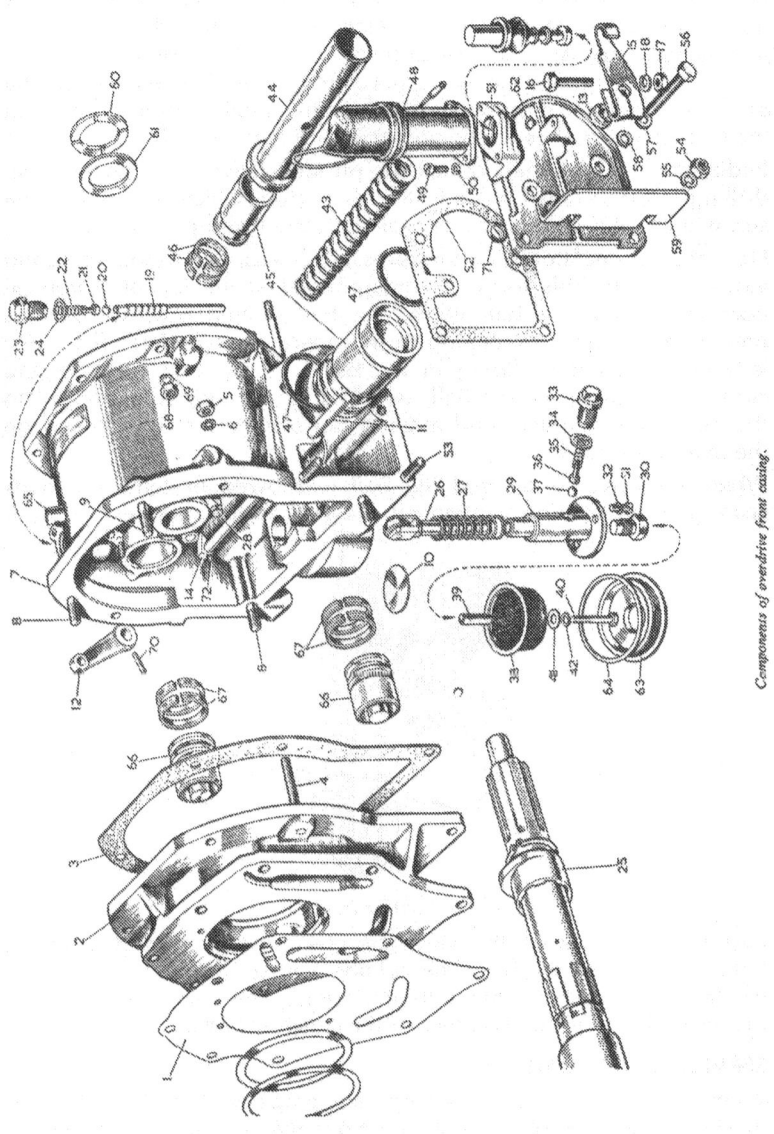

Components of overdrive front casing.

The outer ring of the uni-directional clutch is pressed and riveted into the annulus member. The clutch itself is of the caged roller type, loaded by a lock-type spring made of round wire.

The hydraulic system is supplied with oil by a plunger type pump operated by a cam on the gearbox third motion shaft. The pump body is pressed into the front housing and delivers oil through a non-return valve to the accumulator cylinder, in which a piston moves back against a compression spring until the required pressure is reached when relief holes are uncovered. From the relief holes the oil is led through drilled passages to an annular groove between the two steady bushes on the gearbox third motion shaft.

Radial holes in the shaft collect the oil and deliver it along an axial drilling to other radial holes in the shaft from which it is fed to the sun wheel bush, thrust washers, planet carrier and planet pins.

From the accumulator, oil under pressure is supplied to the operating valve chamber. This forms an enlargement at the top of a vertical bore and contains a ball valve, the ball seating downwards thus preventing oil from circulating to the operating cylinders. The valve is a hollow spindle sliding in the bore, its top end reduced and carrying a seating for the ball, which is then lifted, admitting oil to the operating cylinders and moving the pistons forward to engage the overdrive clutch.

When the valve is lowered the ball is allowed to come on to its seating in the housing, cutting off pressure to the cylinders.

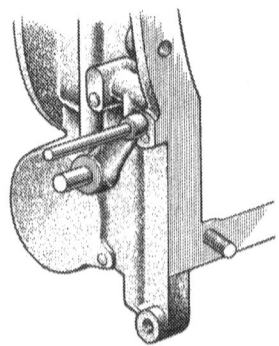

Valve setting lever.

Further movement of the valve brings it out of contact with the ball, allowing the oil from the cylinders to escape down the inside of the valve to discharge into the sump. The cone member then moves back under the influence of the clutch springs.

SERVICING IN POSITION

When the overdrive does not operate properly it is advisable first to check the level of oil and, if below the requisite level, top up with fresh oil and test the unit again before making any further investigations.

Before commencing any dismantling operations it is important that the hydraulic pressure is released from the system. Do this by operating the overdrive 10 to 12 times.

As the unit is fitted with a speed responsive control it will be found more convenient to carry out this operation by moving the valve setting lever manually.

GUIDE TO SERVICE DIAGNOSIS
Overdrive Does Not Engage
1 — Insufficient oil in box.
2 — Electric control not operating.
3 — Leaking operating valve due to foreign matter on ball seat or broken valve spring.
4 — Pump not working due to choked filter.
5 — Pump not working due to broken pump spring.
6 — Leaking pump non-return value due to foreign matter on ball seat or broken valve spring.
7 — Insufficient hydraulic pressure due to leaks or broken accumulator spring.
8 — Damaged gears, bearings or moving parts within the unit requiring removal and inspection of the assembly.

Overdrive Does Not Release
1 — Electric control not operating.
2 — Blocked restrictor jet in valve.
3 — Sticking clutch.
4 — Damaged parts within the unit necessitating removal and inspection of the assembly.

Clutch Slip In Overdrive
1 — Insufficient oil in gearbox.
2 — Worn clutch lining.
3 — Insufficient hydraulic pressure due to leaks.

Clutch Slip in Reverse or Free-Wheel Condition on Over-run
1 — Worn clutch lining.
2 — Blocked restrictor jet in valve.
3 — Insufficient pressure on clutch due to broken clutch springs.

OPERATING VALVE
Having gained access to the unit through the floor, unscrew the valve plug and remove the spring and plunger. The ball valve will then be seen inside the valve chamber. The ball should be lifted 1/32 in. (.794 mm.) off its seat when the overdrive control is operated.

As the unit is fitted with a speed responsive control the appropriate parts of the electrical circuit must be shorted out in order to operate the control.

If the ball does not lift by this amount the fault lies in the control mechanism. Located on the right-hand side of the unit and pivoting on the valve operating cross shaft, which passes right through the housing, is a valve setting lever. In its outer end is a 3/16 in. (4.763 mm.) diameter hole which corresponds with a similar hole in the housing when the unit is in "overdrive" (i.e. when the ball is lifted 1/32 in. off the valve seat.)

If the two holes do not line up, adjust the control mechanism until a 3/16 in. diameter rod can be inserted through the setting lever into the hole in the housing. Check lift of ball after completing the adjustment.

A small magnet will be found useful for removing the ball from the valve chamber. The valve can be withdrawn by inserting the tang of a file into the top, but care must be taken not to damage the ball seating at the end of the valve. Near the bottom of the valve will be seen a small hole breaking through to the center drilling. This is the jet for restricting the exhaust of oil from the operating cylinders. Ensure that this jet is not choked.

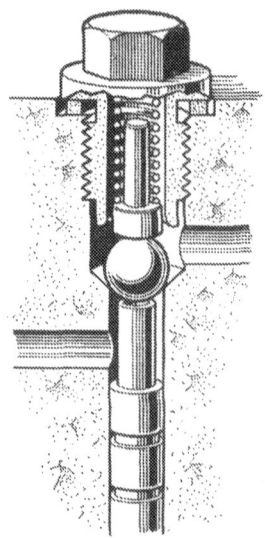

The operating valve.

HYDRAULIC SYSTEM

If the unit fails to operate and the ball valve is found to be seating and lifting correctly check that the pump is functioning.

Jack up the rear wheels of the car, then with the engine ticking over and the valve plug removed, engage top gear. Watch for oil being pumped into the valve chamber. If none appears then the pump is not functioning.

The pump described above, is of the plunger type and delivers oil via a non-return valve to the accumulator. Possible sources of trouble are (1) failure of the non-return valve due to foreign matter on the seat or to a broken valve spring and (2) breakage of the spring holding the pump plunger in contact with the cam.

The pump is self priming, but failure to deliver oil after the system has been drained and refilled indicates that the air bleed is choked causing air to be trapped inside the pump.

In the unlikely event of this happening it will be necessary to remove the pump and clean the flat on the pump body and the bore of the casting into which it fits.

PUMP VALVE

Access to the pump valve is gained through a cover on the left-hand side of the unit. Proceed as follows:—

Solenoid Operated Units

1 — Remove drain plug and drain off oil.
2 — Remove solenoid.
3 — Slacken off clamping bolt in operating lever and remove lever, complete with solenoid plunger.
4 — Remove distance collar from valve operating shaft.
5 — The solenoid bracket is secured by two 5/16 in. (7.938 mm) studs and two 5/16 in. diameter bolts, the heads of which are painted red, **remove the nuts from the studs before touching the bolts. This is important.** The two bolts should now be slackened off together, releasing the tension on the accumulator spring.

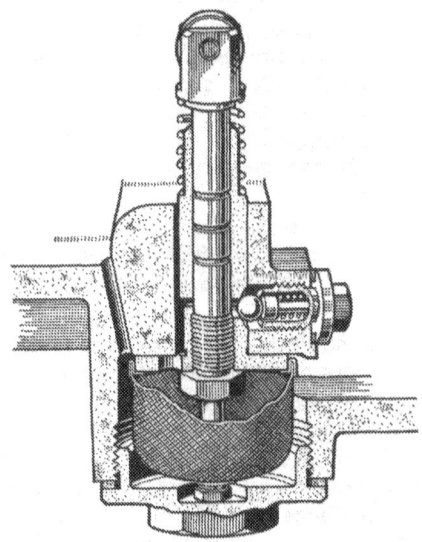

The pump in cut-away form.

6 — Remove the solenoid bracket.
7 — Unscrew the valve cap and take out the spring, plunger and ball. Reassembly is the reverse of the above operations. Ensure that the soft copper washer between the valve cap and pump housing is nipped up tightly to prevent oil leakage.

It will now be necessary to reset the valve operating lever. Proceed as follows:—

Before clamping up the valve shaft rotate the shaft until a 3/16 in. (4.763 mm.) diameter pin can be inserted through the valve setting lever into the corresponding hole in the casing. Leave the pin in position, locking the unit in the overdrive position. Lift the solenoid plunger up to the full extent of its stroke (i.e. to its energized position) and clamp up the operating lever. The solenoid plunger bolt should now drop until it rests on the rubber stop immediately below. This stop gives the desired clearance between the plunger bolt and the boss situated on the solenoid bracket. Remove the pin through the setting lever and operate the lever manually to check that the control operates easily.

DISMANTLING AND REASSEMBLING UNIT
Dismantling

Should trouble arise necessitating dismantling of the unit to a degree further than has already been described, it will be necessary to remove the unit from the car.

Whilst it is possible to lift out the overdrive alone from the car, it is advised that the gearbox and overdrive be removed as a single unit. It is far easier to refit the overdrive to the gearbox when the assembly is on a bench as the extended third motion shaft must be lined up with the splines of the uni-directional clutch.

The unit is split at the adaptor plate which is attached to the front casing by six 5/16 in. (7.938 mm.) studs, two of which are extra long. The four nuts on the shorter studs should be removed before those on the longer ones are touched. The latter should be unscrewed together releasing the compression off the clutch springs. The unit can then be drawn off the mainshaft, leaving the adaptor plate attached to the gearbox.

Remove the clutch springs from their pins. The two bridge pieces against which the operating pistons bear can now be removed. Each is secured by two ¼ in. nuts locked by tab washers. Withdraw the two operating pistons.

As the adaptor plate is now separated from the unit the pump valve can be dismantled without removing the side cover (solenoid bracket) from the casing and there is no need to disturb the latter unless it is necessary to remove the accumulator piston and spring.

Remove the six 5/16 in. (7.938 mm.) nuts securing the two halves of the casing and separate them, removing the brake ring which is spigoted into the two pieces. Lift out the planet carrier assembly. Remove the clutch sliding member complete with the thrust ring and bearing, the sun wheel and thrust washer. Take out the inner member of the uni-directional clutch, the rollers, cage, etc.

Components of overdrive rear casing.

1. Clutch thrust ring.
2. Bridge pieces.
3. Nuts.
4. Locking washers.
5. Clutch spring (long).
6. Clutch spring (short).
7. Front bearing.
8. Circlip (small).
9. Circlip (large).
10. Brake ring.
11. Clutch assembly.
12. Sun wheel assembly.
13. Thrust washer.
14. Uni-directional clutch.
15. Rollers.
16. Outer casing.
17. Securing clip.
18. Thrust washer.
19. Inner bearing.
20. Outer bearing.
22. Rear housing.
21. Spacing washer.
23. Driving flange.
24. Oil seal.
25. Flange nut.
26. Washer.
27. Split pin.
28. Speedometer spindle.
29. Spindle sleeve.
30. Washer.
31. Locking peg.
32. Washer.
33. Oil seal.
34. Spindle adaptor.
35. Overdrive switch.

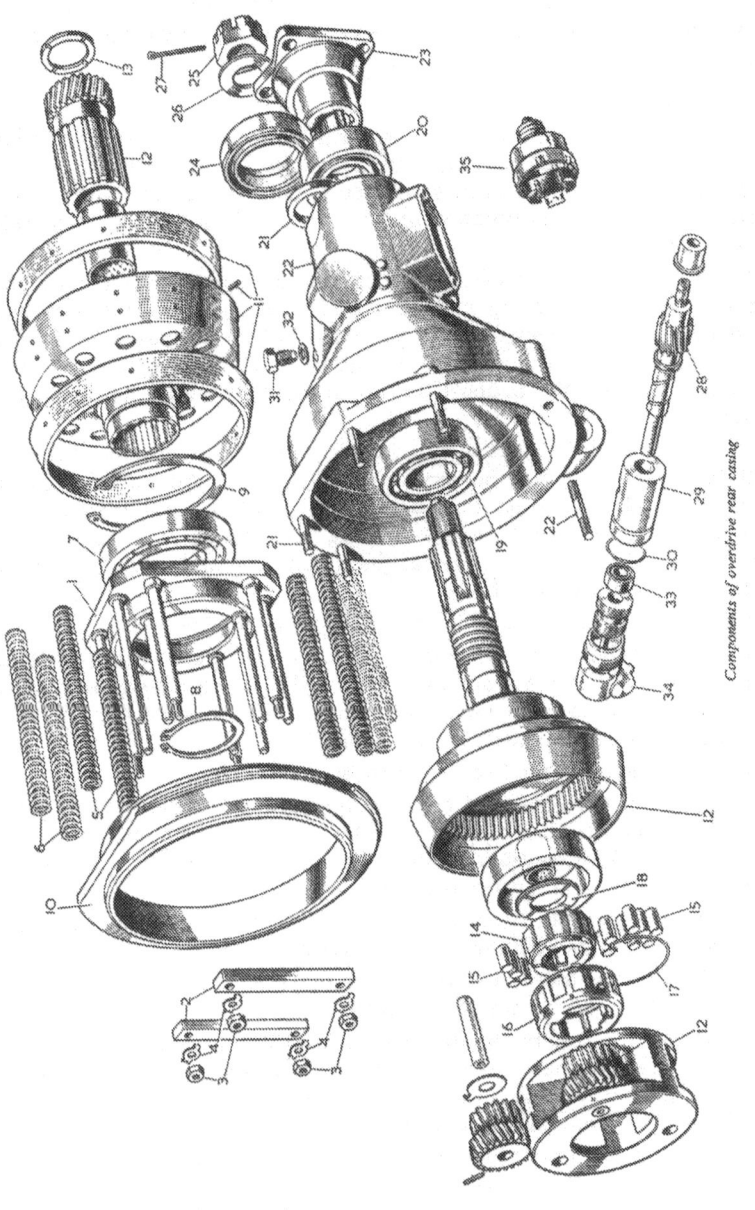

Components of overdrive rear casing

If it is necessary to remove the planet gears from the carrier the three split pins securing the planet bearing shafts must be extracted before the latter can be knocked out.

To remove the annulus, first take off the coupling flange at the rear of the unit, remove the speedometer gear, centrifugal switch, etc., and drive out the annulus from the back. The front bearing will come away on the shaft leaving the rear bearing in the casing.

Inspection

Each part should be thoroughly inspected after the unit is dismantled and cleaned to ensure which parts should be replaced. It is important to appreciate the difference between parts which are worn sufficiently to affect the operation of the unit and those which are merely "worn in."

1 — Inspect the front casing for cracks, damage, etc. examine the bores of the operating cylinders and accumulator for scores and wear. Check for leaks from plugged ends of the oil passages. Ensure that the welch washer beneath the accumulator bore is tight and not leaking. Inspect the support bushes in the centre bore for wear and damage.

2 — Examine the clutch sliding member assembly. Ensure that the clutch linings are not burned or worn. Inspect the pins for clutch springs and bridge pieces and see that they are tight in the thrust ring and not distorted. Ensure that the ball bearing is in good condition and rotates freely. See that the sliding member slides easily on the splines of the sun wheel.

3 — Check the clutch springs for distortion or collapse.

4 — Inspect the teeth of the gear train for damage. If the sun wheel or planet bushes are worn the gears will have to be replaced since it is not possible to fit new bushes in service because they have to be bored true to the pitch line of the teeth.

5 — Examine steel and bronze thrust washers.

6 — See that the rollers of the uni-directional clutch are not chipped and that the inner and outer members of the clutch are free from damage. Make sure that the member is tight in the annulus. Ensure that the spring is free from distortion.

7 — Inspect the ball bearings on the output shaft and see that there is no roughness when they are rotated slowly.

8 — Ensure that there are no nicks or burrs on the mainshaft splines and that the oil holes are open and clean.

9 — Inspect the oil pump for wear on the pump plunger and roller pin. Ensure that the plunger spring is not distorted. Its free length is 2 in. (5.08 cm.). Inspect the valve seat and ball and make sure that they are free from nicks and scratches.

10 — Check the operating valve for distortion and damage and see that it slides easily in its bore in the front casing.

Reassembling the Unit

The unit can be reassembled after all the parts have been thoroughly cleaned and checked to ensure that none are damaged or worn.

Assemble the annulus into the rear casing, not forgetting the spacing washer which fits between a shoulder on the shaft and the rear ball bearing. This washer is available in different thicknesses for selective assembly and should allow no end float of the annulus (output shaft) and no pre-loading of the bearings.
Selective washers are furnished in the following sizes:—
.146 in. ± .0005 in. (3.7084 mm. ± .0127)
.151 in. ± .0005 in. (4.335 mm. ± .0127)
.156 in. ± .0005 in. (3.962 mm. ± .0127)
.161 in. ± .0005 in. (4.089 mm. ± .0127)
Replace the thrust washer and uni-directional clutch inner member with its roller and cage. The fixture (Fig. G.9) is for retaining the rollers in position when assembling the clutch. Ensure that the spring is fitted correctly so that the cage urges the rollers up the ramps on the inner member.

Using tool 18G 178 for assembling the roller clutch.

Fit the pump cam on to the gearbox mainshaft, offer up the front housing to the cover plate and secure temporarily with two nuts. In order to determine the amount of end float of the sun wheel, which should be .008 in. to .014 in. (.203 mm. to .3556 mm.) an extra thrust washer of known thickness should be assembled with the two normally used in front of the sun wheel.
The gear train must be assembled in the following way so that the planet wheels will mesh with the sun wheel and at the same time allow their compound teeth to mesh correctly with the annulus. One tooth on each planet wheel is punch-marked, and the planet wheels must be turned in the carrier so that the punch marks are radially outwards as shown on page 120. With the planet wheels aligned in this way, fit the planet carrier over the sun wheel. The position of the planet wheels in relation to each other ensures that the second set of teeth on the planet wheels will mesh with the annulus teeth. Offer up the assembly to the annulus turning the planet carrier until the locating peg on the inner member of the uni-directional clutch

enters the corresponding hole in the planet carrier. This lines up the splines in the two members.

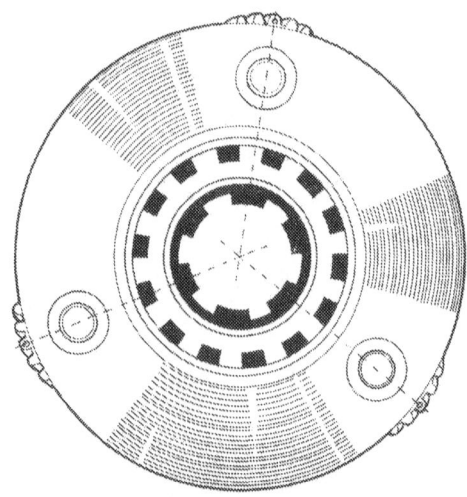

Before assembling the planet carrier to the sun wheel rotate the planet wheels until the punch marks are in the position shown.

Assemble the brake ring to the front casing then offer up the front and rear assemblies, leaving out the clutch sliding member with its springs, etc. The gap between the flanges of the brake ring and rear casing should be measured. This gap will be less than the thickness of the extra thrust washer by the amount of end float of the sun wheel. If this is between the limits specified the unit may be stripped down again and reassembled without the extra thrust washer. The clutch sliding member bridge pieces, etc., must now be replaced. The compression of the springs is taken up on the two long studs between the front casing and adaptor plate.

If the indicated end float is more, or less, than that required it must be adjusted by replacing the steel thrust washer at the front of the sun wheel by one of less or greater thickness, as required. Washers of varying thickness are stocked for this purpose.

Seven sizes are available, as follows:—
.113 in. to .114 in. (2.87 mm. to 2.985 mm.)
.107 in. to .108 in. (2.718 mm. to 2.743 mm.)
.101 in. to .102 in. (2.565 mm. to 2.59 mm.)
.095 in. to .096 in. (2.413 mm. to 2.438 mm.)
.089 in. to .090 in. (2.26 mm. to 2.286 mm.)
.083 in. to .084 in. (2.108 mm. to 2.134 mm.)
.077 in. to .078 in. (1.956 mm. to 1.981 mm.)

Care must be taken to ensure that the thrust washers at the front and rear of the sun wheel are replaced in their correct positions. At the front of the sun wheel the steel washer fits next to the head of the support bush in the housing and the bronze washer between the steel one and the sun wheel. At the rear, the steel washer is sandwiched between the two bronze washers.

OVERDRIVE RELAY SYSTEM
Description
Engagement of overdrive is controlled electrically through a manually operated toggle switch. The circuit shown in Fig. G.11 includes the following components:

i — Relay, model SB40. An electro-magnetic switch used with item (ii) to enable an interlocking safeguard to be incorporated against changing out of overdrive with throttle closed.

ii — Throttle Switch, model RTS1. A lever-operated semi-rotary normally closed switch used in conjunction with item (i) to override the toggle switch under closed throttle conditions.

iii — Gear Switch, model SS10. A small plunger-operated switch allowing overdrive to be engaged only in the two highest forward-gear positions.

iv — Solenoid Unit, model TGS1. An electro-magnetic actuator to engage overdrive mechanism by opening hydraulic control valve.

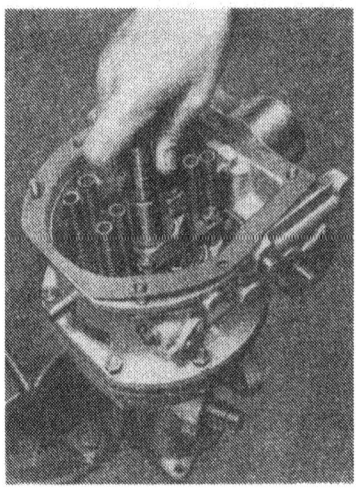

Centralising the gears with dummy mainshaft.

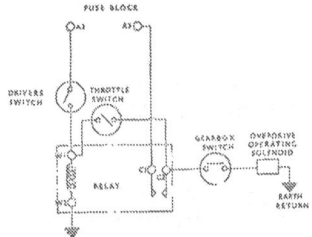

Wiring diagram for the overdrive electrical circuit

Operation

When the toggle switch contacts are closed, current flows by way of the ignition switch and fuse unit supply terminal A3 to energize the relay operating coil. Closure of the relay contacts connect terminal A3 to the gear switch and, providing one of the two higher ratio gears is engaged, will energize the solenoid unit and effect a change from direct drive to overdrive.

Overdrive will be maintained until the solenoid units is de-energized. Change from overdrive to direct drive is effected either by selecting a low gear (when the gear switch contacts will open) or by turning the toggle switch to off with open throttle (when the relay contacts will open).

If effected with closed throttle, a change from overdrive to direct drive could result in a shock to the transmission. An interlocking circuit is therefore incorporated to override the toggle switch under closed throttle conditions. Under these conditions, the throttle switch contacts provide an alternative supply circuit to the relay operating coil.

Maintenance

Regular attention should be paid to wiring and connections. Damaged cabling must be replaced and loose terminals tightened, including the relay and solenoid unit ground connections.

FAULT TRACING

The Solenoid Unit

With engine stopped and neutral gear engaged and ignition switched on, disconnect the solenoid connection. Using a jumper lead, momentarily connect the solenoid to fuse unit supply terminal A3. The solenoid should be heard to operate. If no sound is heard, the solenoid is defective or incorrectly adjusted to the operating linkage. Remake the connection.

The Gear Switch

Engage top gear, depress the throttle pedal and momentarily connect relay terminal C2 to terminal A3. The solenoid should be heard to operate. If no sound is heard, the gear switch is defective. Re-engage neutral gear.

The Relay Coil

Momentarily connect relay terminal W1 to terminal A3. The relay should be heard to operate. If no sound is heard, the relay is defective.

The Toggle Switch

Operate the toggle switch. The relay should be heard to operate. If no sound is heard, the toggle switch is defective.

The Relay Contacts

With top gear engaged, toggle switch closed and throttle switch open, the solenoid should be heard to operate. If no sound is heard, the relay is defective.

The Throttle Switch

Engage top gear and close the toggle switch. Open the toggle switch and slowly depress the accelerator. The solenoid should be energized from zero to one-quarter throttle. If the solenoid is heard to release under one-quarter throttle, the throttle switch is defective.

OVERDRIVE UNIT FOR BN7 AND BT7 CARS

The overdrive units fitted to the BN7 and BT7 cars are basically similar to that described above. The following changes have, however, been made:

1 — A re-designed filter has been fitted and is retained in the body by a boss on the inside of the drain plug. The filter is accessible through the drain plug hole.

2 — New operating pistons have been fitted with synthetic rubber sealing rings and the accumulator piston with three piece cast iron rings.

3 — The pinions are fitted with needle roller bearings in lieu of "Clevite" bushes.

4 — The outer ring of the uni-directional clutch is not riveted.

5 — An additional selective washer 0.160±0.005 in. thick is available.

6 — A re-designed solenoid bracket and adaptor plate has been fitted.

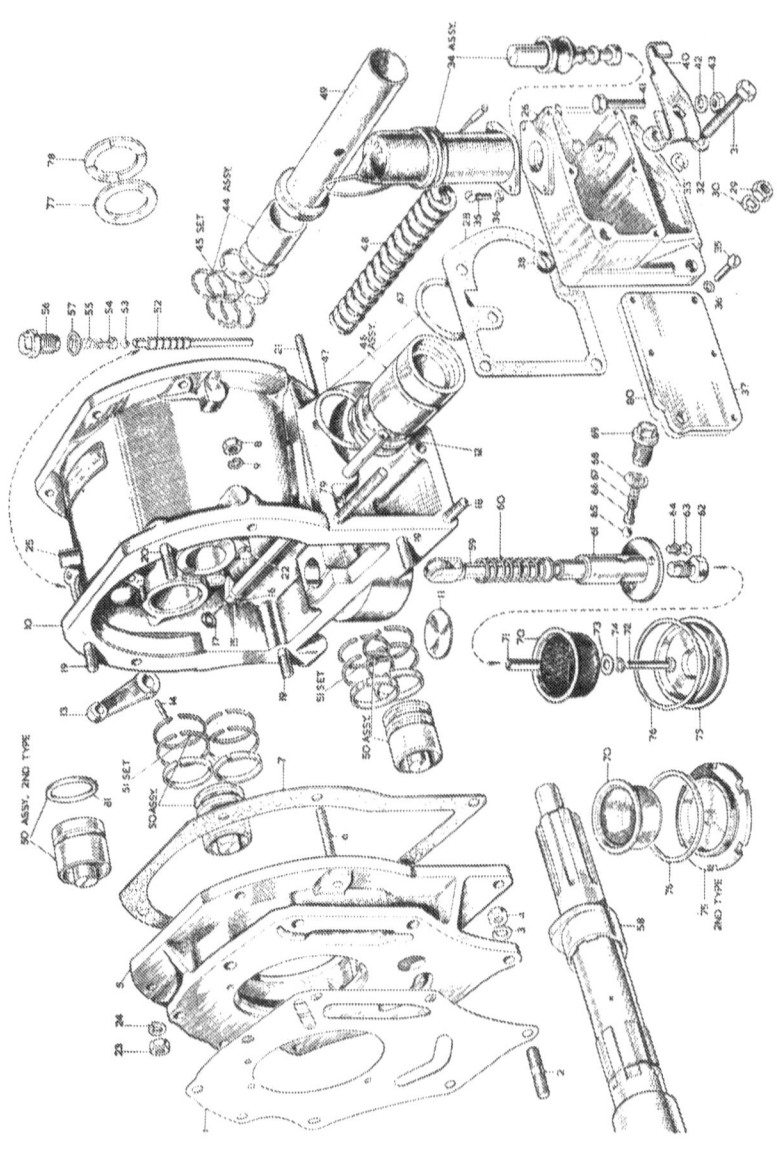

No.	Description	No.	Description	No.	Description
1.	Joint—overdrive unit.	28.	Joint—bracket to case.	55.	Spring for plunger.
2.	Stud—overdrive unit.	29.	Nut—bracket to casing.	56.	Plug for valve—screwed.
3.	Washer for stud (spring).	30.	Washer for nut (spring).	57.	Washer for plug.
4.	Nut for stud.	31.	Screw—bracket to casing.	58.	Cam—oil pump.
5.	Plate—adaptor.	32.	Washer for screw.	59.	Plunger assembly—oil pump.
6.	Stud—adaptor to casing.	33.	Washer for screw (spring).	60.	Spring for plunger.
7.	Joint—adaptor to casing.	34.	Solenoid.	61.	Body—oil pump.
8.	Nut—plate stud to casing.	35.	Screw—solenoid to bracket.	62.	Plug for body—screwed.
9.	Washer for stud (spring).	36.	Washer for screw (spring).	63.	Screw—body to front casing.
10.	Casing—front.	37.	Plate—solenoid bracket cover.	64.	Washer for screw (spring).
11.	Plug.	38.	Seal, oil—valve operating shaft.	65.	Ball valve.
12.	Shaft—valve operating.	39.	Distance collar.	66.	Plunger, ball.
13.	Lever for shaft.	40.	Lever—solenoid.	67.	Spring for plunger.
14.	Pin—lever to shaft.	41.	Screw—lever to spindle.	68.	Washer for valve plug (copper).
15.	Cam—valve operating.	42.	Washer for screw (spring).	69.	Plug—valve.
16.	Pin for cam.	43.	Nut for screw.	70.	Strainer—oil pump.
17.	Seal for shaft.	44.	Piston assembly—accumulator.	71.	Distance tube for strainer.
18.	Stud for solenoid bracket.	45.	Ring—piston.	72.	Bolt for strainer.
19.	Stud for plate—long.	46.	Housing assembly—accumulator.	73.	Washer for bolt.
20.	Stud for plate—short.	47.	Ring, rubber.	74.	Washer for bolt (spring).
21.	Stud—front to rear casing.	48.	Spring—accumulator pressure.	75.	Plug—oil drain.
22.	Peg—oil pump plunger guide.	49.	Tube for spring.	76.	Washer for plug.
23.	Nut—front casing to adaptor plate.	50.	Piston—assembly—operating.	77.	Washer, steel.
24.	Washer for nut (spring).	51.	Ring, piston.	78.	Washer—phosphor bronze.
25.	Breather.	52.	Valve, operating.	79.	Stud for solenoid bracket.
26.	Bracket solenoid.	53.	Ball for valve.	80.	Joint for cover plate.
27.	Stop (rubber).	54.	Plunger, ball.	81.	Ring—piston.

Key to the overdrive front casing components.

DRIVE SHAFT

The propeller shaft and universal joints are of Hardy Spicer manufacture.

The fore and aft movement of the rear axle and other components is allowed for by a sliding spline between the propeller shaft and gearbox unit. Each universal joint consists of a center spider, four needle roller bearings and two yokes.

A nipple is fitted to each center spider for the lubrication of the bearings. The central lubricant chamber is connected to four reservoirs and to the needle roller bearing assemblies.

The needle roller bearings are filled with lubricant on assembly. A nipple is provided on the sleeve yoke of the sliding spline joint for lubrication of the splines.

If a large amount of grease exudes from the cork seals the joint should be dismantled and new seals fitted.

After dismantling, and before reassembly, the inside splines of the sleeve yoke should be smeared liberally with lubricant.

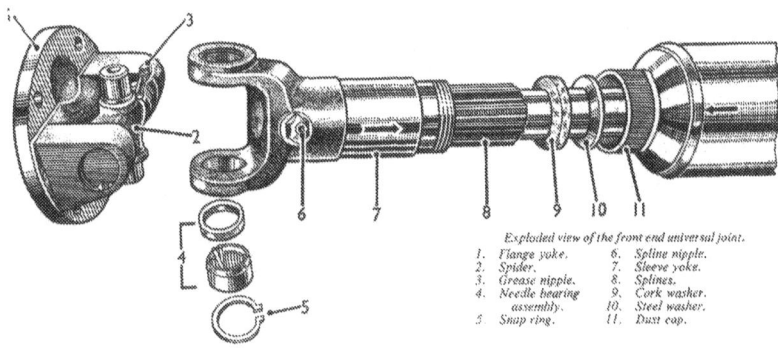

Exploded view of the front end universal joint.
1. Flange yoke.
2. Spider.
3. Grease nipple.
4. Needle bearing assembly.
5. Snap ring.
6. Spline nipple.
7. Sleeve yoke.
8. Splines.
9. Cork washer.
10. Steel washer.
11. Dust cap.

PROPELLER SHAFT ASSEMBLY
Tests for Wear

1 — Wear on the thrust faces is located by testing the lift in the joint, either by hand, or by using a length of wood suitably supported.

2 — Any circumferential movement of the shaft relative to the flange yokes, indicates wear in the needle roller bearings, or the sliding spline.

Removal of Complete Assembly

Before removal of the propeller shaft can be effected, the short length of tunnel immediately to the rear of the gearbox must be removed.

The removal procedure for the propeller shaft is as follows:—

1 — Support the shaft near the sliding joint, then withdraw the bolts

from the gearbox companion flange.

2 — Unscrew, by hand, the dust cap at the rear of the sliding joint. Slide the splined sleeve yoke about half an inch rearwards, thus disengaging the pilot flanges.

3 — Remove the four nuts and bolts securing the rear flange yoke from the axle companion flange and lower the propeller shaft to the ground.

4 — The propeller shaft and the two universals can now be taken to the bench for further dismantling.

Dismantling

The following directions apply to both universal joints of the propeller shaft except for the fact that the front joint can be separated from the shaft, whereas the rear joint has one yoke permanently fixed to the tube.

1 — Clean away the enamel from all the snap rings and bearing faces, to ensure easy extraction of the bearings.

2 — Remove the snap rings by pressing together the ends of the rings and extract with a screwdriver.If the ring does not come out easily, tap the bearing face lightly to relieve the pressure against the ring.

3 — Hold the splined end of the shaft in one hand and tap the radius of the yoke with a lead or copper hammer, when it will be found that the bearing will begin to emerge. If difficulty is experienced, use a small bar to tap the bearing from the inside, taking care not to damage the race itself. Turn the yoke over and extract the bearing with the fingers, being careful not to lose any of the needles.

4 — Repeat this operation for the other bearing, and the splined yoke can be removed from the spider.

5 — using a support and directions as above remove the spider from the other yoke.

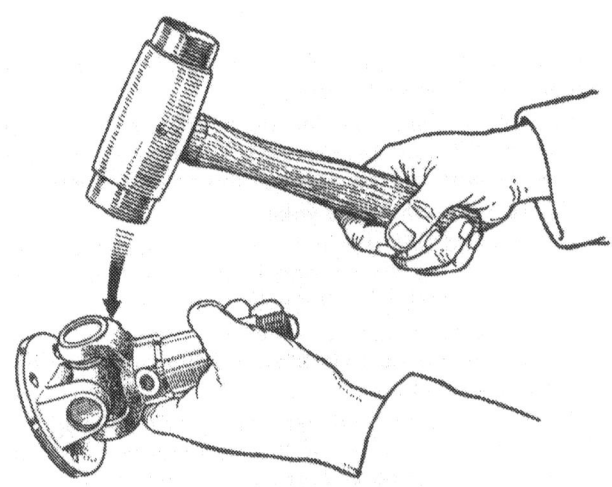

Tapping the joint to extract bearing.

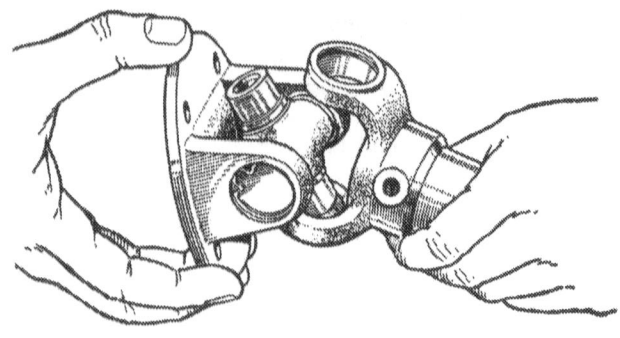

Separating the joint.

Examination and Checking for Wear

After long usage the parts most likely to show signs of wear are the bearing races and the spider journals of the universal joints. Should looseness or stress marks be observed, the assembly should be renewed complete, as no oversize journals or bearings are provided. It is essential that bearing races are a light drive fit in the yoke trunnions. Should any ovality be apparent in the trunnion bearing holes, new yokes must be fitted.

With reference to wear of the cross holes in a fixed yoke, which is part of the tubular shaft assembly, only in cases of emergency should this be replaced. It should normally be renewed with a complete tubular shaft assembly. The other parts likely to show signs of wear are the splined sleeve yoke, or splined stub shaft. A total of .004 in. circumferential movement, measured on the outside diameter of the spline, should not be exceeded. Should the splined stub shaft require renewing, this must be dealt with in the same way as the fixed yoke, i.e. a replacement tubular shaft assembly fitted.

Reassembly

1 — See that all drilled holes in the journals of the universal joints are cleaned out and filled with lubricant.

2 — Assemble the needle rollers in the bearing races and fill with lubricant. Should difficulty be experienced in assembly, smear the walls of the races with grease to retain the needle rollers in place.

3 — Insert the spider in the flange yoke.

4 — Using a soft-nosed drift about 1/32 in. smaller in diameter than the hole in the yoke, tap the bearing in position. It is essential that bearing races are a light drive in the yoke trunnion.

5 — Repeat this operation for the other three bearings. The spider journal shoulders should be coated with shellac prior to fitting the retainers to ensure a good seal.

6 — If the joint appears to bind, tap lightly with a wooden mallet which will relieve any pressure of the bearings on the end of the journals. When replacing the sliding joint on the shaft, be sure that the trunnions in the sliding and fixed yoke are in line. This can be

checked by observing that arrows marked on the splined sleeve yoke and the splined stub shaft are in line. It is advisable to renew cork washers and washer retainers on spider journals, using a tubular drift.

Replacing the Shaft Assembly

1 — Wipe the companion flange and flange yoke faces clean, to ensure that the pilot flange registers properly and the joint faces bed evenly all around.

2 — Insert the bolts, and see that the nuts are tightened evenly all round and are securely locked.

3 — The dust cap must be screwed up by hand as far as possible. The sliding joint is always placed towards the front of the car.

REAR AXLE

LUBRICATION

For the lubrication of the hypoid axle use lubricants only from approved sources. Do not, in any circumstances mix brands of hypoid lubricant. If there is any doubt as to the oil previously used, drain and flush the axle before finally filling up with new hypoid oil. Do not use kerosene as a flushing medium. On a new car the oil should be drained and the axle refilled at 500 miles (800 km.) **and subsequently every 6,000 miles (9600 km.). Failure to do this will eventually lead to axle breakdown.**
The filler plug is situated on the rear side of the axle, and the drain plug is in the bottom of the banjo casing.

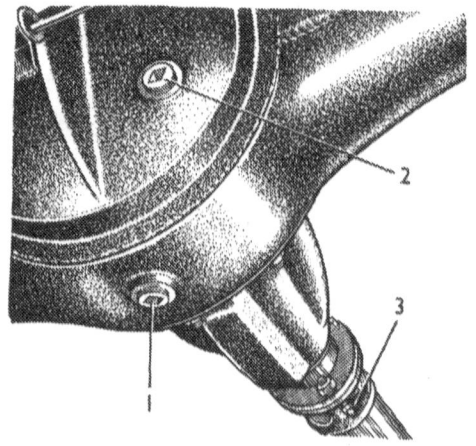

Rear axle.
1. Drain plug. 2. Filler plug. 3. Propeller shaft universal nipple.

AXLE UNIT

To Remove and Replace

1 — Loosen the wheel nuts or hub caps, then jack-up the car and place supports under frame members just forward of the rear springs front anchorage. Take off both wheels after removing the wheel nuts or hub caps.

2 — Working from under the car, unscrew the four self-locking nuts and remove the bolts (U.N.F.) securing the propeller shaft flange to axle pinion flange.

3 — Disconnect the handbrake cable from the axle. This is accomplished by unscrewing it from its link to the brake balance lever, and unscrewing the nut holding its outer casing to the axle.

4 — The hydraulic brake pipe at the rear axle is detached from the flexible pipe at the union just forward of the right hand shock

absorber.

5 — Unscrew the nuts securing the shock absorber links to the axle mounting brackets. Do not attempt to remove the links as this operation will prove much easier when freeing the axle.

6 — Remove the self-locking nuts from the spring clips ("U" bolts) which secure the axle to the springs. Observe that a fibre pad is situated between the axle and spring.

7 — Disconnect the tiebar at its axle anchorage by unscrewing its securing nuts.

8 — With the axle free, the connecting links from the shock absorbers should be detached.

9 — Remove the rubber block fixed between the axle and the left hand chassis frame. It is not necessary to detach the corresponding block on the right hand chassis frame.

10 — The complete axle should be removed from the right-hand side of the car. Take care not to damage other components, particularly the fuel pump.

11 — Installing the axle is the reverse of the above operations.

On re-assembling, it is advisable to jack-up the springs to meet the axle thus locating the spring center bolt properly. Remember to fit the fibre pad.

When assembling is complete adjust the handbrake if required and bleed the hydraulic brake system all round.

AXLE SHAFTS
To Remove and Replace

1 — Loosen the wheel nuts or hub cap of the wheel concerned before jacking-up the car.

2 — Remove the wheels after further unscrewing the wheel nuts or hub caps.

3 — Take out the two drum locating screws, using a screwdriver.

Note — If wire wheels are fitted it will be necessary to remove the five self-locking nuts, which secure the rear hub extension, to gain access to the two drum locating screws.

4 — The drum can be tapped off the hub and brake linings, provided the handbrake is released and the brake shoes are not adjusted so closely as to bind on the drum.

Should the brake linings hold the drum when the handbrake is released, it will be found necessary to slacken the brake shoe adjuster a few notches.

5 — Remove the axle shaft retaining screw and draw out the axle shaft by gripping the flange outside the hub. It should slide easily but if it is tight on the studs it may need gently prising with a screwdriver inserted between the flange and the hub. Should the paper washer be damaged it must be renewed when re-assembling.

HUBS

To remove and replace several special Service Tools are required.

1 — Remove the drum, axle shaft and bearing spacer.

2 — Knock back the tab of the locking washer and unscrew the nut with Service Tool 18G 258.

3 — Tilt the lock washer to disengage the key from the slot in the threaded portion of the axle casing; remove the washer.

4 — The hub can then be withdrawn with a suitable extractor such as Service Tool 18G 220 with adaptors 'A', 'D' and 'E'. The bearing and oil seal will be withdrawn with the hub.

5 — Fit a new oil seal using Service Tool 18G 134 and adaptor 18G 134AQ.

6 — The bearing is not adjustable and is replaced in one straightforward operation.

When re-assembling it is essential that the outer face of the bearing spacer should protrude from .001 in. (.025 mm.) to .004 in. (.091 mm.) beyond the outer face of the hub and the paper washers, when the bearing is pressed into position. This ensures that the bearing is gripped between the abutment shoulder in the hub and the driving flange of the axle shaft.

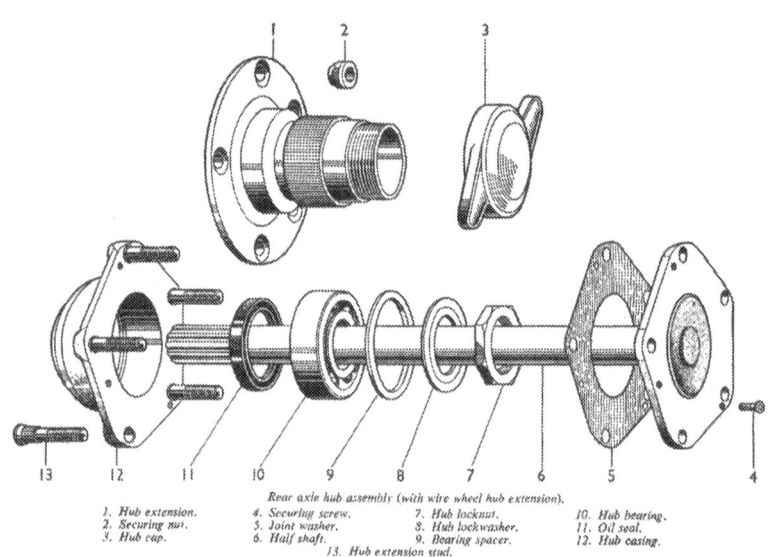

Rear axle hub assembly (with wire wheel hub extension).
1. Hub extension.
2. Securing nut.
3. Hub cap.
4. Securing screw.
5. Joint washer.
6. Half shaft.
7. Hub locknut.
8. Hub lockwasher.
9. Bearing spacer.
10. Hub bearing.
11. Oil seal.
12. Hub casing.
13. Hub extension stud.

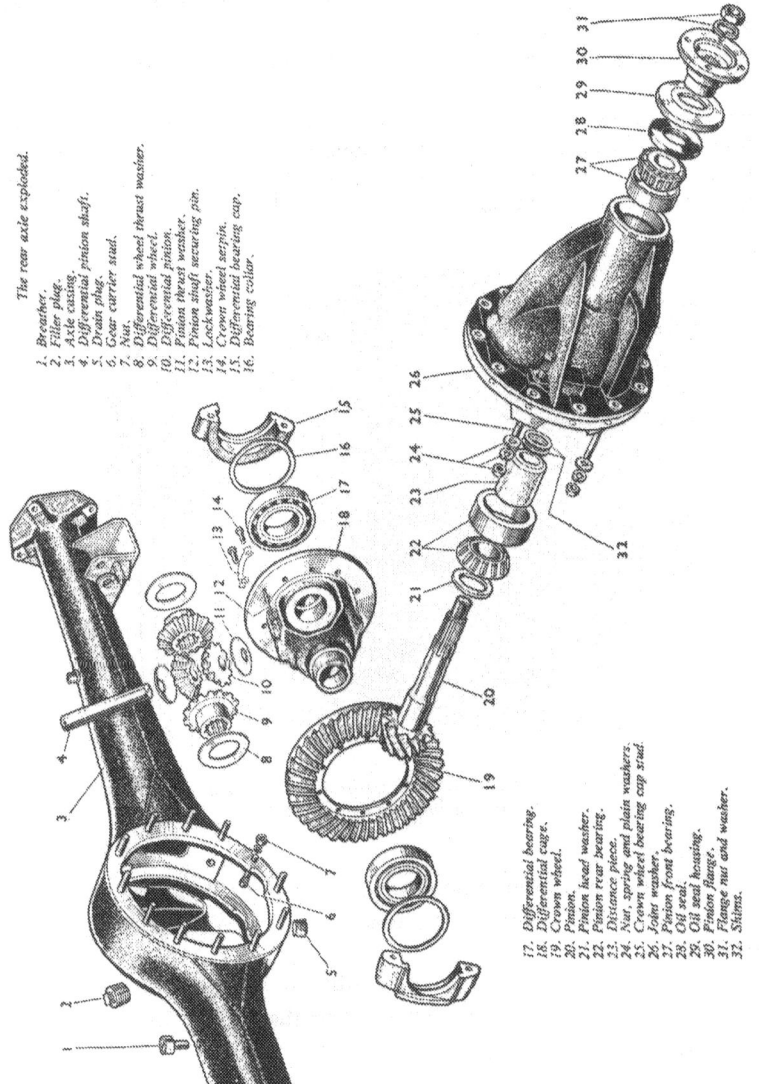

The rear axle exploded.

1. Breather.
2. Filler plug.
3. Axle casing.
4. Differential pinion shaft.
5. Drain plug.
6. Gear carrier stud.
7. Nut.
8. Differential wheel thrust washer.
9. Differential wheel.
10. Differential pinion.
11. Pinion thrust washer.
12. Pinion shaft securing pin.
13. Lockwasher.
14. Crown wheel setpin.
15. Differential bearing cap.
16. Bearing collar.
17. Differential bearing.
18. Differential cage.
19. Crown wheel.
20. Pinion.
21. Pinion head washer.
22. Pinion rear bearing.
23. Distance piece.
24. Nut, spring and plain washers.
25. Crown wheel bearing cap stud.
26. Joint washer.
27. Pinion front bearing.
28. Oil seal housing.
29. Oil seal.
30. Pinion flange.
31. Flange nut and washer.
32. Shims.

REAR SPRINGS

The road springs are of the semi-elliptical type. The rear ends pivot in shackles to allow for variation in the effective lengths of the springs as they are flexed on load or rebound. The front ends of the springs are mounted in rigid brackets on the chassis longitudinal members. Driving and braking forces are transmitted from the axles to the chassis by this end of the springs.

Two rubber buffers attached to the axle limit any excessive upward or bump movement of the axle.

The rear spring dampers are of the lever, hydraulic type and are mounted to brackets on the chassis longitudinal members. The levers are attached to brackets on the axle. A filler plug is located in the top plate of each rear damper.

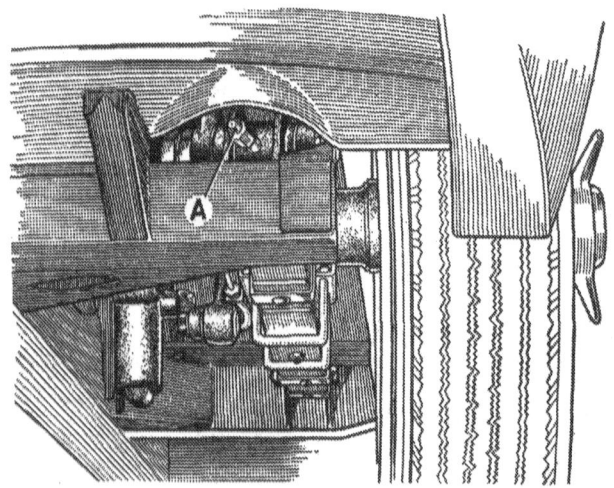

This illustration shows the position of the rear spring lubricator beneath the luggage compartment.

Maintenance

1 — Examine and tighten, if necessary the spring "U" bolts.

2 — Examine the oil level in the rear spring dampers and top up if necessary.

3 — Clean the springs and wipe them with an oily rag.

4 — Examine the springs for fractures and the bushes for wear.

To Remove

1 — Jack up the car on that side from which the spring is to be removed.

2— Pack up the chassis rear cross member with suitable supports, placing the supports as near to the spring rear anchorage as possible.

3 — Place a screw jack under the center of the spring to relieve the tension.

4 — Remove the respective wheel.

5 — Using a box spanner release the four self-locking nuts from the "U" bolts which secure the spring to the axle tube.

6 — Detach the nut and spring washer on the inside of the upper rear shackle, and the locknut, spring washer and nut on the inside of the lower rear shackle.

7 — Remove the shackle inside connecting link and extract the top and bottom shackle pins, together with the outside link.

8 — At the forward end of the spring detach the anchor pin by removing the nut and spring washer on the inside of the pin and drive the pin clear.

9 — Remove the supporting jack from under the spring to withdraw the latter from the car.

Spring rear shackle assembly in exploded form.

SHOCK ABSORBERS

The shock absorbers are of the hydraulic double acting piston type. All the working parts are submerged in oil. They are carefully set before dispatch and cannot be adjusted without special equipment. Any attempt to dismantle them will seriously affect their operation and performance. Should adjustment or repair be necessary they must be returned to their makers.

Maintenance

The maintenance of the hydraulic shock absorbers should include a periodical examination of their anchorage to the body frame and axle brackets. The fixing bolts and nuts must be tightened as necessary.

The cheese-headed screws securing the cover-plates must be kept fully tightened to prevent leakage of the fluid.

When checking the fluid level every 6,000 miles (9600 km.) all road dirt must be carefully cleared away from the vicinity of the filler plugs before the plugs are removed. This is most important as it is absolutely vital that no dirt or foreign matter should enter the operating chamber.

The correct fluid level is just below the filler plug threads.

The use of Armstrong Super (thin) Shock Absorber Oil is recommended. When this is not available any good quality mineral oil to Specification S.A.E. 20/20 W is acceptable. This alternative is not suitable for low temperature operation and is deficient in various other ways.

To Remove

1 — Remove the nut and spring washer that secure the shock absorber lever to the link arm.

2 — Withdraw the two fixing setpins from the shock absorber body and chassis bracket.

3 — Remove the shock absorber, threading the lever over the link arm bolt.

To Replace

The replacement of a rear shock absorber is a reversal of the removal procedure. Ensure that the link is above the arm when refitting the unit to the chassis and axle. When handling shock absorbers that have been removed from the chassis, it is important to keep the assemblies upright otherwise air may enter the working chamber and so cause erratic resistance.

Connecting Link Bushes

The rubber bushes integral with both ends of the connecting link which joins the shock absorber to the rear axle cannot be renewed. When these bushes are worn the arm must be renewed complete.

TIE-ROD ASSEMBLY

A tie-rod that is mounted in rubber bushes between a bracket welded to the axle casting and a bracket welded to the chassis frame prevents lateral motion between the axle and the frame.

To renew the rubber bushes, remove the self-locking nuts, washers and outer bushes from the ends of the tie-rod, free the rear axle and remove the rod. Then remove the inner rubber bushes.

Replacement of the tie-rod is a reversal of this procedure.

STEERING

The steering gear is a unit of extreme simplicity. The steering tube revolves a cam, which, in turn, engages with a taper peg fitted to a rocker shaft. This assembly is enclosed in an oil tight casing which carries two ball bearings at either end of the cam. These bearings are designed to carry radial and thrust loads.

When the steering wheel is turned the tube revolves the cam, which, in turn, causes the taper peg to move over a predetrmined arc, thus giving the rocker shaft its desired motion. Attached to the rocker shaft is a steering side and cross tube lever, which links up with the steering linkage.

The steering is of the "three cross tube" type, having a center cross tube connecting the steering side and cross tube lever to the arm on the idler shaft. Two shorter side tubes, one on either side, connect the steering arms to the steering gear and idler levers respectively.

Showing the front suspension, steering layout and lubrication points.
1. Cross tube connections.
2. Side rod inner connections.
3. Lower link.
4. Side rod outer connections.
5. Swivel pin.
6. Shock absorber.
7. Steering idler.
8. Anti-roll bar (no lubrication required).

MAINTENANCE

Lubrication of the grease nipples on the steering connections and swivel bearings is most important to maintain accurate steering.
Every 1,000 miles (1600 km.) charge the following points with lubricant:—

a — Steering rods and cross tube — 6 nipples.

b — Lower wishbone arm outer bearing — 2 nipples.

c — Swivel pin bushes — 4 nipples.

The steering box and steering idler should be topped up with recommended oil to the top of the filler plug opening every 1,000 miles (1600 km.).

ADJUSTMENTS IN THE VEHICLE

The following adjustments maintain the performance of the steering at its maximum and consist of aligning the front wheels and taking up backlash in the steering gear. Proceed as detailed below.

1 — Front wheel alignment is governed by four factors — camber, castor, swivel pin inclination and wheel toe-in. The correct camber and swivel pin angles are built into the front suspension and will change only if the suspension is distorted by accidental damage. It is most important that the front wheels should toe-in 1/16 in. (1.58

mm.) to 1/8 in. (3 mm.), and this is governed by the angle of the *track-rod* arms and the length of the track-rod. An adjustment is provided so that the track-rod may be lengthened or shortened to maintain the correct alignment. The track-rod should not be adjusted to correct a bent track-rod arm.

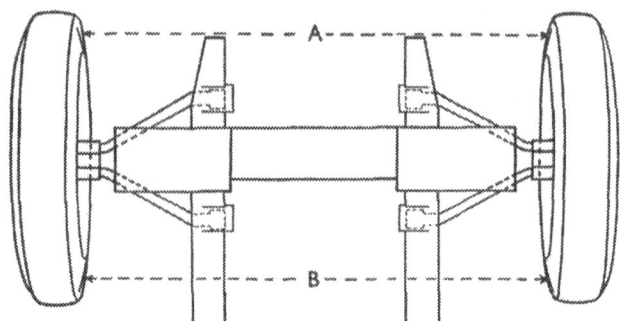

The toe-in must be adjusted so that A is $\frac{1}{16}$ in. to $\frac{1}{8}$ in. less than B.

The track is best adjusted by means of an optical alignment gauge. The cross tube is threaded right-hand at one end and left-hand at the other, so that the track adjustment can be made by simply rotating the tube in the required direction after releasing the locknuts. Always re-tighten the locknuts at each end of the cross tube after an adjustment has been made.

The side-rods are non-adjustable.

When adjusting the track the following precautions should be observed:—

a — The car should have come to rest from a forward movement. This ensures as far as possible that the wheels are in their natural running position.

b — It is preferable for alignment to be checked with car laden.

c — With conventional base-bar tire alignment gauges measurements in front of and behind the wheel centers should be taken at the same points on the tires or rim flanges. This is achieved by marking the tires where the first reading is taken and moving the car forwards approximately half a road wheel revolution before taking the second reading at the same points. With the optical gauge two or three readings should be taken with the car moved forwards to different positions — 180° road wheel turn for two readings and 120° for three readings. An average figure should then be calculated.

Wheels and tires vary laterally within their manufacturing tolerances, or as the result of service, and alignment figures obtained without moving the car are unreliable.

2 — Steering cam bearing adjustment should be carried out to eliminate all perceptible end play. To adjust the cam bearings, proceed as follows:—

a — From underneath the vehicle disconnect the side rod from the steering lever to free the gear of all loads.

b — Disconnect the flashing indicator switch and horn push cables at the snap connectors behind the radiator grille and, from inside the vehicle, gently draw out the indicator switch and horn button until the cables have been drawn into the stator tube, being thus protected from oil.

c — Place an oil tray under the steering box.

d — Remove the nut and olive from the end cover and remove the end cover by unscrewing the four retaining bolts.

e — Add or remove shims as necessary to obtain the correct adjustment. The steering wheel should turn freely when held lightly at the rim with the thumb and forefinger, but should have no end play.

3 — Rocker-shaft adjustment should be carried out after adjusting the cam bearings (described above).

a — With the side rod still disconnected from the steering lever, slacken the adjusting screw locknut and screw in the adjusting screw.

b — Check for backlash by exerting a light pressure on the lower end of the steering lever alternatively in both directions, while an assistant turns the steering wheel slowly from lock to lock. It will be noticed that the amount of slackness is not constant, there being less slackness in the center than in the full lock position. If slackness appears at all positions of the drop arm, the adjusting screw should be screwed in farther. After further adjustment, test again in the same manner. The correct adjustment is such that a "tight spot" will barely be apparent as the steering wheel is removed past the center position, with no backlash at the steering droparm. At this position tighten the adjusting screw locknut.

c — Refill the steering box with the correct grade of oil.

d — Reconnect the side rod.

STEERING GEAR ASSEMBLY

To Remove

1 — Remove the horn quadrant.

2 — Pry off the circlip, exposed to view, and then release the locking ring behind the steering wheel hub.

3 — Pull the steering wheel clear of the column, followed by the telescopic spring and locating collar.

4 — From behind the fascia release the two-piece clamping bracket supporting the top end of the column.

5 — Remove the radiator.

6 — Remove the radiator grille.

7 — There are two sealing plates, one on each side of the scuttle, through which the steering column passes, release each plate by undoing the four metal thread screws.

8 — Jack up the front of the car and remove the front wheels.

9 — Disconnect the cross tube and side rod from the steering lever.

10 — Unscrew the three nuts and bolts securing the steering box mounting bracket to the chassis.

11 – Maneuver the steering column together with the steering box downwards and forwards out of the radiator grille opening.

To Replace

The replacement of the steering gear is a reversal of the procedure "To Remove," but observe the following precautions:—

1 – Carefully align the steering column so that no bending stress is imposed upon it before tightening the support brackets.

2 – Make sure that the steering wheel is in the center of travel and the front wheels are in the straight ahead position when installing the side rod.

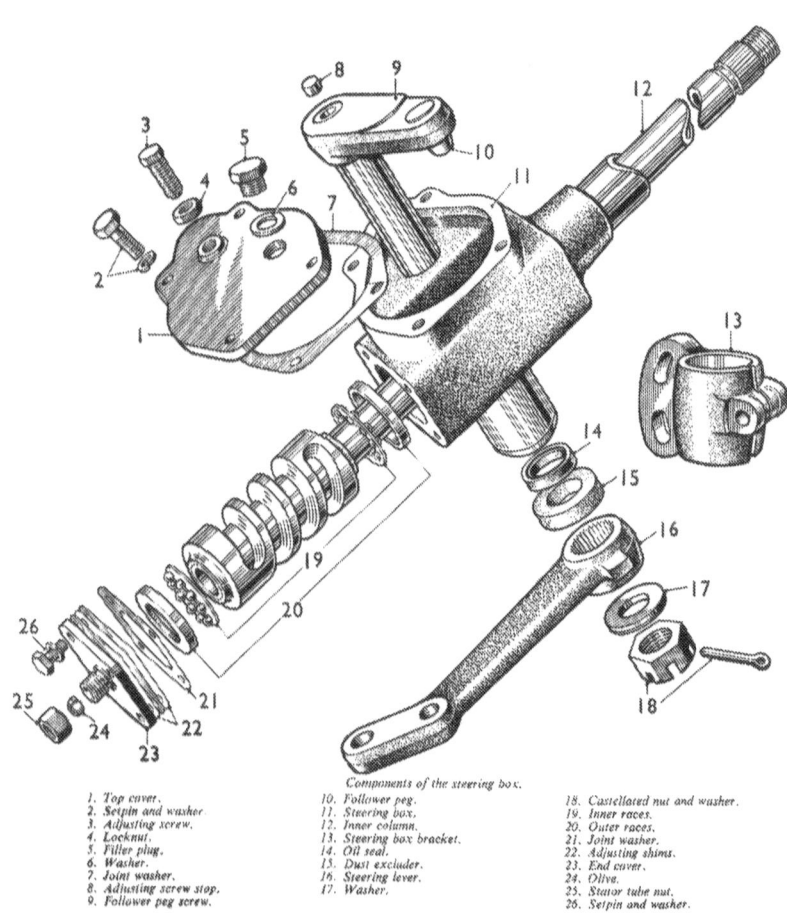

Components of the steering box.

1. Top cover.
2. Setpin and washer.
3. Adjusting screw.
4. Locknut.
5. Filler plug.
6. Washer.
7. Joint washer.
8. Adjusting screw stop.
9. Follower peg screw.
10. Follower peg.
11. Steering box.
12. Inner column.
13. Steering box bracket.
14. Oil seal.
15. Dust excluder.
16. Steering lever.
17. Washer.
18. Castellated nut and washer.
19. Inner races.
20. Outer races.
21. Joint washer.
22. Adjusting shims.
23. End cover.
24. Olive.
25. Stator tube nut.
26. Setpin and washer.

SUSPENSION

INDEPENDENT FRONT SUSPENSION

The independent front suspension is known as the "wishbone" type, since the top and bottom linkages roughly conform to the shape of a wishbone. Between these two wishbones is the coil spring, held under compression between the top spring plate and the lower spring plate which is secured to the lower wishbone by four bolts. The top wishbone is formed by the lever arms of a double-acting hydraulic shock absorber which is anchored to the top spring plate bracket by four bolts. At the swivel end, the top wishbone is secured to the swivel pin trunnion by means of a fulcrum pin and tapered rubber bushes. The bottom wishbone is secured by a single lower link spindle and tapered rubber bushes to two mounting plates, bolted to the front suspension member, and by two screwed bushes and a screwed fulcrum pin to the lower end of the swivel pin.

Checking for Wear

The following tests should be made to check for wear in various components of the front suspension unit.

1 — Wear of the swivel pin, or bushes, or both, may be checked by jacking up the front of the car and endeavoring to rock the wheel by grasping opposite points of the tire in a vertical position. If any sideways movement can be detected between the swivel axle assembly, the swivel pin or the swivel pin bushes are worn and must be stripped for examination.

2 — Up and down, or sideways movement of the shock absorber cross shaft, relative to the shock absorber casting, denotes wear of the shock absorber shaft bearings which can only be remedied by refitting a new shock absorber. These bearings are best checked when the suspension is dismantled and when with some freedom of movement, it is possible to move the top wishbone arms, which are attached at their inner ends of the shock absorber cross shaft.

3 — The rubber bearing bushes used for the upper wishbone arm outer bearings and for the lower wishbone arm inner bearings may in time deteriorate and need renewing. Excessive sideways movement in either of these bearings would denote softening of the rubber bushes.

4 — The screwed bushes or the screwed trunnion fulcrum pin of the lower wishbone arm outer bearing assembly may develop excess free play due to wear of either of these parts. This assembly can best be checked when the suspension has been dismantled.

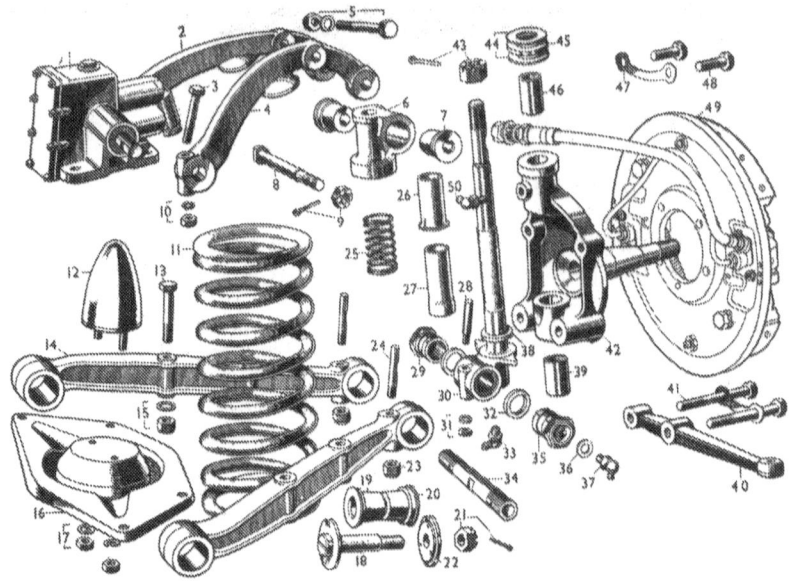

Components of the independent front suspension.

1. Shock absorber.
2. Rear top wishbone arm.
3. Clamping bolt for front wishbone arm.
4. Front top wishbone arm.
5. Joining bolt for top wishbone arms.
6. Upper trunnion link.
7. Trunnion rubber bearing.
8. Upper trunnion fulcrum pin.
9. Fulcrum locking nut and split pin.
10. Nut and washer for clamping bolt.
11. Coil spring.
12. Rebound rubber bumper.
13. Spring plate bolt.
14. Rear lower wishbone arm.
15. Simmonds nut and lockwasher.
16. Spring plate.
17. Rebound bumper nut and washer.
18. Fulcrum pin for inner lower bearing.
19. An inner lower rubber bearing.
20. An outer lower rubber bearing.
21. Fulcrum pin nut and split pin.
22. Fulcrum pin special washer.
23. Nut for bush cotter.
24. Bush cotter.
25. Swivel pin dust cover spring.
26. Upper dust cover.
27. Lower dust cover.
28. Cotter for fulcrum pin.
29. Rear screwed bush.
30. Swivel pin and lower trunnion.
31. Nut and washer.
32. Cork ring.
33. Trunnion oil nipple.
34. Screwed fulcrum pin.
35. Front screw bush.
36. Flat washer.
37. Oil nipple.
38. Cork ring.
39. Swivel axle lower bush.
40. Steering arm.
41. Steering arm setpin.
42. Swivel axle.
43. Swivel pin nut and split pin.
44. Staybrite washers.
45. Oilite washer.
46. Swivel axle upper bush.
47. Back plate setpin lockwasher.
48. Back plate setpin.
49. Back plate assembly.
50. Swivel pin oil nipple.

CASTOR AND CAMBER ANGLES AND SWIVEL PIN INCLINATION

The castor and camber angles and the swivel pin inclination are three design settings of the front suspension assembly. They have a very important bearing on the steering and general riding of the car. Each of these settings is determined by the machining and assembly of the component parts during manufacture. They are not therefore adjustable.

However, should the car suffer damage to the suspension affecting these settings, the various angles must be verified to ascertain whether replacements are necessary.

Camber Angle

This is the outward tilt of the wheel and a rough check can be made by measuring the distance from the outside wall of the tire, immediately below the hub, to a plumb line hanging from the outside wall of the tire above the hub. The distance must be the same on both wheels. Before making this test, it is very important to ensure that the tires are in a uniform condition and at the same pressure. Also that the car is unladen and on level ground.

Damage to the upper and lower wishbone arms may well affect the camber angle.

Castor Angle
This is the tilt of the swivel pin when viewed from the side of the car. This also is only likely to be affected by damage to the upper and lower wishbone arms.

Swivel Pin Inclination
This is the tilt of the swivel pin when viewed from the front of the car and is again only likely to be affected by damage to the wishbone arms.

A useful tool which can be used for checking these settings is the Dunlop "wheel camber, castor and swivel gauge." With the car standing on level ground this gauge will give readings enabling the castor, camber and swivel pin angles to be quickly verified.

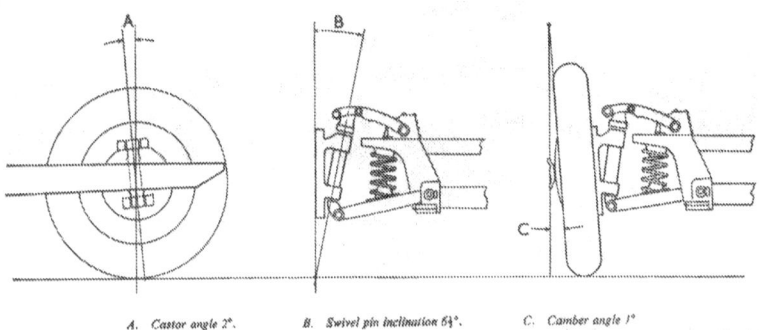

A. Castor angle 2°.   B. Swivel pin inclination 6¼°.   C. Camber angle 1°

FRONT HUBS
(Disc Wheels)
To Check for Wear
The inner and outer ball bearings of the front hub are **non-adjustable**, the amount of thrust being determined by a distance piece. To check for wear of these bearings, the car should be jacked until the wheel of the front hub is clear of the ground. Then grasp the tire with both hands in the vertical position and rock the wheel. Movement between the wheel and the back plate denotes wear of the hub bearings. Should a very positive movement be apparent, the front hub bearings will need renewing.

To Remove and Dismantle
1 — Jack the car until the wheel is clear of the ground and then place blocks under the independent suspension spring plate. Lower the car on to the blocks.

2 — Remove the wheel and the countersunk screw holding the brake drum. If the drum appears to bind on the brake shoes, the shoe adjusters should be slackened.

3 — Lever off the hub cap, and then extract the split pin from the swivel axle locking nut. Using a box wrench and tommy bar remove

the axle nut and ease the flat washer, under the nut, clear of the axle thread.

4 — The front hub can now be withdrawn by using an extractor which fits over the wheel studs. The hub is withdrawn complete with the inner and outer bearings, the distance piece and the oil seal. Should the inner bearing race remain on the swivel axle it can be removed by carefully inserting a narrow rod into the two small holes, in turn, in each side of the swivel axle and tapping the race lightly.

5 — With the hub removed, the outer bearing and the distance piece (spacer) can be dismantled by inserting a drift through the inner bearing and gently tapping the outer bearing clear on the hub. The inner bearing and oil seal can then be removed by inserting the drift from the opposite side of the hub.

6 — The removal of the brake backplate is described fully in the section on brakes.

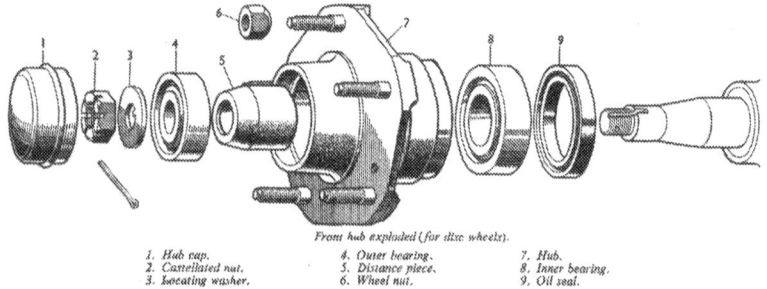

From hub exploded (for disc wheels).

1. Hub cap.
2. Castellated nut.
3. Locating washer.
4. Outer bearing.
5. Distance piece.
6. Wheel nut.
7. Hub.
8. Inner bearing.
9. Oil seal.

To Assemble and Replace

1 — Insert the inner ball bearing race into the hub with the side of the race marked "thrust" facing the distance piece.

2 — Pack the hub with **recommended** grease and then insert the distance piece so that the domed end faces the outer bearing.

3 — Replace the outer bearing so that the thrust side faces the distance piece. Use a soft metal drift to replace both bearings, tapping them gently and alternately on diametrically opposite sides of the bearing to ensure they move evenly into their respective housings on the hub.

4 — Replace the hub oil seal over the inner bearing so that the hollow side of the seal faces the bearing. Renew the seal if it is damaged in any way.

5 — Replace the hub on the swivel axle, using a hollow drift which will bear evenly on both the inner and outer races of the outer hub bearing. Gently tap the hub into position until the inner race bears against the shoulder on the swivel axle.

6 — Place the swivel axle flat washer into position and tighten the nut. The split pin should be inserted to lock the nut.

7 — Tap the hub cap on to the hub after first packing the cap with grease.

8 — Replace the brake drum and secure with the countersunk screw.

It is important that the drum is fully home before this screw is tightened and, if necessary, the drum should be pressed in position by tightening two wheel nuts.

9 — Refit the wheel. The wheel nuts are best finally tightened when the car is off the jacking blocks, but re-adjust the brake shoes if necessary before the car is lowered to the ground.

FRONT HUBS
(Wire Wheels)
To Check for Wear

The inner and outer bearings of the front hub are of the taper roller type and are therefore **adjustable.** To check for wear of these bearings the car should be jacked up until the wheel of the front hub to be checked, is clear of the ground. Movement between the wheel and the back plate denotes wear of the hub bearings. Should a very positive movement be apparent, the front hub bearings will need renewing.

To Remove and Dismantle

1 — Jack up the car until the wheel is clear of the ground and then place blocks under the independent spring plate. Lower the car on to the blocks.

2 — Remove the knock-on hub cap (direction of rotation marked on cap) and pull the wheel off the splines.

3 — Release the nuts and washers holding the brake drum, then gently tap the brake drum clear of the front hub assembly. If the drum appears to bind on the brake shoes, the shoe adjusters should be slackened.

4 — Use an extractor to extract the grease retaining cup from within the hub.

5 — Straighten the end of the split pin and then pry it out through the hole provided in the hub.

6 — Using a box wrench and tommy bar remove the hub securing nut and flat washer from the swivel axle.

7 — Withdraw the front hub using an extractor. It is preferable to

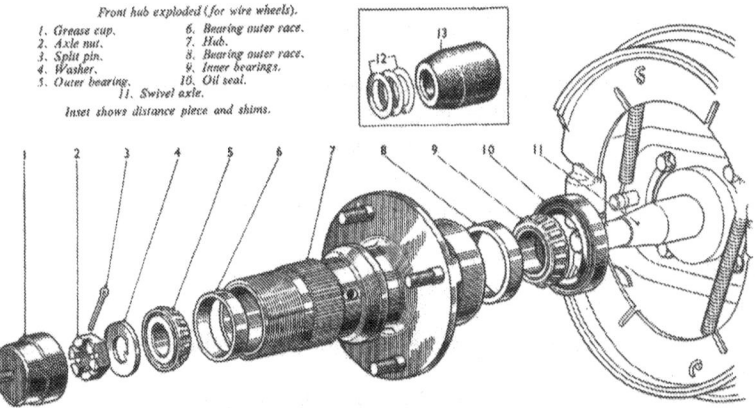

Front hub exploded (for wire wheels).
1. Grease cup.
2. Axle nut.
3. Split pin.
4. Washer.
5. Outer bearing.
6. Bearing outer race.
7. Hub.
8. Bearing outer race.
9. Inner bearings.
10. Oil seal.
11. Swivel axle.
Inset shows distance piece and shims.

use an extractor which screws into position on the hub cap thread, but an extractor which locates over the hub studs may also be used. The hub is withdrawn complete with the inner and outer bearings and oil seal.

8 — With the hub removed, dismantle the outer bearing by inserting a drift through the inner bearing and gently tapping the outer bearing clear of the hub. The inner bearing and oil seal can then be removed by inserting the drift from the opposite side of the hub.

Re Reassemble and Replace

The end-float in the hub bearings must be checked and adjusted whenever the hub has been dismantled for attention or when play in the hub bearings has become excessive. The end-float is adjustable by means of shims situated between the outer bearing and the bearing distance piece.

1 — Press the two bearing outer rings into the hub. Insert the inner race and rollers of the inner bearing and the bearing spacer into the hub, packing the assembly with grease.

2 — Fit the oil seal to the hub and mount the hub assembly on the stub axle. Position the inner race and rollers of the outer bearing, suitably greased, and in the hub **without fitting shims at this stage.**

3 — Fit the stub axle nut and washer. Tighten the nut and at the same time rotate the hub back and forth until there is noticeable drag. This ensures that the bearing cones are properly seated.

4 — Unscrew and remove the stub axle nut. Exract the washer and the center of the outer bearing. Insert a sufficient thickness of shims **to produce an excessive amount of end-float.** Note the total thickness of shims used. Replace the bearing center, the washer, and tighten the stub axle nut.

5 — Measure accurately the total amount of end-float in the bearings. Remove the stub axle nut, washer, and outer bearing center. Reduce the number of shims to eliminate end-float, while still allowing the hub to rotate freely, when the stub axle nut has been refitted and tightened to a torque wrench reading of 40 to 70 lb/ft. (5.53 to 9.68 kg.m.). Latitude for this reading is given so that the nut may be aligned with the split pin hole in the stub axle.

6 — Insert a new split pin through the hole provided in the hub and lock the stub axle nut.

7 — Pack the retaining cap with grease and, using a drift, tap it gently but firmly up against the outer bearing.

8 — Replace the brake drum and secure with the four spring washers and self-locking nuts.

9 — Grease the wheel hub splines, refit the road wheel and replace the knock-on hub cap.

SHOCK ABSORBERS
To Remove

1 — Jack up the car and place stands under the chassis in safe positions.

2 — Remove the road wheel. Place a jack beneath the outer end of

the lower wishbone arm and raise it until the shock absorber arms are clear of their rebound rubber.

3 — Remove the clamp bolt connecting the two shock absorber arms together.

4 — Remove the split pin and castellated nut on the upper fulcrum pin and withdraw the pin.

5 — One arm of each shock absorber unit is secured to the shock absorber spindle by a clamp bolt. When the clamp bolt has been removed the arm may be partially withdrawn. This allows the trunnion link and its rubber bushes to be separated easily from the shock absorber arms.

6 — Retrieve the trunnion link rubber bushes.

7 — Once the four shock absorber fixing bolts and their spring washers have been extracted the unit may be removed from car.

NOTE — The jack must be left in position under the suspension wishbone while the top link remains disconnected in order to keep the coil spring securely in position and to avoid straining the steering connections.

To Replace

Replacement is a reversal of the above procedure, but attention must be given to the following points:

1 — Having bolted the shock absorber to the chassis frame and before fitting the upper trunnion fulcrum pin, work the arms of the unit three or four times through their full travel to expel any air which may have found its way into the operating chamber.

2 — The fulcrum pin bushes must be renewed if softening of the rubber or side movement is evident.

3 — Fit the trunnion with its bushes between the shock absorber arms and refit the fulcrum pin before pushing the loosened arm home on the shock absorber spindle and replacing the clamp bolt.

4 — Tighten the fulcrum pin nut and the clamp bolt connecting the two shock absorber arms only when the load is on the suspension, i.e., with the jack in position under the lower suspension arm or a 2 in. 5.08 mm.) distance piece interposed between the shock absorber arm and the chassis frame.

FRONT HUBS WITH DISC BRAKES

The inner and outer bearings of the front hub are of the taper roller type and are therefore **adjustable.** To check for wear of these bearings the car should be jacked up until the wheel of the front hub to be checked is clear of the ground. Movement between the brake disc and the steering arm denotes wear of the hub bearings or incorrect adjustment. Should a very positive movement be apparent, the front hub bearings will need renewing. The amount of movement present may be checked by a dial gauge.

To Remove and Dismantle

1 — Jack up the car until the wheel is clear of the ground and then place blocks under the spring plate. Lower the car on to the blocks.

2 — Remove the "knock-on" hub cap (direction of rotation marked on

cap) and pull the wheel off the splines.

3 — Remove the brake calliper unit.

4 — Use an extractor to extract the grease retaining cup from within the hub.

5 — Straighten the end of the split pin and then pry it out through the hole provided in the hub.

6 — Using a box wrench and tommy bar remove the hub securing nut and flat washer from the swivel axle.

7 — Withdraw the front hub using an extractor. Use an extractor which screws into position on the hub cap thread. Do not attempt to remove the hub by pulling on the brake disc. The hub is withdrawn complete with the inner and outer bearings and oil seal.

8 — With the hub removed, dismantle the outer bearing by inserting a drift through the inner bearing and gently tapping the outer bearing clear of the hub. The inner bearing and oil seal can then be removed by inserting the drift from the opposite side of the hub.

To Reassemble and Replace follow procedure given for front hubs with wire wheels.

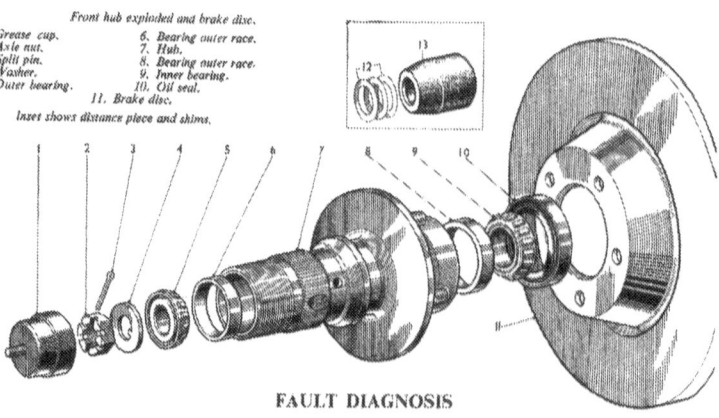

Front hub exploded and brake disc.
1. Grease cup.
2. Axle nut.
3. Split pin.
4. Washer.
5. Outer bearing.
6. Bearing outer race.
7. Hub.
8. Bearing outer race.
9. Inner bearing.
10. Oil seal.
11. Brake disc.
Inset shows distance piece and shims.

FAULT DIAGNOSIS

Symptom	No.	Possible Fault
(a) Wheel Wobble	1	Unbalanced wheels and tyres
	2	Slack steering connections
	3	Incorrect steering geometry
	4	Excessive play in steering gear
	5	Broken or weak front springs
	6	Loose idler mounting or worn idler shaft
	7	Worn hub bearings
	8	Loose or broken shackles
(b) Wander	1	Check 2, 3, 4 and 8 in (a) Broken spring clips
	2	Front suspension and rear axle mounting points out of alignment
	3	Uneven tyre pressures
	4	Uneven tyre wear
	5	Weak shock absorbers or springs
(c) Heavy Steering	1	Check 3 in (a) Excessively low tyre pressures
	2	Insufficient lubricant in steering box
	3	Insufficient idler lubrication
	4	"Dry" steering connections
	5	Out of track
	6	Incorrectly adjusted steering gear
	7	Misaligned steering column

BRAKES

CARS WITH DRUM BRAKES

The brakes on all four wheels are hydraulically operated by foot pedal application, directly coupled to a master cylinder in which the hydraulic pressure of the brake operating fluid is originated. A supply tank cast integrally with the master cylinder provides a reservoir by which the fluid is replenished, and a pipe line consisting of tube, flexible hose and unions, interconnect the master cylinder and the wheel cylinders.

The pressure generated in the master cylinder by application with the foot pedal is transmitted with equal and undiminished force to all wheel cylinders simultaneously. This moves the pistons outwards, which in turn expand the brake shoes thus producing automatic equalization, and efficiency in direct proportion to the effort applied at the pedal.

When the pedal is released the brake shoe springs return the shoes which then return the wheel cylinder pistons, and therefore the fluid back into the pipe lines and master cylinder.

An independent mechanical linkage actuated by a handbrake, mounted on the propeller shaft tunnel, operates the rear wheels by mechanical expanders attached to the rear wheel cylinder bodies.

The front brakes are of the two leading shoe types with sliding shoes which ensure automatic centralization of the brake shoe in operation. The rear brakes are also fitted with sliding shoes, and incorporate the handbrake mechanism.

Front Brakes

The front brakes are operated by two wheel cylinders situated diametrically opposite each other on the inside of the backplate and interconnected by a bridge pipe on the outside.

Each wheel cylinder consists of a light alloy body containing a spring seal support, seal, steel piston and edges of both shoes making initial contact with the drum. The shoes are allowed to slide and centralize during the actual braking operation which distributes the braking force equally over the lining area ensuring high efficiency and even lining wear.

Adjustment for lining wear is by means of two knurled snail cam adjusters, each operating against a peg at the actuating end of each shoe. Both adjusters turn clockwise to expand the shoes.

The brake shoes rest on supports formed in the backplate and are held in position by two return springs which pass from a hole in the abutment end of each web to a peg fixed to the backplate.

The bleed screw which is incorporated in one cylinder, is provided with a steel ball, this is normally seated firmly on a valve opening in the cylinder. A dust cover it fitted over the screw nipple to exclude dirt and with the removal of this cover and an anti-clockwise turn of the screw the fluid may escape.

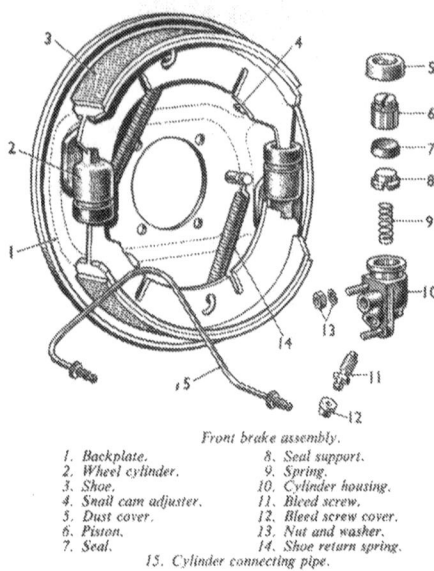

Front brake assembly.

1. Backplate.
2. Wheel cylinder.
3. Shoe.
4. Snail cam adjuster.
5. Dust cover.
6. Piston.
7. Seal.
8. Seal support.
9. Spring.
10. Cylinder housing.
11. Bleed screw.
12. Bleed screw cover.
13. Nut and washer.
14. Shoe return spring.
15. Cylinder connecting pipe.

Rear Brakes

The rear brake shoes are not fixed but are allowed to slide and centralize with the same effect as in the front brakes. They are hydraulically operated by a single acting wheel cylinder incorporating the handbrake mechanism. At the cylinder end the leading shoe is located in a slot in the piston while the trailing shoe rests in a slot formed in the cylinder body. At the adjuster end they rest in slots in the adjuster links. Both shoes are supported on the backplate and are held in position by two return springs fitted from shoe to shoe with the shorter spring nearer the adjuster.

The wheel cylinder consists of a light alloy die casting into the end of which moves a piston, with seal in a highly finished bore. In the other end of the housing a slot is machined to carry the trailing shoe. The pivoted handbrake lever projects through the backplate at right angles and operates on the leading shoe. The cylinder is attached to the backplate by a spring clip allowing it to slide laterally.

A bleed screw is incorporated in the cylinder housing with a rubber dust cap over the nipple end.

Adjustment for lining wear is made by the brake shoe adjuster. This has a steel housing which is spigotted and bolted firmly to the inside of the backplate. The housing carries two opposed steel links, the outer end slotted to carry the shoes, and the inclined inner faces bearing on inclined faces of the hardened steel wedge.

The wedge has a threaded spindle with a square end which projects on the outside of the backplate, enabling a wrench to be used for adjustment purposes, by rotating the wedge in a clockwise direction, the links are forced apart and the fulcrum of the brake shoes expanded.

When the brake is applied, the piston under the influence of the hydraulic pressure, moves the leading shoe and the body reacts by sliding on the backplate to operate the trailing shoe.

The handbrake lever is pivoted in the cylinder body, and when operated the lever tip expands the leading shoe, and the pivot moves the cylinder body and with it the trailing shoe.

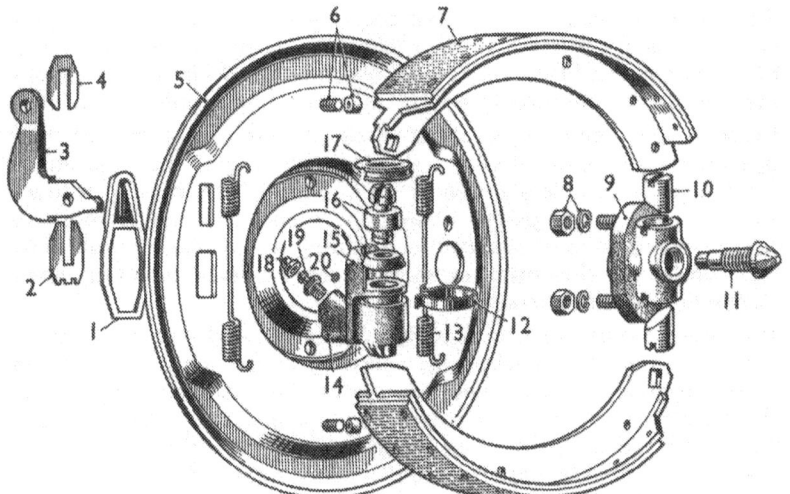

Rear brake backplate exploded.

1. Rubber seal.
2. Wheel cylinder locking plate.
3. Handbrake lever.
4. Wheel cylinder locking plate.
5. Backplate.
6. Steady post.
7. Brake shoe.
8. Nut and spring washer.
9. Adjuster body.
10. Adjuster tappets.
11. Adjuster wedge.
12. Dust cover clip.
13. Shoe return spring.
14. Pipe orifice.
15. Cylinder body.
16. Piston.
17. Dust cover.
18. Bleed nipple dust cover.
19. Bleed nipple.
20. Bleed valve ball.

Handbrake

The handbrake operates on the rear wheels only and is applied by a pull-up type of lever situated on the propeller shaft tunnel. The cable from the control is attached to the compensator mounted on the rear axle. From compensator to the brake levers are transverse rods which are non-adjustable.

The handbrake linkage is set when leaving the works and should not require any attention. Only when a complete overhaul is necessary should the handbrake linkage require re-setting.

When this is correct the rear shoes should be locked to the drums, the handbrake control just slightly applied, and the cable slackness just removed, by means of adjusting the sleeve nut at the front end of the longitudinal cable.

Replenishment of Hydraulic Fluid

Inspect the supply tank at regular intervals and maintain at the indicated level by the addition of Girling Brake Fluid.

Great care should be exercised when adding brake fluid, to prevent dirt or foreign matter entering the system.

IMPORTANT — Serious consequences may result from the use of incorrect fluids, and on no account should any other than Girling Brake Fluid be used. This fluid has been specially prepared and is unaffected by high temperature or freezing.

Bleeding the Hydraulic System

Bleeding is necessary any time a portion of the hydraulic system has been disconnected, or if the level of the brake fluid has been allowed to fall so low that air has entered the master cylinder.

With all the hydraulic connections secure and the supply tank topped up with the fluid, remove the rubber cap from the left hand rear bleed nipple and fit the bleed tube over the bleed nipple, immersing the free end of the tube in a clean jar containing a little brake fluid.

Unscrew the bleed nipple about three-quarters of a turn and then operate the brake pedal with a slow full stroke until the fluid entering the jar is completely free of air bubbles. Then, during a down stroke of the brake pedal, tighten the bleed screw sufficiently to seat the ball, remove bleed tube and replace the bleed nipple dust cap. **Under no circumstances must excessive force be used when tightening the bleed screws.**

This process must now be repeated for each bleed screw at each of the three remaining backplates, finishing at the wheel nearest the master cylinder. Always keep a careful check on the supply tank during bleeding, since it is most important that a full level is maintained. Should air reach the master cylinder from the supply tank, the whole of the bleeding operation must be repeated.

After bleeding, top up the supply tank to its correct level of approximately three-quarters full.

Never use fluid that has been bled from a brake system for topping up the supply tank, as this brake fluid may be to some extent aerated. Such fluid must be allowed to stand for at **least** twenty-four hours before it is used again. This will allow the air bubbles in the fluid time to disperse.

Great cleanliness is essential when dealing with any part of the hydraulic system, and especially so where the brake fluid is concerned. Dirty fluid must never be added to the system.

NOTE — **It is advisable to turn all the brake shoe adjusters to their full "off" position before bleeding. After bleeding adjust brakes as described below.**

Adjusting the Brake Shoes

The brakes are adjusted for lining wear, **only** at the brakes themselves, and on no account should any alteration be made to the handbrake cable for this purpose.

Front Brakes. A separate snail cam adjuster is provided for each shoe. Jack up the car until the wheel to be adjusted is clear of the ground, then fully release both the hexagon head adjuster bolts on the outside of the backplate by turning anti-clockwise with an open-ended wrench.

Turn one of the adjuster bolts clockwise until the brake shoe concerned touches the brake drum, then release the adjuster until the shoe is just free of the drum. Repeat the process for the second adjuster and shoe.

Spin the wheel to ensure that the brake shoes are quite free of the drum. Repeat the whole procedure for the second front wheel.

Showing the location of the two brake shoe adjusters on a front brake backplate.

Rear Brakes. One common adjuster is provided for both shoes and the adjustment of both rear wheels is identical.

Release the handbrake and jack up the car. Turn the square end of the adjuster on the outside of each rear backplate in a clockwise direction until a resistance is felt. Slacken two clicks when the drum should rotate freely.

FRONT BRAKES

Replacing Brake Shoes

NOTE — Always fit Girling "Factory Lined" replacement shoes. These have the correct type of lining and are accurately ground to size. When fitting replacement shoes, fit a new set of shoe return springs.

1 — Jack up the car and remove road wheels, hub extensions and brake drums.

2 — Lift one shoe out of the abutment slot of one wheel cylinder, then release from the piston slot of the other. (It will be found quite simple to remove the shoe return springs). To prevent the wheel cylinder pistons from expanding it is advisable to place a rubber band round each cylinder. Repeat with the second shoe.

3 — Clean down the backplate, check wheel cylinders for leaks and freedom of motion.

4 — Check adjusters for easy working and turn back (anti-clockwise) to full "off" position. Lubricate where necessary with **Girling (White)**

Brake Grease.

5 — Smear the tips of the brake shoe supports on the backplate, and the operating and abutment ends of the new shoes with **Girling (White) Brake Grease.** The (white) brake grease must not be allowed to contact hydraulic cylinders, pistons or rubber parts. Keep all grease off the linings on new replacement shoes and do not handle more than necessary.

6 — Fit new shoe return springs to the new shoes. Place the hooked end of the spring through the hole in the shoe web and the swan neck through the hole in the back plate near the abutment end of the same shoe. Each shoe can be replaced independently. Remove rubber bands from cylinder.

7 — Make sure the drums are clean and free from grease, etc., then re-fit.

8 — Adjust the brakes as described under "Running Maintenance."

9 — Re-fit the road wheels and lower the car to the ground.

REAR BRAKES
Replacing Brake Shoes

Proceed in stages as described for front brakes, paragraphs 1 to 9, substituting the details in the following paragraphs for those bearing the same number.

2 — Lift one of the shoes out of the slots in the adjuster link and wheel cylinder piston. Both shoes can then be removed complete with springs. Place a rubber band round the wheel cylinder to keep piston in place.

6 — Fit the two new shoe return springs to the new shoes (with the shorter spring at adjuster end) from shoe to shoe and between shoe web and backplate. Locate one shoe in the adjuster link and wheel cylinder piston slots, then pry over the opposite shoe into its relative position. Remove rubber band.

NOTE — The first shoe has the lining positioned towards the heel of the shoe and on the second shoe towards the toe or operating end in both left-hand and right-hand brake assemblies. Several hard applications of the brake pedal should be made to ensure all the parts are working satisfactorily and the shoes bedding to the drums, then the brakes should be adjusted as described.

Immediately after fitting replacement shoes it is advisable to slacken one further click on the brake adjuster to allow for possible lining expansion, reverting to normal adjustment afterwards.

BRAKE PEDAL
To Remove

1 — The brake and clutch pedal linkages are mounted in a common bracket and thus have to be released as a unit.

2 — Inside the car disconnect the brake and clutch cylinder levers from their master cylinder push rods by removing the clevis pins.

3 — Working under the bonnet, unscrew the six securing setpins sufficiently to allow the brake and clutch pedal linkage bracket to be withdrawn from inside the car.

4 — Release the brake and clutch pedal return springs.

5 — Unscrew the nut securing the brake and clutch pedal shaft and withdraw the shaft to release the brake and clutch pedal levers together with their distance piece.

6 — Inspect the lever bushes for wear and renew if necessary. Replacement is the reverse of the procedure.

MASTER CYLINDER
Description
The master cylinder consists of an alloy body with a polished finish bore, and reservoir with cap. The inner assembly is made up of the push rod, dished washer, circlip, plunger, plunger seal, spring thimble, plunger return spring, valve spacer, spring washer, valve stem and valve seal. The open end of the cylinder is protected by a rubber dust cover.

Dismantling the Brake Master Cylinder
1 — Release the master cylinder push rod from the brake pedal.

2 — Disconnect the pressure pipe union from the cylinder and remove the securing bolts, then the master cylinder and fluid reservoir may be withdrawn complete from the car.

3 — Remove the filler cap and drain out the fluid. Pull back the rubber dust cover and remove the circlip with a pair of long nosed pliers. The push rod and dished washer can then be removed.

4 — When the push rod has been removed the plunger with seal attached will be exposed; remove the plunger assembly complete. The assembly can be separated by lifting the thimble leaf over the shouldered end of the plunger.

5 — Depress the plunger return spring allowing the valve stem to slide through the elongated hole of the thimble thus releasing the tension on the spring.

6 — Remove the thimble, spring and valve complete.

7 — Detach the valve spacer, taking care not to lose the spacer spring washer which is located under the valve head. Remove the seal.

8 — Examine all parts, especially the seals, for wear or distortion and replace with new parts where necessary.

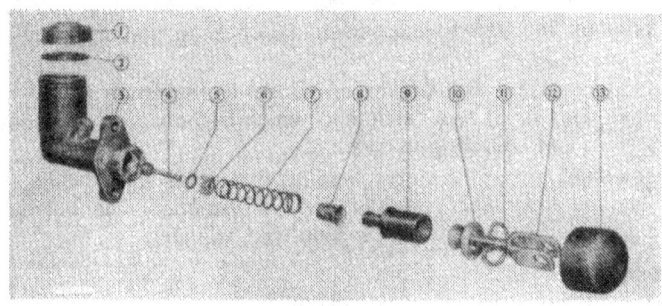

Components of the master cylinder and reservoir.
1. Filler cap.
2. Washer.
3. Master cylinder.
4. Valve stem.
5. Spring washer.
6. Valve spacer.
7. Return spring.
8. Thimble.
9. Plunger.
10. Dished washer.
11. Circlip.
12. Push.
13. Dust cover.

Assembling the Brake Master Cylinder

1 — Replace the valve seal so that the flat side is correctly seated on the valve head.

2 — The spring washer should then be located with the dome side against the underside of the valve head, and held in position by the valve spacer the legs of which face towards the valve seal.

3 — Replace the plunger spring centrally on the spacer, insert the thimble into the spring and depress until the valve stem engages through the elongated hole of the thimble, making sure the stem is correctly located in the center of the thimble. Check that the spring is still central on the spacer.

4 — Refit a new plunger seal with the flat of the seal seated against the face of the plunger. Insert the reduced end of the plunger into the thimble until the thimble leaf engages under the shoulder of the plunger. Press home the thimble leaf.

5 — Smear the assembly with the recommended brake fluid, and insert the assembly into the bore of the cylinder valve end first, easing the plunger seal lips into the bore.

6 — Replace the push rod with the dished side of the washer under the spherical head, into the cylinder followed by the circlip which engages into the groove machined in the cylinder body.

7 — Replace the rubber dust cover and refit the whole unit into its aperture in the scuttle, not forgetting to fit the packing washer first. Secure the unit by means of the two bolts on the flange and refit the pressure pipe union into the cylinder.

8 — Reconnect the push rod fork with its corresponding hole in the brake pedal lever, securing it with the circlip.

9 — Bleed the hydraulic system.

CARS WITH DISC BRAKES

The brakes on all four wheels are hydraulically operated by foot pedal application, the pedal being directly coupled to a master cylinder in which the hydraulic pressure of the brake operating fluid is originated.

Steel pipe lines, unions and flexible hoses convey the hydraulic pressure from the master cylinder to each wheel cylinder.

The cable actuated hand brake mechanism operates the rear brake shoes only by mechanical expanders attached to the brake cylinder bodies.

Girling calliper type disc brakes are fitted to the front wheel hubs. Each brake consists of two carriers to which friction pads are bonded. The system is self adjusting in operation.

The rear brakes are of the single leading shoe type with sliding shoes which ensure automatic centralization in operation. Manual adjustment is provided by means of a wedge type adjuster.

Front Brakes

The front brake unit consists of a hub mounted disc rotating with the wheel, and a braking unit rigidly attached to the swivel axle at the rear. The brake unit is a calliper which straddles the disc and houses two horizontally opposed blind cylinders and the friction pads. Within each cylinder is a rubber sealing ring positioned by a groove in the cylinder body, and a piston protected by a dust cover. A segmental friction pad bonded to a steel backplate is inserted between each piston and the disc. The pads and backplates are secured by retaining pins and spring clips. The pads are self adjusting in operation and should need no attention between replacements.

If any part of the hydraulic system is disconnected the brake lines must be bled, the bleed screw is fitted at the top of the calliper housing on the inside.

NOTE — The bridge bolts joining the two halves of the calliper together should not be removed.

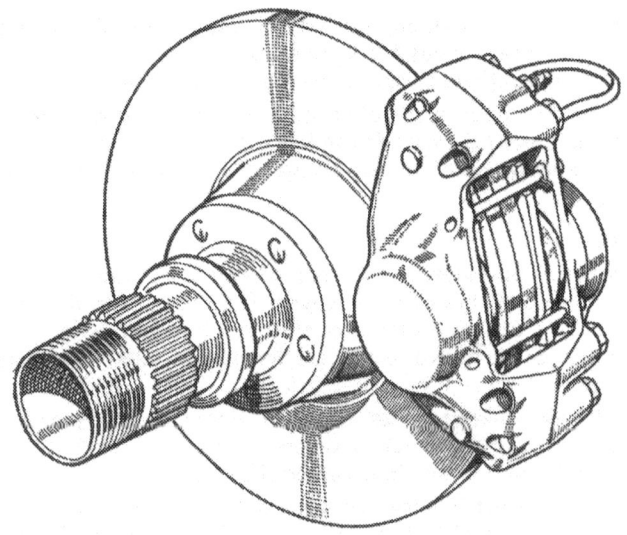

Front disc brake and hub assembly.

Rear Brakes

The brake shoes are allowed to slide and centralize during the actual braking operation which distributes the braking force equally over the lining area ensuring high efficiency and even lining wear. They are hydraulically operated by a single acting wheel cylinder incorporating the handbrake mechanism. At the cylinder end the leading shoe is located in a slot in the piston while the trailing shoe rests in a slot formed in the cylinder body. At the adjuster end the shoes rest in slots in the adjuster links. Both shoes are supported on the backplate and are held in position by the two return springs fitted from shoe to shoe with the shorter spring nearer the adjuster.

The wheel cylinder consists of a light alloy die casting with a highly finished bore in which moves the piston and seal. A slot is machined in the other end of the cylinder body to carry the trailing shoe and at right angles projecting through the backplate is pivoted the handbrake lever. The cylinder is attached to the backplate by a spring clip allowing it to slide laterally.

A bleed screw is incorporated in the cylinder housing with a rubber dust cap cover over the nipple.

Adjustment for lining wear is made by the brake shoe adjuster. This has a steel housing which is spigotted and bolted firmly to the inside of the backplate. The housing carries two opposed steel links, the outer end slotted to carry the shoes, and the inclined inner faces bearing on inclined faces of the hardened steel wedge.

The wedge has a threaded spindle with a square end which projects on the outside of the backplate, enabling a wrench to be used for adjustment purposes, by rotating the wedge in a clockwise direction, the links are forced apart and the fulcrum of the brake shoes expanded.

When the brake is applied, the piston under the influence of the hydraulic pressure, moves the leading shoe and the body reacts by sliding on the backplate to operating the trailing shoe.

The handbrake lever is pivoted in the cylinder body, and when operated the lever tip expands the leading shoe, and the pivot moves the cylinder body which in turn moves the trailing shoe against the brake drum.

Handbrake

The handbrake operates on the rear wheels only and is applied by the lever alongside the gearbox cover. The cable from the control is attached to the compensator mounted on the rear axle. From the compensator to the brake levers are transverse rods which are non-adjustable.

The handbrake linkage is set when leaving the works and should not require any attention. Only when a complete overhaul is necessary should the handbrake linkage require re-setting.

When this is correct the rear shoes should be locked to the drums, the handbrake control just slightly applied, and the cable slackness just removed, by adjusting the sleeve nut at the front end of the cable.

MAINTENANCE

This section should be used in conjunction with the drum brake section particular attention being given to — **"Replenishment of Hydraulic Fluid"** and **"Bleeding the Hydraulic System."**

Front brake adjustment

Wear on the front disc brake friction pads is automatically compensated during braking operations, manual adjustment is therefore not required. In order to maintain peak braking efficiency and at the same time obtain the maximum life from the friction pads, they should be examined at every 3,000 miles (4800 km.) service and if the wear on one pad is greater than the other their operating positions should be changed over.

Rear Brakes are adjusted for wear only at the brakes themselves and on no account should any alteration be made to the handbrake cable for this purpose.

One common adjuster is provided for both shoes and the adjustment for both wheels is identical.

Release the handbrake and jack up the car. Turn the end of the adjuster on the outside of each brake backplate in a clockwise direction until a resistance is felt. Slacken two notches when the drum should rotate freely.

Replacing Friction Pads

When wear has reduced the thickness of the pads to approximately 1/8 in. (3.18 mm.) they must be renewed. Under no circumstances should a pad be allowed to wear below 1/16 in. (1.59 mm.).

1 — Jack up the car and remove the road wheels.

2 — Remove the spring clips locking the retaining pins in position and draw them back. Pull out the friction pad assemblies.

3 — Clean down the callipers and inspect for fluid leaks.

4 — Push in the pistons to the bottom of the cylinder bores with a suitable lever.

5 — Slip in the new pads and locate them in position with the retaining pins and secure with the spring clips.

6 — Press the brake pedal hard once or twice in order to settle the hydraulic system.

REMOVING A CALLIPER UNIT
To Remove

1 — Unscrew the brake pipe union nut in front of its support bracket, disconnect and blank off the pipe.

2 — Remove the two nuts securing the brake hose support bracket and remove the bracket.

3 — Unscrew the two calliper retaining bolts and remove the calliper assembly complete.

Replacement is the reverse of the procedure.

NOTE — Tightening the retaining bolts to a torque reading of between 45 to 50 lb.ft. (6.22 to 6.91 kg.m.).

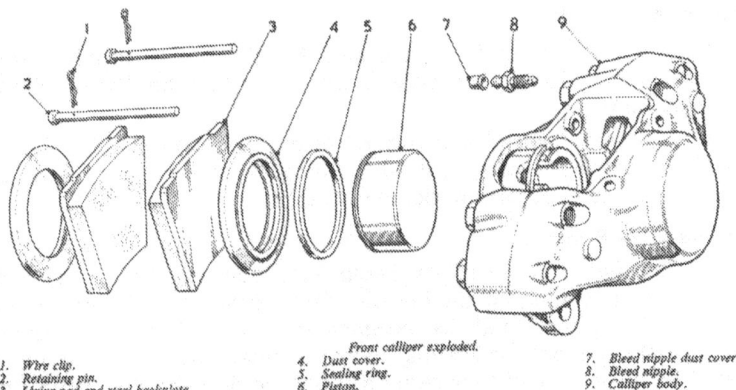

Front calliper exploded.

1. Wire clip.
2. Retaining pin.
3. Lining pad and steel backplate.
4. Dust cover.
5. Sealing ring.
6. Piston.
7. Bleed nipple dust cover.
8. Bleed nipple.
9. Calliper body.

DISMANTLING A CALLIPER UNIT

1 — Remove the calliper from the vehicle
2 — Withdraw the brake pads as described on page 159 but do not push the pistons to the bottom of their bores.
3 — It is recommended that the unit is thoroughly cleaned before proceeding with dismantling.
4 — Force the pistons out of their bores by connecting the flexible hose to a fluid supply and applying pressure to eject the pistons. Alternatively, push back the dust seal and insert two suitable levers into the seal groove and pull the piston out with an even pressure. Taking care not to damage the groove and piston surfaces.
5 — Disengage the dust cover and remove the internal seal, by inserting a blunt blade along its side and easing it out. Renew the dust cover and internal seal if they show signs of wear.
Clean internally with methylated spirits only and allow to dry. Use brake fluid to clean rubber parts.
NOTE — No attempt should be made to remove the bridge bolts joining the two halves of the calliper.

ASSEMBLING A CALLIPER UNIT

1 — Fit the internal seal into the groove in the cylinder bore with the scraping edge (smaller diameter) innermost.
2 — Locate the lip of the dust cover in the outer groove.
3 — Smear the piston with brake fluid and push it into the bore, closed end first.
4 — Push the piston right home and then engage the outer edge of the cover with the groove in the piston body.
5 — Refit the pad assemblies and lock in position with the retaining pins.
6 — Refit the calliper unit taking care that the disc passes between the two pads.
7 — Connect the brake hose and bleed the system. Check for leaks with the brake fully applied.

THE BRAKE DISC

A check should be made to ascertain that the disc is running true. As maximum efficiency can only be attained when the disc run-out is at a minimum.
It must be remembered that run-out at the disc may also be due to the hub bearings being out of adjustment, this item should be checked carefully before condemning a disc.

To Check for Run-out

Clamp the dial indicator to a suitable fixed point on the vehicle with the needle pad bearing on the disc face. Run-out must not exceed .004 in. (.102 mm) total, as excessive run-out will cause knocking back of the pistons which may create judder and increased pedal travel. If there is doubt concerning this condition the disc should be replaced.

To Remove

1 — Remove the calliper unit but do not disconnect the hydraulic supply hose. A spacer should be placed between the pads in order to hold the pistons in position.

2 — Dismantle the hub assembly.

3 — The disc is held to the hub by five nuts and spring washers, after removing these the two components may be separated.

To Replace

1 — Assembling the brake disc to the hub is a reversal of the procedure.

2 — Replace the hub on the swivel axle.

3 — Check for run-out as detailed above.

4 — Replace the calliper assembly.

5 — Refit the wheel and replace the hub cap.

Scoring of brake discs is not detrimental, provided that the scoring is concentric, even, and not excessive. If it is thought advisable however, the discs may be reground. No more than .040 in. (1.02 mm.) may be removed from each disc; i.e. after grinding the thickness must not be less than .380 to .375 in. (0.65 to 9.40 mm.).

The faces must run true to within .002 in. (.051 mm.) and the thickness must be parallel to within .001 in. (.025 mm.).

REAR BRAKES

Maintenance and repair of rear brakes and the balance of the hydraulic system on disc braked cars is the same as for cars with all drum brakes. Therefore, follow the procedures outlined previously under the heading CARS WITH DRUM BRAKES.

FAULT DIAGNOSIS

Symptom	No.	Possible Fault
(a) Spongy Pedal (loss of fluid pressure)	1 2 3 4 5	Leak in system Master cylinder plunger worn Wheel cylinder leaking Air in system Lining not "down" on shoe
(b) Excessive Pedal Depression	1 2 3	In (a) check 1 and 4 Excessive lining wear Extremely low brake fluid level Too much pedal free movement
(c) Brakes Grab or Pull to Side	1 2 3 4 5 6 7 8 9 10	Brake backplate loose on axle Scored, cracked or distorted drum High spots on drum Incorrect shoe adjustment Oily or wet linings Rear axle or front suspension anchorage loose Worn or loose rear spring anchorage Worn steering connections Different grades or types of lining fitted Uneven tyre pressures
(d) Dragging Brakes	1 2 3 4 5 6 7	In (c), check 3 Wheel cylinder piston seized Weak or broken brake shoe return springs Master cylinder by-pass port restricted Too little pedal free movement Handbrake mechanism seized Supply tank overfilled Filler cap air vent choked
(e) Springy Pedal	1 2 3	Linings not "bedded-in" Brake drums weak or cracked Master cylinder fixing loose
(f) Brakes Inefficient	1	In (c), check 4 In (d), check 7 Incorrect type of linings fitted

DISC BRAKE

Symptom	No.	Possible fault
(c) Brakes Grab or Pull to Side	1 2 3	Disc out of true Calliper loose Pad loose in calliper
(d) Dragging Brakes	1 2	Excessive pad wear Pressure build up in fluid supply.
(f) Brakes Inefficient	1 2	Disc out of true Incorrect grade of lining pad.

ELECTRICAL SYSTEM

The 12-volt electrical equipment incorporates compensated voltage control for the charging circuit. The positive ground system of wiring is employed.

Battery details may be found in **"General Data."**

The generator is mounted on the right of the cylinder block and driven by an endless belt from the crankshaft pulley. A rotatable mounting enables the bolt tension to be adjusted.

The voltage control unit adjustment is sealed and should not normally require attention. The fuses are carried in external holders mounted in an accessible position on the right-hand side of the engine compartment together with spare fuses.

The starter motor is mounted on the flywheel housing on the right-hand side of the engine unit and operates on the flywheel through the usual sliding pinion device.

The headlamps employ the double-filament dipping system. Both lamps are fitted with double-filament bulbs, both dipping according to the regulations existing in the countries concerned.

BATTERY

The battery is a 12-volt lead-acid type, having six cells, each cell consisting of a group of positive and negatives plates immersed in a solution of sulphuric acid (electrolyte).

Maintenance

The purpose of the following operations is to maintain the performance of the battery at its maximum.

1 — The battery and the surrounding parts should be kept dry and clean, particularly the tops of the cells as any dampness could cause a leakage between the securing strap and the battery negative terminal, resulting in a partially discharged battery. Clean off any corrosion from the battery bolts, strap and tray with diluted ammonia, afterwards painting the affected parts with anti-sulphuric paint.

2 — Remove the vent plugs and check that they are not perished or cracked, otherwise leakage of electrolyte will occur. Clean out the vent holes, if necessary, with a piece of wire.

3 — The electrolyte levels should be maintained **just above** the tops of the separators by adding distilled water. Never add acid.

4 — Check the terminal posts. If they are corroded, remove the cables and clean with diluted ammonia. Smear the posts with petroleum jelly before remaking the connections and ensure that the cable terminal screws are secure.

5 — Test the condition of the battery cells by using a hydrometer. All the readings should be uniform.

The specific gravity readings and their indications are as follows:

Climates below 90°F. (32°C.)

1.270 to 1.290	Cell fully charged.
1.90 to 1.210	Cell about half discharged.

1.110 to 1.130   Cell fully discharged.
           Climates frequently above 90°F. (32°C.)
1.210 to 1.230   Cell fully charged.
1.130 to 1.150   Cell about half discharged.
1.050 to 1.070   Cell fully discharged.

These figures are given assuming an electrolyte temperature of 60°F. (16°C.). If the temperature of the electrolyte exceeds this, .002 must be added to hydrometer readings for each 5°F. rise to give the true specific gravity. Similarly .002 must be subtracted from hydrometer readings for every 5°F. below 60°F.

To Remove

1 — Raise the boot lid to again access to the battery.
2 — Disconnect both cables from the battery.
3 — Release the battery clamp and lift out the battery.

Charging from an External Source

The length of time for a used battery to remain on charge before it can be accepted as fully charged depends entirely on the specific gravity before charging commences and the charging rate. The charging should continue until all cells are gassing freely and evenly and the specific gravity is each of the six cells has reached a maximum, i.e. has shown no further rise in four hours. The specific gravity at the end of charging should be within the limits given, and should not vary more than .005 from the values given.

Do not allow the temperature of the electrolyte to exceed the maximum permissible temperature, i.e. 100°F. 38°C.) in climates ordinarily below 90°F. (32°C.), or 120°F. (49°C.) in climates frequently above 90°F. (32°C.). If this temperature is reached the charge should be suspended to allow the temperature to fall at least 10°, otherwise the life of the battery will be shortened.

To Install

The installation of the battery is a reversal of the procedure **"To Remove."** Smear the terminal posts and cable connections with petroleum jelly and tighten the terminal screws sufficiently to prevent the cables from moving on the terminal posts when tested by hand.

GENERATOR

The generator is a shunt-wound two-pole two-brush machine, arranged to work in conjunction with a compensated voltage control regulator unit. A fan, integral with the driving pulley, draws cooling air through the generator, inlet and outlet holes being provided in the end brackets of the unit.

The output of the generator is controlled by the regulator and is dependent on the state of charge of the battery and the loading of the electrical equipment in use. When the battery is in a low state of charge, the generator gives a high output, whereas if the battery is fully charged, the generator gives only sufficient output to keep the battery in good condition without any possibility of overcharging. In addition, an increase in output is given to balance the current taken by lamps and other accessories when in use. Further, a high boosting charge is given for a few minutes immediately after starting up, thus quickly restoring to the battery the energy taken from it by the electric starting motor.

Lubrication

Every 3,000 miles (4800 km.) inject a few drops of medium viscosity (S.A.E. 30) engine oil into the hole marked "oil" at the end of the bearing housing.

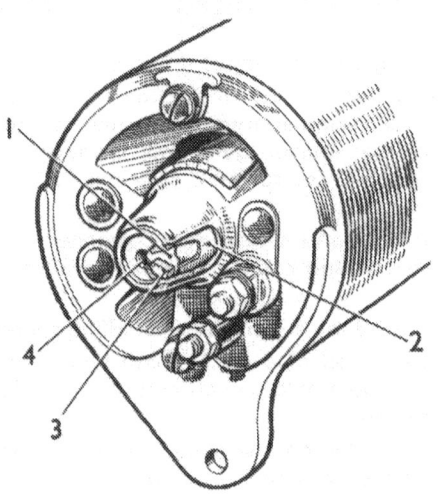

Fig. N.9. generator lubrication.
1. Aluminium disc.
2. Porous bronze bush.
3. Felt ring.
4. Oil hole.

Inspection of Brushgear and Commutator

Periodically inspect the brush-gear and commutator. Access to the brushgear on earlier generators is gained by removing the metal band cover from around the yoke. Some generators are now produced without brush-gear inspection windows in the yoke and it is necessary to unscrew the two through bolts and withdraw the commutator end bracket before access to the brush-gear can be gained.

Check that the brushes move freely in their holders by holding back the brush springs and pulling gently on the flexible connectors. If a brush is inclined to stick, remove it from its holder and clean its sides with a solvent-moistened cloth. Be careful to replace brushes in their original positions in order to retain the "bedding." Brushes which have worn so that they will not "bed" properly on the commutator must be renewed.

The commutator should be clean, free from oil or dirt, and should have a polished appearance. If it is dirty, clean it by pressing a fine dry cloth against it while the engine is slowly turned over by hand. If the commutator is very dirty, moisten the cloth with solvent.

Belt Adjustment

Occasionally inspect the generator driving belt and adjust if necessary to take up any undue slackness by turning the generator on its mounting. Care should be taken to avoid overtightening the belt, which should have sufficient tension only to drive without slipping. See that the generator is properly aligned, otherwise undue strain will be thrown on the bearings.

TESTING IN POSITION TO LOCATE FAULT IN CHARGING CIRCUIT

In the event of a fault in the charging circuit, adopt the following procedure to locate the cause of the trouble.

1 — Inspect the driving belt and adjust if necessary.

2 — Check that the generator and control box are connected correctly. The larger generator terminal must be connected to control box terminal "D," and the smaller generator terminal to control box terminal "F." Check the control box terminal "E" and associated ground cable for tightness.

3 — Switch off all lights and accessories, disconnect the cables from the generator terminals and connect the two terminals with a short length of wire.

4 — Start the engine and set to run at normal idling speed.

5 — Clip the negative lead of a moving coil voltmeter, calibrated 0 to 20 volts, to one generator terminal, and the other lead to a good ground point on the yoke.

6 — Gradually increase the engine speed, when the voltmeter reading should rise rapidly without fluctuation. Do not allow the voltmeter reading to reach 20 volts and do not race the engine in an attempt to increase the voltage. It is sufficient to run the generator up to a speed of 1,000 r.p.m. If there is no reading, check the brushgear as described in (7) following.

If there is a low reading of approximately ½ to 1 volt, the field winding may be at fault (see "Field Coils"). If there is a reading of 4 to 5 volts, the armature winding may be at fault.

NOTE — Excessive sparking at the commutator in the above test indicates a defective armature which should be replaced.

7 — Remove the cover band (when fitted) and examine the brushes and commutator. Hold back each of the brush springs and move the brush by pulling gently on its flexible connector. If the movement is sluggish, remove the brush from its holder and ease the sides by lightly polishing on a smooth file. Always replace brushes in their original position.

If the brushes are badly worn, new brushes must be fitted and bedded to the commutator. The minimum permissible length of brush is 7/16 in.

Test the brush spring tension with a spring scale. The tension of the springs when new is 36 to 44 oz. In service it is permissible for this value to fall to 30 oz. before performance may be affected. Fit new springs if the tension is low. If the commutator is blackened or dirty, clean it by holding a solvent moistened cloth against it while the engine is turned slowly by hand cranking. Re-test the generator as in

(6); if there is still no reading on the voltmeter there is an internal fault and the complete unit, if a spare is available, should be replaced. Otherwise the unit must be dismantled for internal examination.

When reassembling a "windowless" yoke generator, the brushes must first be held clear of the commutator in the usual way, i.e., by partially withdrawing the brushes from their brush-boxes until each brush is trapped in position by the side pressure of its spring. The brushes can be released on to the commutator with a small screwdriver or similar tool when the end bracket is assembled to within about half-an-inch of the yoke. Before closing the gap between end bracket and yoke, see that the springs are in correct contact with the brushes.

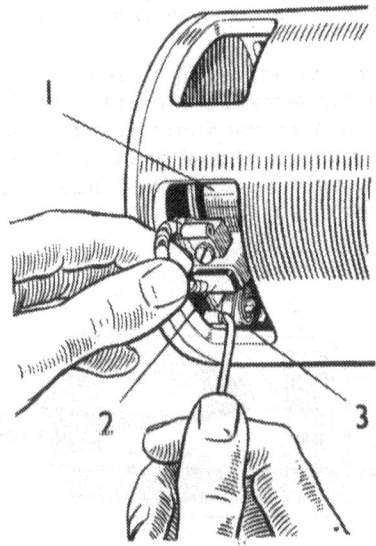

Removing a generator brush from its holder.
1. Commutator.   2. Brush.   3. Brush spring.

8 — If the generator is in good order, remove the link from between the terminals and restore the original connections, taking care to connect the larger generator terminal to control box terminal "D," and the smaller terminal to control box terminal "F."

GENERATOR ASSEMBLY
To remove

1 — Disconnect the two leads to the generator.

2 — Disconnect the high tension lead and the two low tension leads to the coil.

3 — Slacken the nut securing the sliding link and the two bolts holding the generator to its mounting bracket.

4 — Push the generator downwards to slacken the fan belt so that the latter can then be removed.

5 — Remove the setpin from the upper end of the sliding link and *take out the nuts and bolts from the mounting bracket.*

6 — Lift the generator clear of the engine.

7 — Unscrew the two nuts securing the coil to its bracket on the generator and remove the coil.

To Dismantle

1 — Take off the driving pulley.

2 — On earlier type generators, remove the cover band, hold back the brush springs and remove the brushes from their holders.

3 — Unscrew and withdraw the two through bolts.

4 — The commutator end bracket can now be withdrawn from the generator yoke.

5 — The driving end bracket together with the armature can now be lifted out of the yoke.

6 — The driving end bracket, which on removal from the yoke has withdrawn with it the armature and armature shaft ball bearing, need not be separated from the shaft unless the bearing is suspected and requires examination, or the armature is to be replaced; in this event the armature should be removed from the end bracket by means of a hand press.

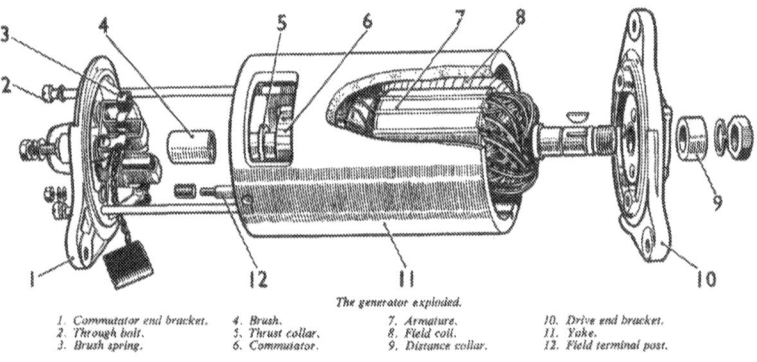

The generator exploded.

1. Commutator end bracket.
2. Through bolt.
3. Brush spring.
4. Brush.
5. Thrust collar.
6. Commutator.
7. Armature.
8. Field coil.
9. Distance collar.
10. Drive end bracket.
11. Yoke.
12. Field terminal post.

THE STARTER

To Test on Vehicle

1 — Switch on the lamps and operate the starter control. If the lights go dim, but the starter is not heard to operate, an indication is given that current is flowing through the starter windings but that the starter pinion is possibly jammed in the geared ring on the flywheel. This was probably caused by the starter being operated while the engine was still running. In this case the starter must be removed from the engine for examination.

2 — Should the lamps retain their full brilliance when the starter switch is operated, check that the switch is functioning. If the switch is in order, examine the connections at the battery, starter switch and starter, and also check the wiring between these units. Con-

tinued failure of the starter to operate indicates an internal fault, and the starter must be removed from the engine for examination.

Sluggish action of the starter is usually caused by a poor connection in the wiring which produces a high resistance in the starter circuit. Check as described above.

Damage to the starter drive is indicated if the starter is heard to operate but does not crank the engine.

To Remove and Replace

Release the starter cable from the terminal and unscrew the two starter securing bolts. Maneuver the starter forwards below the oil filter and lift clear of the engine.

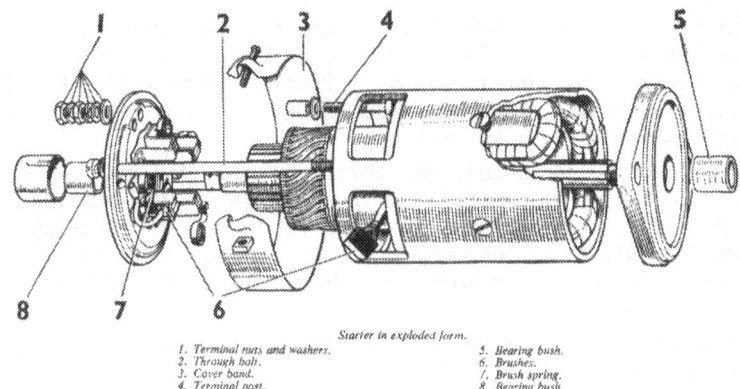

Starter in exploded form.

1. *Terminal nuts and washers.*
2. *Through bolt.*
3. *Cover band.*
4. *Terminal post.*
5. *Bearing bush.*
6. *Brushes.*
7. *Brush spring.*
8. *Bearing bush.*

Examination of Commutator and Brush Gear

1 — Remove the starter cover band and examine the brushes and the commutator.

2 — Hold back each of the brush springs and move the brush by pulling gently on its flexible connector. If the movement is sluggish remove the brush from its holder and ease the sides by lightly polishing on a smooth file. Always replace brushes in their original positions. If the brushes are worn so that they no longer bear on the commutator, or if the brush flexible lead has become exposed on the running face, they must be renewed.

3 — If the commutator is blackened or dirty, clean it by holding a solvent-moistened cloth against it while the armature is rotated.

4 — Secure the body of the starter in a vise and test by connecting it with heavy-gauge cables to a 12-volt battery. One cable must be connected to the starter terminal and the other held against the starter body or end bracket. Under these light load conditions the starter should run at a very high speed.

If the operation of the starter is still unsatisfactory, it should be dismantled for detailed inspection and testing.

To Dismantle

1 — Take off the cover band at the commutator end, hold back the brush springs and take out the brushes.

2 — Extract the split pin at the driving end and remove the nut (left-hand thread), spring, washer, pinion and sleeve, restraining spring and collar and spring sleeve.

3 — Remove the terminal nuts and washers from the terminal post and screw out the two through-bolts.

4 — Remove the commutator end bracket, the attachment bracket and the armature.

Commutator

A commutator in good condition will be smooth and free from pits and burned spots. Clean the commutator with a cloth moistened with gasoline.

Field Coils

The field coils can be tested for an open circuit by connecting a 12-volt battery, having a 12-volt bulb in one of the leads, to the tapping point of the field coils to which the brushes are connected and the field terminal post. If the lamp does not light, there is an open circuit in the wiring of the field coils.

Lighting of the lamp does not necessarily mean that the field coils are in order, as it is possible that one of them may be grounded to a pole shoe or to the yoke. This may be checked by removing the lead from the brush connector and holding it on a clean part of the starter yoke. Should the bulb now light it indicates that the field coils are grounded.

Should the above tests indicate that the fault lies in the field coils, they must be renewed.

Armature

Examination of the armature will in many cases reveal the cause of failure, e.g. conductors lifted from the commutator due to the starter being engaged while the engine is running and causing the armature to be rotated at an excessive speed. A damaged armature must in all cases be renewed — no attempt should be made to machine the armature core or to true a distorted armature shaft.

CONTROL BOX

This unit contains the cut-out and voltage regulator. The regulator controls the generator output in accordance with the load on the battery and its state of charge. When the battery is discharged, the generator gives a high output so that the battery receives a quick recharge, which brings it back to its normal state in the minimum time.

On the other hand, if the battery is fully charged the generator will give a trickle charge only, which is sufficient to keep the battery in good condition without over charging, thus avoiding damage to the plates.

The regulator also causes the generator to give a controlled boosting charge immediately after starting up, which quickly restores to the battery the energy taken from it when starting. After about 30 minutes running, the output of the generator falls to a steady rate, best suited to the particular state of charge of the battery.

The cut-out is an automatic switch for connecting and disconnecting the battery with the generator. This is necessary because the battery would otherwise discharge through the generator with the engine stopped or running at low speed.

Regulator Adjustment

The regulator is carefully set during manufacture, and in general it should not be necessary to make any further adjustment. If however, the battery does not keep in a charged condition, or if the generator output does not fall when the battery is fully charged, the setting should be checked, and if necessary corrected.

It is important, before altering the regulator setting when the battery is in a low state of charge, to check that its condition is not due to a battery defect or to slipping of the generator belt.

Checking and Adjusting the Electrical Setting

The electrical setting can be checked without removing the cover from the control box.

1 — Withdraw the cables from the terminals marked "A" and "A.1" at the control box and join them together. Connect the negative lead of a moving coil (0 to 20 volts) voltmeter, to control box terminal "D" and connect the other lead to terminal "E."

2 — Slowly increase the speed of the engine until the voltmeter needle "flicks" and then steadies. This should occur at a voltmeter reading between the limits given for the appropriate temperature of the regulator. If the voltage at which the reading becomes steady is outside these limits the regulator must be adjusted.

3 — Shut off the engine and remove the control box cover. Release the locknut securing the regulator adjusting screw and turn the adjusting screw in a clockwise direction to raise the setting, or in an anti-clockwise direction to lower the setting. Turn the screw a fraction at a time and tighten the locknut. Repeat this procedure until the desired setting is obtained.

4 — Adjustment of the regulator open circuit should be completed within 30 seconds otherwise overheating of the shunt winding will cause false settings to be made. A generator run at high speed on open circuit will build up a high voltage, therefore when adjusting the regulator do not run the engine up to more than half throttle or a false setting will be made. Remake the original connections.

Mechanical Setting

The mechanical settings of the regulator, shown on page 172 are accurately adjusted before leaving the factory, and provided that the armature carrying the moving contact is not removed, these settings should not be tampered with. If however, the armature has been removed, the regulator will have to be reset. To do this, proceed as follows:—

1 — Slacken the fixed contact locking nut (3), and unscrew the contact until it is well clear of the armature moving contact. Slacken the voltage adjusting screw lockinug nut (7) and unscrew the adjuster until it is well clear of the armature tension spring. Slacken the two armature assembly securing screws (2).

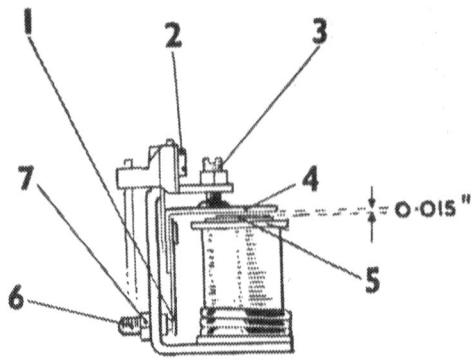

Regulator mechanical setting.
1. Armature tension spring.
2. Armature securing screws.
3. Fixed contact adjustment screw.
4. Armature.
5. Core face and shim.
6. Voltage adjusting screw.
7. Lock nut.

2 — Insert a .015 in. feeler gauge (which should be wide enough to completely cover the core face), between the armature and the core shim. Take care not to turn up, or damage the edge of the shim. Press the armature squarely down against the gauge and re-tighten the two armature securing screws.

3 — With the gauge still in position, screw the adjustable contact down until it just touches the armature contact. Tighten the locking nut and remove the feeler gauge. Reset the voltage adjusting screw as described under "Electrical Setting."

Cleaning Regulator Contacts

After periods of long service it may be found necessary to clean the regulator contacts. Fine carborundum stone or fine emery cloth may be used. Carefully wipe away all traces of dust or other foreign matter, using a clean fluffless cloth moistened with denatured alcohol.

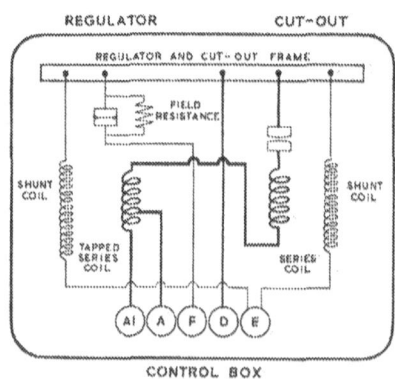

Internal connections of the control box.

Cut-Out Electrical Setting

If the regulator is correctly set but the battery is still not being charged the cut-out may be out of adjustment. To check the voltage at which the cut-out operates remove the control box cover and connect the voltmeter between the terminals "D" and "E." Start the engine and slowly increase its speed until the cut-out contacts are seen to close, noting the voltage at which this occurs. This should be 12.7 to 13.3 volts.

If operation of the cut-out takes place outside these limits, it will be necessary to adjust. To do this:—

1 — Slacken the locknut (2), securing the cut-out adjusting screw and turn the screw in a clockwise direction to raise the voltage setting, or in an anti-clockwise direction to reduce the setting. Turn the screw a fraction at a time and then tighten the locknut.

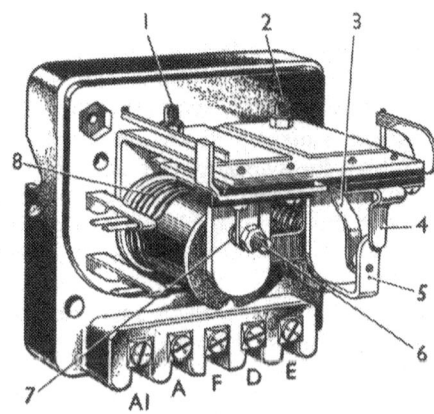

Control box.

1. Regulator adjusting screw.
2. Cut-out adjusting screw.
3. Fixed contact blade.
4. Stop arm.
5. Armature tongue and moving contact.
6. Regulator moving contact.
7. Fixed contact.
8. Regulator series windings.

2 — Test after each adjustment by increasing the engine speed and noting the voltmeter readings at the instant of contact closure. Electrical settings of the cut-out, like the regulator, must be made as quickly as possible because of temperature rise effects. Tighten the locknut after making the adjustment.

3 — Adjustment of the drop-off voltage (8.5 to 11 volts) is effected by carefully bending the fixed contact blade. If the cut-out does not operate there may be an open circuit in the wiring of the cut-out and regulator unit, in which case the unit should be removed for examination or renewal.

Cut-out Mechanical Setting

If for any reason the cut-out armature has to be removed from the frame, care must be taken to obtain the correct air gap settings on reassembly. These can be obtained as follows:—

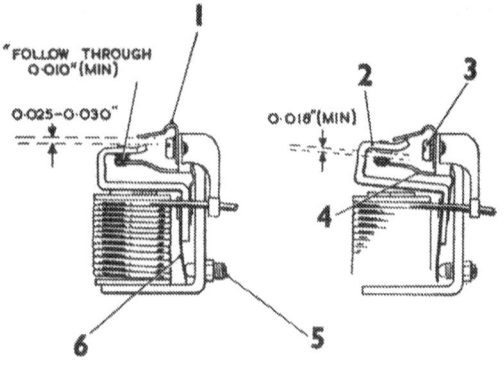

Cut-out mechanical setting.

1. Stop arm.
2. Armature tongue and moving contact.
3. Armature securing screw.
4. Fixed contact blade.
5. Cut-out adjusting screw.
6. Armature tension spring.

1 — Slacken the adjusting screw locking nut and unscrew the adjusting screw (5) until it is well clear of the armature tension spring (6). Slacken the two armature assembly securing screws (3).

2 — Press the armature squarely down against the copper sprayed core face and re-tighten the two armature assembly securing screws.

3 — Using a pair of round-nosed pliers, adjust the gap between the armature stop-arm and the armature tongue by bending the stop-arm. The gap must be .025 in. to .030 in. when the armature is pressed squarely down on the core face.

4 — Similarly, the insulated contact blade must be bent so that, when the armature is pressed squarely down against the core face, there is a minimum "follow through," or contact deflection of .010 in. The contact gap, when the armature is in the free position must be .018 in. minimum. Reset the cut-out adjusting screw as described under "Cut-out Electrical Setting."

Cleaning Cut-out Contacts

If the contacts appear rough or burnt, place a strip of fine glass paper between, and with them closed by hand, draw the paper through. This should be done two or three times with the rough side towards each contact. Wipe away all dust or other foreign matter, using a clean fluffless cloth moistened with denatured alcohol.

Do not use emery cloth or carborundum stone for cleaning the cut-out contacts.

FUSE UNIT

The fuse unit, which is mounted on the bulkhead under the engine cowl, is an open insulated moulding carrying two single-pole cartridge-type fuses which are held by spring clips between grub-screw-type terminal blocks. Two spare fuses are carried in recesses in the fuse unit base and are positioned by a common retaining spring. The fuse which bridges the terminal blocks (A1—A2) is to protect general auxiliary circuits, e.g. the horn and interior lamps, which are independent of the ignition switch. The other fuse, bridging terminal blocks (A3—A4), is to protect ignition auxiliary circuits, e.g. the fuel gauge, windscreen wiper motor and flashing indicators, which only operate when the ignition is switched on.

To Replace

1 — Ensure all fuses are serviceable.

2 — Reconnect the cables to the appropriate terminals on the fuse unit in accordance with the color code given in the wiring diagram.

3 — Secure the fuse unit to the bulkhead.

4 — Reconnect the battery cables and test the circuits concerned.

THE FLASHER UNIT

The Lucas flasher unit is situated in the engine compartment and is operated by a self-cancelling steering column direction switch, a warning lamp being provided in the center of the facia panel.

The unit is contained in a small cylindrical metal container, one end of which is rolled over on to an insulated plate carrying the mechanism and three terminals. The unit depends for its operation on the linear expansion of a length of wire which becomes heated by an electric current flowing through it. This actuating wire controls the movement of a spring-loaded armature attached to a central steel core and carrying a moving contact.

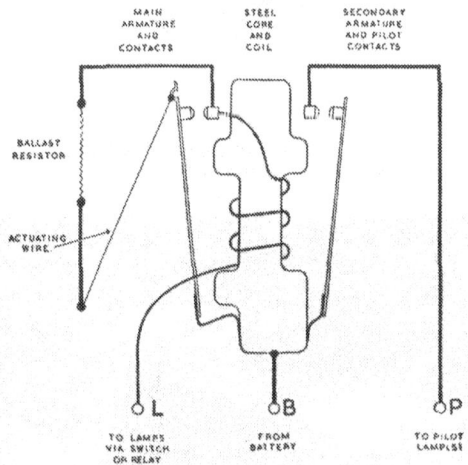

Functions of Warning Lamp

The warning lamp not only serves to indicate that the flasher unit is functioning correctly but also gives warning of any bulb failure occurring in the external direction-indicator lamps — since a reduction in bulb current flowing through the coil reduces the electromagnetic effect acting on the secondary armature and so prevents closure of the pilot light contacts.

The Brake Switch Overriding Relay

When stop-light filaments are used also as direction lights, it is essential that responses to the flasher unit should override simultaneous applications of the brake switch. In the event of simultaneous applications being made, the relay allows the appropriate stop-light filament to flash and the other to remain steadily illuminated as long as the brake pedal is depressed.

Operation of the direction-indicator switch to right or left first energizes the appropriate relay operating coil which effects movement of its associated armature in the direction shown by the arrow. By this means, flasher unit terminal 'L' is connected to relay terminals '2' and '3' (or '6' and '7') and, thus, to the indicating lamps. As long as the relay coil remains energized, connection to the brake lamp on the corresponding side is interrupted.

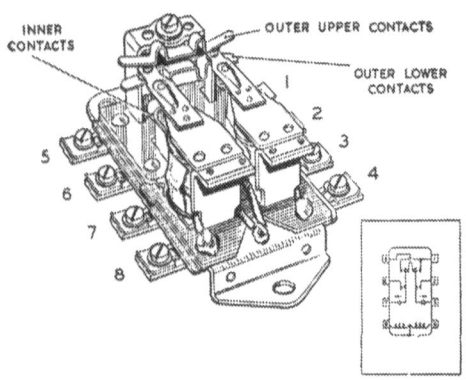

Brake switch overriding relay, model DB10, with cover removed and (inset) internal connections.

The location of the brake switch overriding relay

Checking Faulty Operation

In the event of trouble occurring with a flashing light direction-indicator system, the following procedure should be followed:—

1 — Check the bulbs for broken filaments.

2 — Refer to the vehicle wiring diagram and check all flasher circuit connections.

3 — Switch on the ignition.

4 — Check with a voltmeter that flasher unit terminal 'B' is a battery voltage with respect to ground.

5 — Connect together flasher unit terminals 'B' (or 'X') and 'L' and operate the direction-indicator switch. If the flasher lamps now light, the flasher unit is defective and must be replaced.

6 — If the lamps do not light in test (5), check the brake switch overriding relay as follows:—

a — Temporarily link relay terminal '1' to terminals '2' and '3'.

b — Temporarily link relay terminal '1' to terminals '6' and '7'.

c — If the lamps do flash in test (6), the relay is defective and requires either re-setting, see "Checking and Re-setting Air Gaps."

d — Direction-indicator switches are best checked by substitution.

Maintenance

Flasher units cannot be dismantled for subsequent reassembly. A defective unit must therefore be replaced, care being taken to reconnect as the original.

The cover of the brake switch overriding relays can be withdrawn for checking air-gap settings. No further dismantling is possible. In the event of defective coils or contacts occurring, relays must be replaced as complete units, care being taken to reconnect as the original.

Similarly, defective direction-indicator switches are normally replaceable only as complete units.

Replacement of Flasher Unit

When replacing a flasher unit or installing a flashing light system, it is advisable to test the circuits before connections to flasher terminals 'L', 'B' and 'P' are made. When testing, join the cables normally connected to these terminals together and operate the direction-indicator switch. In the event of a wrong connection having been made, the ignition auxiliaries fuse will blow but no damage will be done to the flasher unit.

Flasher units must be handled with care. Factory-made settings, though good for conditions of normal automobile duty, can be thrown off balance by rough handling.

WINDSHIELD WIPERS

Maintenance

1 — An inspection should be made of the rubber wiping elements which after long service become worn and should be renewed.

2 — The rubber grommet or washer around the wheel-box spindle should be lubricated with a few drops of glycerine.

3 — Denatured alcohol should be used to remove oil, tar spots and other stains from the windshield. It has been found that the use of some silicone and wax-based polishes for this purpose can be detrimental to the rubber wiping elements.

4 — The gearbox and cable rack are packed with grease during manufacture and need no further lubrication.

Checking Switching Mechanism

If the wiper fails to park or parks unsatisfactorily, the limit switch in the gearbox cover should be checked. Unless the limit switch is correctly set, it is possible for the wiper motor to overrun the open circuit position and continue to draw current.

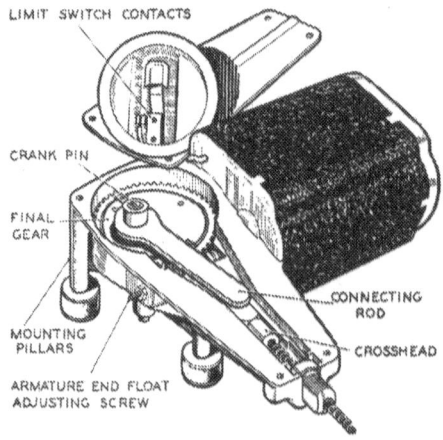

Wiper motor gearbox cover removed (Model D.R.2)

Resetting the Limit Switch

Slacken the four screws securing the gearbox cover and observe the projection near the rim of the limit switch. Position the projection in line with the groove in the gearbox cover. Turn the limit switch 25° in an anti-clockwise direction and tighten the four securing screws. If the wiping blades are required to park on the opposite side of the screen, the limit switch should be turned back 180° in a clockwise direction.

Fitting a Blade to a Wiper Arm

Pull the wiper arm away from the windshield and insert the curved "wrist" of the arm into slotted spring fastening of the blade. Swivel the two components into engagement.

Fitting a Wiper Arm to Driving Spindle

1 — First ensure that the wiper spindles are in the correct parking position by switching on the ignition and turning the wiper control on and then off.

2 — To fit the arms, press the headpieces on to the spindles at the correct parking angle until the retaining clip is heard to snap over

the end of the spindle drum.

3 — Switch off the wiper control. The arms should come to rest in the correct parking position.

Adjusting

Correct operation can be obtained by adjusting the position of the arms relative to the spindles. If necessary the position of the arms may be adjusted by removing and re-engaging them with the splined driving spindles, the angular pitch of the splines being 5°.

Do not attempt to turn the arms whilst in position, but press back the retaining clip in the headpiece and withdraw the arms from the driving spindles. Refit in the desired position. The above adjustment may affect the self-parking position. If so, it may be corrected by adjustment of the limit switch position, as described above.

If the arms and blades are required to come to rest on the opposite side, the limit switch should be turned through 180°. It should be noted that the switch cover is designed for turning through a sector only and not through 360°. This feature prevents unnecessary twisting of the external flexible connections.

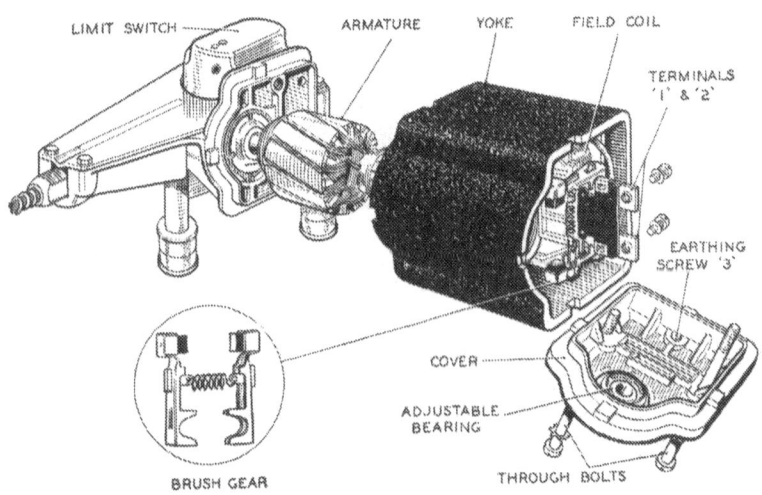

Wiper motor exploded.

IGNITION SWITCH

The ignition switch is a rotary barrel-type Yale lock located centrally on the facia panel. Operation of the switch is carried out by inserting the ignition key into the lock and turning it in a clockwise direction. In addition to controlling the primary circuit of the ignition coil the switch also operates as a master switch for the ignition, fuel gauge and pump, and the flashing indicators.

To Test in the Vehicle

Test the ignition switch in the manner described on page 57.

To Remove

1 — Unscrew the locknut securing the switch to the instrument panel and release the electrical connections at the rear of the switch.

2 — Remove the switch from the instrument panel.

DIRECTION INDICATOR WARNING LAMP

To Remove and Dismantle

1 — Pull out the bulb holder with bulb from the rear of the warning lamp.

2 — Unscrew the bulb.

3 — To release the green lens unscrew the chrome retaining ring situated on the front of the facia panel.

To Reassemble and Install

The reassembly and installation is the reversal of the procedure "To Remove and Dismantle."

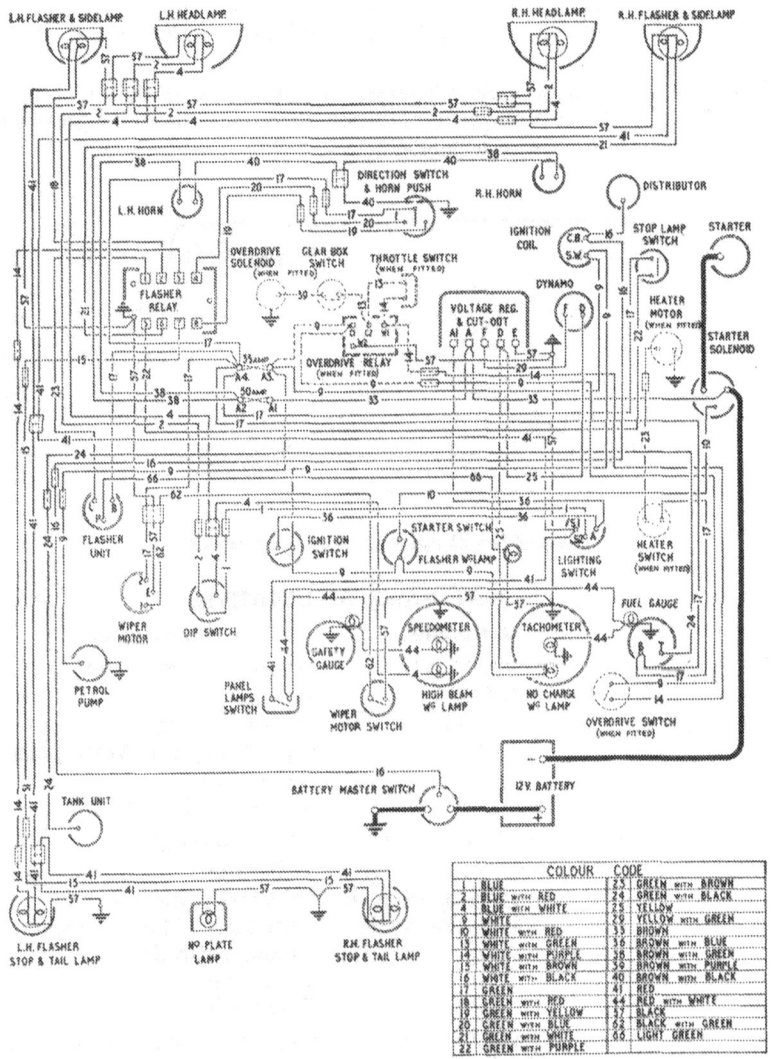

Wiring diagram.

MAINTENANCE

CARE OF TIRES

To obtain the best tire mileage and to obviate irregular wear on the front tires, it is essential that the wheels be interchanged diagonally with the rear wheels and the spare wheel every 3,000 miles (4800 km.). Disc wheel nuts should be tightened to a torque wrench reading of 60 lb/ft. Knock off hubcaps should not be excessively overtightened and splines should be kept greased.

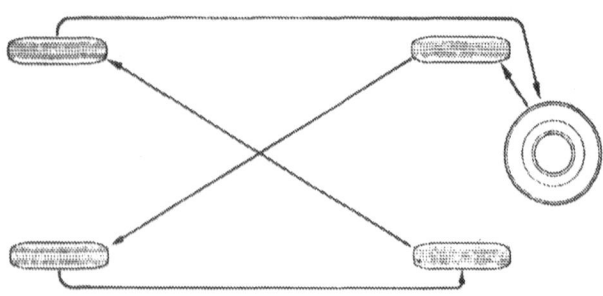

System of tyre changing to regularize tyre wear.

PART NAME ALTERNATIVES

	Part name	Alternatives
ENGINE	Gudgeon pin	Piston pin. Small-end pin. Wrist pin.
	Scraper ring	Oil control ring.
	Core plug	Expansion plug. Welch plug. Sealing disc.
	Oil sump	Oil pan. Oil reservoir.
CONTROLS	Mixture control	Choke. Strangler.
GEARBOX	Gear lever	Shift lever.
	Change speed fork	Shift fork. Selector fork.
	First motion shaft	Clutch shaft. First reduction pinion. Main drive pinion. Drive gear.
	Layshaft	Countershaft.
AXLE	Crown wheel	Ring gear. Spiral drive gear.
	Bevel pinion	Small pinion. Spiral drive pinion.
	'U' bolts	Spring clips.
	Axle shaft	Half-shaft. Hub driving shaft.
	Differential gear	Sun wheel.
	Differential pinion	Planet wheel.
STEERING	Swivel pin	Pivot pin. Steering pin. King pin.

	Stub axle	Swivel axle.
	Track-rod	Cross-tube.
	Draglink	Side tube. Steering connecting rod.
ELECTRICAL	Dynamo	Generator.
	Control box	Voltage regulator. Cut-out. Voltage control.
EXHAUST	Silencer	Muffler.
BODY	Bonnet	Hood.
	Wing	Mudguard. Fender.

FROST PRECAUTIONS

Steps must be taken to prevent the water in the cooling system from freezing during frosty weather. Water, when it freezes, expands, with the result that there is a very considerable risk of bursting either the radiator, heater element, or the cylinder block by the pressure generated. Since no provision is made for draining the heater unit, draining the radiator and cylinder block is not a sufficient safeguard.

The cooling system is of the sealed type and relatively high temperatures are developed in the radiator upper tank. For this reason anti-freeze solutions having an alcohol base are unsuitable owing to their high evaporation rate producing a rapid loss of coolant and a consequent interruption of circulation.

Only anti-freeze of the ethylene glycol type incorporating the correct type of corrosion inhibitor is suitable and owners are recommended to use Bluecol, Shell Snowflake, Esso Anti-freeze, or any other anti-freeze that conforms to specification B.S.3151 or B.S. 3152.

The recommended quantities of anti-freeze for different degrees of frost are:

Down to	Down to
7° F. (= 14° C.)	0° F. (= 18° C.)
15% solution	20% solution
Quantity 3 pints (1.71 litres)	Quantity 4 pints (2.27 litres)

Where temperatures below 0° F. (−18° C.) are likely to be encountered, a solution of at least 25 per cent of anti-freeze must be used to ensure immunity from trouble. Consult your local Dealer on this matter.

First decide what degree of frost protection is required before adding the anti-freeze.

Make sure that the cooling system is watertight and examine all joints, renewing any defective rubber hose.

Before adding anti-freeze to the cooling system it is advisable to clean the cooling system thoroughly by swilling out the water passages with a hose inserted in the filler, and with the drain taps open.

Avoid excessive topping up, otherwise there is a risk of losing valuable anti-freeze due to expansion of the solution. Top up only when the system is at its normal running temperature.

Generally speaking, anti-freeze is not injurious to cellulose paint pro-

vided it is wiped off in reasonable time.
Radiator anti-freeze must not be used in the windshield washing equipment.

Mk. II

TRIPLE CARBURETORS

1. Jet adjusting nut
2. Throttle adjusting screw.
3. Fast idle adjusting screw.
4. Jet locking nut.
5. Float chamber securing nut.
6. Jet link.
7. Jet head.
8. Vacuum ignition take-off.

Healey 3000 Mk. II

The carburetors fitted to the Healey 3000 Mk. II are triple S.U. type H.S.4. Each carburetor is mounted on an individual manifold secured to the cylinder head by three studs and nuts, and interconnected by an external balance pipe running above the manifolds.

The H.S.4. carburetor is of the automatically expanding choke type in which the size of the main air passage (or choke) over the jet, and the effective area of the jet, are variable according to the degree of throttle opening used on the engine against the prevailing road conditions (which may differ widely from light cruising to heavy pulling). Therefore, to serve the complete throttle range a single jet only is used, being a simple metal tube sliding in a single bearing bush, fed by fuel along a small diameter nylon tube leading direct from the base of the float-chamber. The jet is varied in effective area by a tapered fuel metering needle.

Adjustments

Slow-running is governed by the setting of the jet adjusting nuts and the throttle adjusting screws, all of which must be correctly set and synchronized if satisfactory results are to be obtained.

Before blaming the carburetor setting for incorrect slow-running make certain that the trouble is not caused by badly adjusted distributor contact points, faulty plugs, incorrect valve clearance, or faulty valves and springs.

Slow running adjustment and synchronization

After the first 1,000 miles (1,600 km.) or so when the engine is fully run in, the slow running may require adjustment. This must only be carried out when the engine has reached its normal running temperature.

As the needle size is determined during engine development, tuning of the carburetors is confined to correct idling setting. Slacken the actuating arms on the throttle spindle inter-connection. Close all throttles fully by unscrewing the throttle adjusting screws, then open each throttle by screwing down the idling adjustment screws one turn.

Remove pistons and suction chambers, and disconnect the jet control cables. Screw the jet adjusting nuts until each jet is flush with the bridge of its carburetor, or as near to this as possible (all jets being in the same relative position to the bridge of their respective carburetors). Replace the pistons and suction chamber assemblies, and check that the pistons fall freely on to the bridge of the carburetors (by use of the piston lifting pins). Turn down the jet adjusting nut two complete turns (12 flats).

Re-start the engine, and adjust the throttle adjusting screws to give the desired idling speed, by moving each throttle adjusting screw an equal amount. By listening to the hiss in the intakes, adjust the throttle adjusting screws until the intensity of the hiss is similar on all intakes. This will synchronize the throttle setting.

When this is satisfactory, the mixture should be adjusted by screwing each jet adjusting nut up or down by the same amount, until the fastest idling speed is obtained consistent with even firing. During this adjusting, it is necessary that the jets are pressed upwards to ensure that they are in contact with the adjusting nuts.

As the mixture is adjusted the engine will probably run faster, and it may therefore be necessary to unscrew the throttle adjusting screws a little, each by the same amount, to reduce the speed.

Now check the mixture strength by lifting the piston of the front carburetor by approximately 1/32 in. (.75 mm.) when if:

(a) the engine speed increases, this indicates that the mixture strength of the front carburetor is too rich.

(b) the engine speed immediately decreases, this indicates that the mixture strength of the front carburetor is too weak.

(c) the engine speed momentarily increases very slightly, then the mixture strength of the front carburetor is correct.

Repeat the operation at the center and rear carburetors, and after adjustment re-check the front carburetor, since all carburetors are inter-dependent.

When the mixture is correct the exhaust note should be regular and even. If it is irregular with a splashy type of misfire and colorless exhaust, the mixture is too weak. If there is a regular or rhythmical type of misfire in the exhaust beat, together with a blackish exhaust, then the mixture is too rich.

The carburetor throttle on each carburetor is operated by a lever and pin, with the pin working in a forked lever attached to the throttle spindle. A clearance exists between the pin and the fork, which must be maintained when the throttle is closed and the engine idling, to prevent any load from the accelerator linkage being transferred to

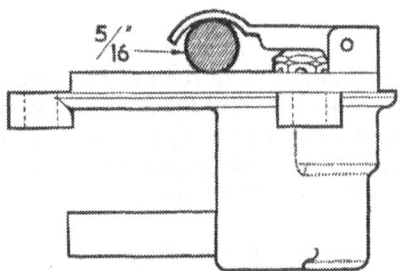

the throttle butterfly and spindle.

To set this clearance: with the throttle shaft levers free on the throttle shaft, put a .012 in. (.305 mm.) feeler between each throttle shaft stop at the top and the carburetor heat shield. Move each throttle shaft lever downwards in turn until the lever pin rests lightly on the lower arm of the fork in the carburetor throttle lever. Tighten the clamp bolt of the throttle shaft lever at this position. When all three carburetors have been dealt with, remove the feelers. The pins on the throttle shafts should then have clearance in the forks.

Re-connect the choke cables, ensuring that the jet heads return against the lower face of the jet adjusting nuts when the choke control is pushed fully in.

Pull out the mixture control knob on the dash panel to its maximum movement without moving the carburetor jets (about ⅝ in.) (15.87 mm.) and adjust the fast idle cam screws to give an engine speed of about 1,000 r.p.m. when hot.

The Float-chamber

The position of the forked lever in the float-chamber must be such that the lever of the float (and therefore the height of the fuel at the jet) is correct.

This is checked by inserting a 5/16 in. (7.94 mm.) round bar between the forked lever and the machined lip of the float-chamber lid. The prongs of the lever should rest on the bar when the needle is on its seating. If this is not so, the lever should be reset at the point where the prongs meet the shank. Care must be taken not to bend the shank, which must be perfectly flat and at right angles to the needle when it is on its seating.

Jet centering

To check the jet for concentricity with the jet needle, set the jet head and the jet adjusting nut in the uppermost position, lift the suction piston with the piston lifting pin and allow the piston to fall. It should fall freely and a definite soft metallic click will be heard as the base of the piston strikes the jet bridge.

If this does not happen with the jet raised, but does occur when the jet is lowered, the jet bearing and jet must be recentered as follows: —

Disconnect the link between the jet head and carburetor lever by removing the small Phillips retaining screw from the jet head.

Unscrew the union securing the jet feed tube into the base of the float chamber and withdraw the jet from the jet bearing, complete with feed tube.

Unscrew the jet adjusting nut and remove the lock spring; screw up the nut to its fullest extent and refit the jet head and feed tube.

Slacken the jet locking nut until the jet bearing is just free to rotate with finger pressure. Remove the piston damper from the top of the suction chamber body and gently press down the piston on to its stop.

Tighten the jet locking nut, at the same time ensuring that the jet head is held firmly in its uppermost position and at its correct angular relation to the float chamber.

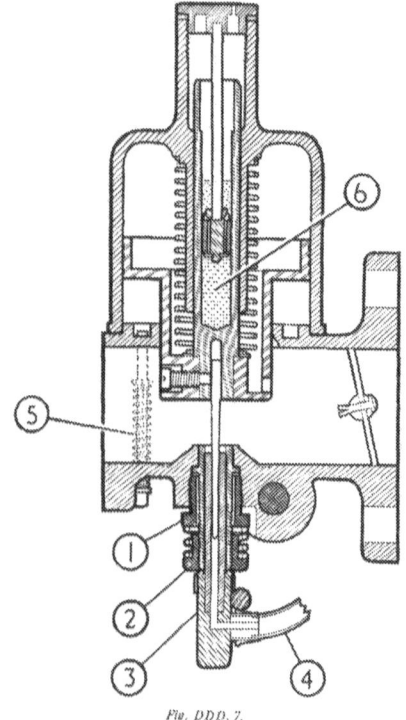

Fig. D.D.D. 7.

1. *Jet locking nut.*
2. *Jet adjusting nut.*
3. *Jet head.*
4. *Feed tube from float chamber*
5. *Piston lifting pin.*
6. *Damper reservoir.*

Repeat the check for concentricity both with the jet raised and lowered. If the result is not satisfactory the recentering operation must be repeated until the correct result is obtained.

When the operation is completed, replace the adjusting nut lock spring and the jet operating link.

This adjustment is best effected with the carburetors removed from the engine.

Float needle sticking

If the engine runs unevenly, apparently through lack of fuel, when there is plenty in the tank and the pump is working properly, the probable cause is a sticking float needle. An easy test for this is to disconnect the pipe from the electric pump to the carburetor and switch the ignition on and off quickly while the end of the pipe is directed onto a pad of cloth or into a container.

If fuel is delivered, starvation is almost certainly being caused by the float needle sticking to its seating, and the float chamber lid(s) should therefore be removed and the needle and seating cleaned and refitted.

At the same time it will be advisable to clean out the entire fuel feed system as this trouble is caused by foreign matter in the fuel, and unless this is removed it is likely to recur. It is of no use whatever renewing any of the component parts of the carburetor(s), and the only cure is to make sure that the fuel tank and pipe lines are entirely free from any kind of foreign matter or sticky substance capable of causing this trouble.

Piston sticking

The piston assembly comprises the suction disc and the piston forming the choke, into which is inserted the hardened and ground piston rod which engages in a bearing in the center of the suction chamber and in which is, in turn, inserted the jet needle. The piston rod running in the bearing is the only part which is in actual contact with any other part, the suction disc, piston, and needle all having suitable clearances to prevent sticking. If sticking does occur the whole assembly should be cleaned carefully and the piston rod lubricated with a spot of thin oil. No oil must be applied to any other part except the piston rod. A sticking piston can be ascertained by removing the piston damper and lifting the piston by pressing the piston lifting pin; the piston should come up quite freely and fall back smartly onto its seating when released. On no account should the piston return spring be stretched or its tension altered in an attempt to improve its rate of return.

FLOAT CHAMBER OVERFLOW PIPES

Flexible plastic overflow pipes were fitted to each carburetor float chamber from Power Unit No. 29E-H-1092. The float chamber lids were modified to incorporate short overflow nozzles on to which the flexible pipes are a push fit. The overflow pipes may be fitted with the modified lids to earlier 3000 Mk. II cars.

CARBURETORS WITH NYLON FLOATS

Carburetors fitted to later 3000 Mk. II cars incorporated float chambers equipped with nylon floats in place of the metal floats used previously. The nylon floats are integral with the float levers which are attached to the float chamber lids. The nylon float and lever assembly may be interchanged with the earlier metal float and separate lever. Red aluminum tags were used for a time to identify carburetors modified in this way.

To check the float lever, hold the float chamber lid and float assembly upside down and place a ⅛ in. (3.18 mm.) diameter bar across *the diameter* of the machined lip of the float chamber lid, parallel with the float lever hinge pin, and under the float lever. The face of the float lever should just rest on the bar when the needle valve is fully on its seating. If it does not do this, carefully reset the angle made between the straight portion of the float lever and its hinge until the correct position is obtained.

REVISED LOCATION OF FUEL PUMP

From Car No. 17547 (BN7) and 17352 (BT7) the fuel pump and fuel lines were transferred from the left-hand side to the right-hand side of the car. The repositioning of these components isolates them from the exhaust system and diminishes any possibility of fuel vaporization. This change involved the introduction of new fuel pipes between the tank and the pump, and between the pump and the flexible pipe leading to the carburetors, new petrol pipe fittings, and associated body modifications.

On the BT7 the fuel pump is now accessible when the right-hand rear seat pan has been removed.

Access to the fuel pump on the BN7 is obtained in the same way as before although it is now located on the right-hand side.

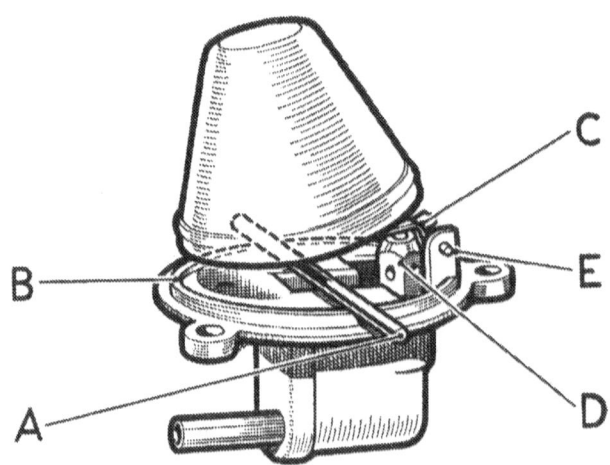

Checking the nylon float level.

A. ⅛ *in. diameter bar.*
B. *Machined lip.*
C. *Float lever resetting point.*
D. *Needle valve assembly.*
E. *Hinge pin.*

BJ7 ~ MODEL CARBURETORS

The Austin-Healey 3000 Mk. II Sports Convertible (Series BJ7) is equipped with twin S.U. carburetors, type HS6. Each carburetor is attached by four studs and nuts to a detachable one-piece six port induction manifold. The carburetor float chambers incorporate nylon floats and are fitted with flexible overflow pipes.

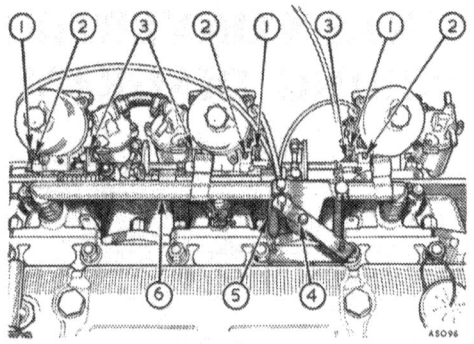

1. Fast idling adjusting screws.
2. Throttle adjusting screws.
3. Throttle operating levers.
4. Choke cable relay lever.
5. Throttle return spring.
6. Balance tube.

The construction and servicing of the HS6 carburetor are basically similar to that of the HS4 type.

Water and dirt in the carburetor

Should this be suspected, lift the piston with a pencil when the jet can then be seen. Flood the carburetor and watch the jet; if fuel does not flow freely there is a blockage. To remedy this start the engine, open the throttle, and block up the air inlet momentarily, keeping the throttle open until the engine starts to race.

If the jet is completely blocked and the engine will not run correctly, the jet must be removed and thoroughly cleaned.

Float-chamber flooding

This is indicated by fuel flowing from the drain hole in the top of the float chamber lid below the main fuel feed pipe, and is generally caused by grit between the float chamber needle and its guide. The float-chamber lid should be removed and the needle and its guide thoroughly cleaned.

CARBURETOR REMOVAL

Turn the battery master switch to the 'off' position

Disconnect the fuel feed pipe from the front carburetor, the two snap-lock ball joints from the accelerator relay shaft, and the three throttle return springs.

Release the three mixture control cables from the carburetor levers. Slacken the retaining clip and remove the engine breather hose from the rear air cleaner. Pull off the rubber connector for the vacuum ignition control pipe from the top of the rear carburetor body. Remove the two nuts, spring washers and plain washers securing each carburetor flange and withdraw the three carburetors as one unit.

Detach the throttle interconnecting shafts, remove the fuel pipes and separate the carburetors.

Refitting is a reversal of the removing procedure.

The throttle linkage must be checked and re-adjusted if necessary after refitting.

BJ7~ SPORTS CONVERTIBLE WIRING DIAGRAM

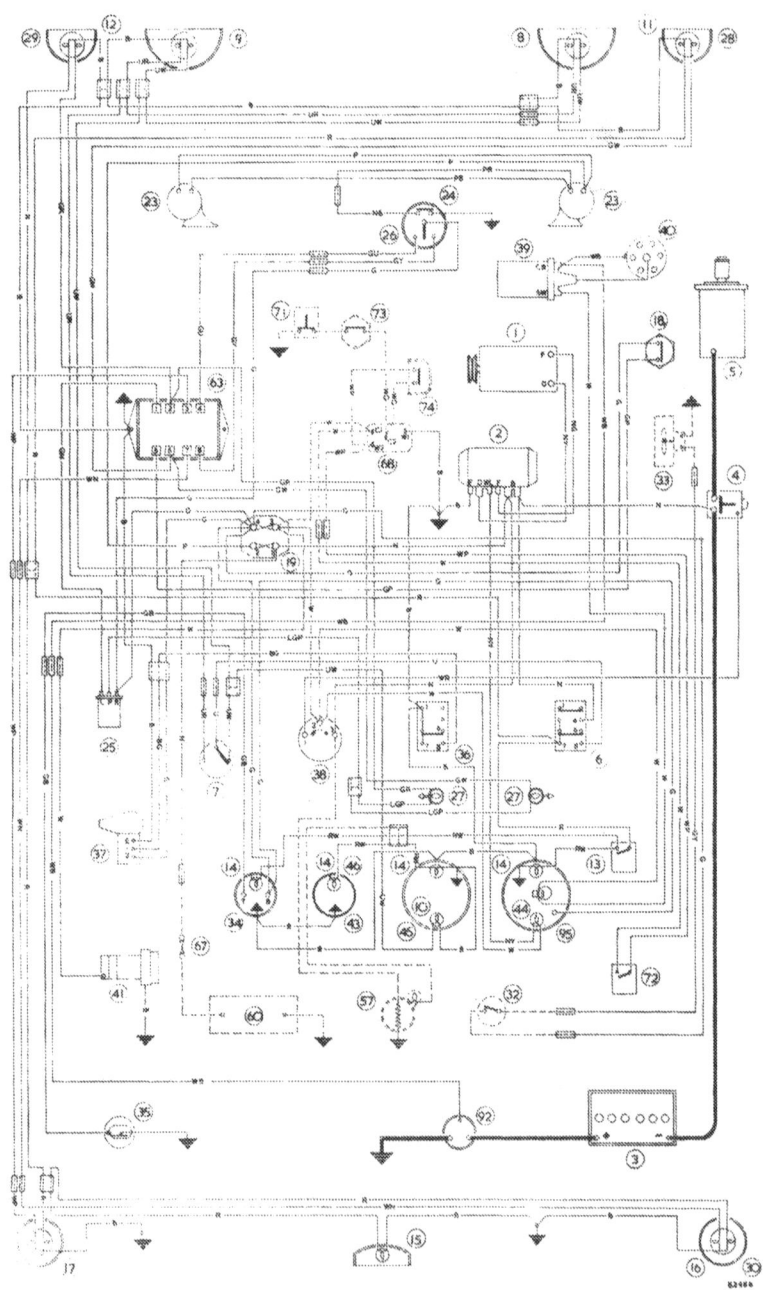

KEY TO WIRING DIAGRAM

No.	Description	No.	Description

1. Dynamo.
2. Control box.
3. Battery.
4. Starter solenoid.
5. Starter motor.
6. Lighting switch.
7. Headlight dip switch.
8. R.H. headlamp.
9. L.H. headlamp.
10. Main-beam warning light.
11. R.H. pilot lamp.
12. L.H. pilot lamp.
13. Panel light switch.
14. Panel lights.
15. Number-plate illumination lamp.
16. R.H. stop and tail lamp.
17. L.H. stop and tail lamp.
18. Stop light switch.
19. Fuse unit (50 amps. '1–2', 35 amps. '3–4').
23. Horns.
24. Horn-push.
25. Flasher unit.
26. Direction indicator switch.
27. Direction indicator warning lights.
28. R.H. front flasher lamp.
29. L.H. front flasher lamp.
30. R.H. rear flasher lamp.
31. L.H. rear flasher lamp.
32. Heater motor switch.
33. Heater motor.*
34. Fuel gauge.
35. Fuel gauge tank unit.
36. Windscreen wiper motor switch.
37. Windscreen wiper motor.
38. Ignition/starter switch.
39. Ignition coil.
40. Distributor.
41. Fuel pump.
43. Oil pressure gauge.
44. Ignition warning light.
45. Speedometer.
46. Water temperature gauge.
57. Cigar lighter.*
60. Radio.*
63. Flasher relay.
67. Fuse (radio circuit).*
68. Overdrive relay.*
71. Overdrive solenoid.*
72. Overdrive manual control switch.
73. Overdrive gear switch.*
74. Overdrive throttle switch.*
92. Battery cut off switch.
95. Revolution counter.

CABLE COLOUR CODE

B.	Black.	G.	Green.	W.	White.
U.	Blue.	P.	Purple.	Y.	Yellow.
N.	Brown.	R.	Red.	L/G.	Light Green.

When a cable has two colour code letters the first denotes the main colour and the second denotes the tracer colour, or, alternatively, the first may signify the intensity of the colour and the second the actual colour.

All items marked thus * fitted as optional extra, circuits shown dotted.

CONTROLS

Gear lever

The four forward gears and the reverse gear are engaged by moving the lever to the position indicated in the illustration inset. Earlier cars, with the longer side-mounted gear lever, have the same gear positions.

To engage the reverse gear move the lever to the left of the neutral position until resistance is felt, apply side pressure to the lever to overcome the resistance and then pull it backwards to engage the gear.

Synchromesh engagement is provided on second, third, and fourth gears.

Ensure that the gear lever is in the neutral position before attempting to start the engine.

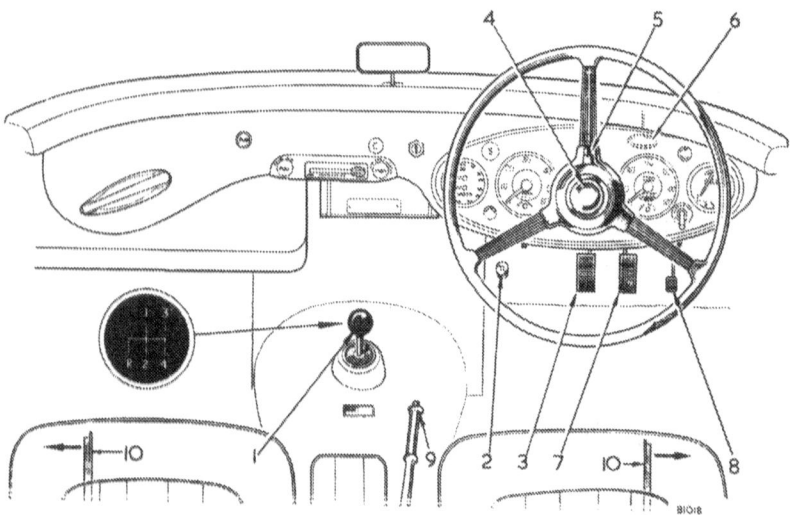

The Controls (right-hand drive.)

1. Gear lever.
2. Dip switch.
3. Clutch pedal.
4. Horn button.
5. Direction indicator switch.
6. Bonnet lock control.
7. Brake pedal.
8. Accelerator pedal.
9. Hand brake.
10. Seat adjuster.

Brake pedal

The centre pedal operates the hydraulic brakes on all four wheels and also the twin stop warning lights when the ignition is switched on.

Clutch pedal

The left-hand pedal operates the clutch. Do not allow the foot to rest on the clutch pedal while driving as this will cause excessive wear of the release mechanism.

Choke or mixture control

To enrich the mixture and assist starting when the engine is cold pull out the knob marked 'C'. Push it inwards to the normal running position as soon as the engine is warm enough to run without the rich mixture.

The first one or two notches of movement operate only the throttle control. This initial movement can be used to give a fast engine idling speed and prevent stalling when driving at low speeds before the engine has fully warmed up.

CONTROLS

This will not be detrimental, but do not run the engine for any length of time with the control withdrawn to any greater extent.

Note.—This control is not fitted to earlier cars having an automatic choke control built into the carburetter.

Hand brake

Situated on the right-hand side of the propeller shaft tunnel, between the seats. To release, pull rearwards slightly and depress the knob in the end of the lever with the thumb, then push fully forward. The hand brake works on the rear wheels only.

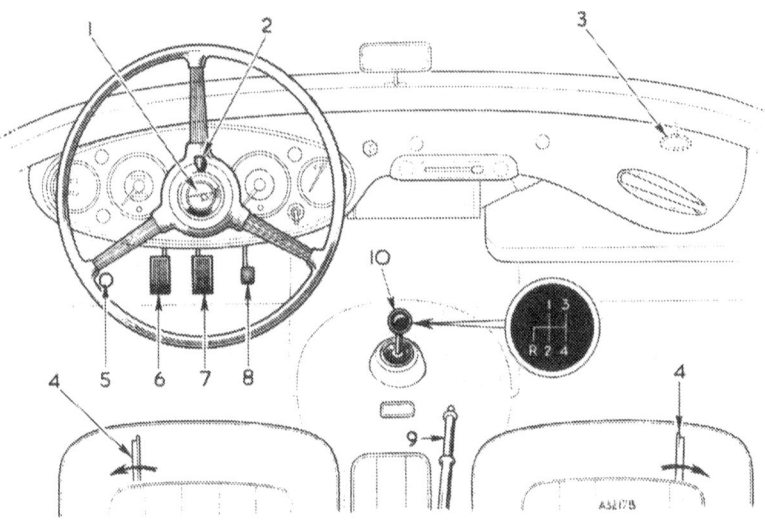

The Controls (left-hand drive)

1. Horn button.
2. Direction indicator switch.
3. Bonnet lock control.
4. Seat adjuster.
5. Dip switch.
6. Clutch pedal.
7. Brake pedal.
8. Accelerator pedal.
9. Hand brake.
10. Gear lever.

Overdrive switch (when fitted)

The switch is mounted on the fascia panel with the two positions clearly marked.

Dip switch

This is situated to the left of the clutch pedal. To dip the headlight beams depress the switch. Press the switch again to return them to the straight ahead position.

Ignition switch

Turn the key clockwise to switch on the ignition. Do not leave the switch 'on' when the engine is not running—the warning light is a reminder.

The fuel pump and gauge are brought into action by this switch, which is also the master switch for the windshield wipers, direction indicators, and heater blower motor.

CONTROLS

Starter switch
Press in the button marked 'S' to start, and release it as soon as the engine fires. If the engine fails to start after a few revolutions, do not operate the starter again until the crankshaft is stationary.

Direction indicator switch
The flashing direction indicators are controlled from the centre of the steering wheel. Normally, after the car has turned a corner, the control is automatically returned to the vertical position and the indicators switched off, but when only a slight turn has been made it may be necessary to return the switch manually.

Horn button
The horns are sounded by pressing the button at the centre of the steering wheel.

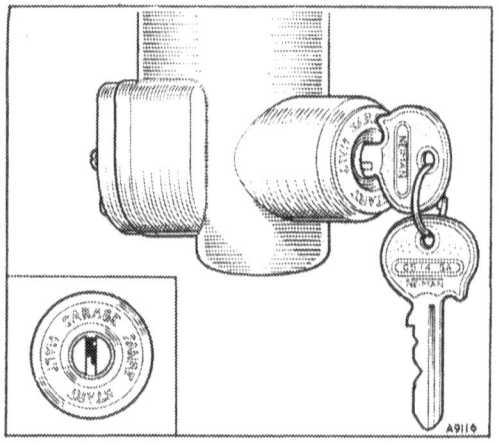

The ignition/starter switch and steering column lock, with the four key positions shown inset.

Ignition/starter switch and steering column lock
Cars exported to Germany and Sweden are equipped with a combined ignition/starter switch and steering column lock mounted centrally below the steering column.

The switch has four key positions (see illustration). The key supplied may be removed or inserted when the lock is in the 'HALT' or 'GARAGE' positions. Removing the key when the lock is in the 'HALT' position locks the steering column so that the steering wheel cannot be turned. To unlock the steering column, insert the key and turn to the 'GARAGE' position. If the key is removed when the lock is in the 'GARAGE' position the steering remains free.

Turning the key clockwise to the 'FARHT' position switches on the ignition. Further clockwise movement against spring pressure to the 'START' position operates the starter motor. As soon as the key is released it will return to the 'FARHT' position.

INSTRUMENTS AND SWITCHES

Lighting switch

Pull out knob marked 'SIDE-HEAD' to switch on the pilot, tail and number-plate lights.

Turn the knob clockwise and pull out again to switch on the headlights. The headlight beams are raised and lowered by the foot dip switch.

Panel light switch

Slide the switch to the right to illuminate the instruments. The panel lights operate only when the pilot lights are 'on'.

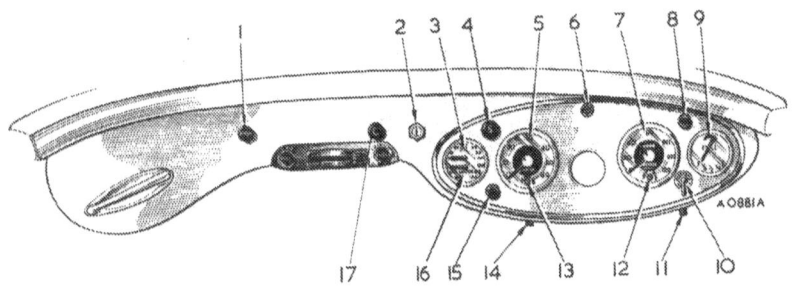

The Instruments and Switches (right-hand drive)

1. Windshield washer control.
2. Ignition switch.
3. Oil pressure gauge.
4. Starter switch.
5. Tachometer.
6. Flasher warning light.
7. Speedometer.
8. Lighting switch.
9. Fuel gauge.
10. Overdrive switch.
11. Trip distance setting knob.
12. Headlight beam warning light.
13. Ignition warning light.
14. Panel light switch.
15. Windshield wiper switch.
16. Water temperature gauge.
17. Choke control.

Battery master switch

This switch, situated in the luggage compartment, is fitted as an anti-theft device. The luggage compartment must of course be locked after the switch has been turned to the 'off' position.

Speedometer

In addition to indicating the vehicle road speed this instrument records the trip and total distances. The trip figures at the top of the speedometer face can be reset to zero by pushing up the knob at the bottom of the speedometer and turning it to the right.

Tachometer

This instrument indicates the revolutions of the engine per minute and thus assists the driver to use the most effective engine speed range for maximum performance in any gear.

INSTRUMENTS AND SWITCHES

Fuel gauge

When the ignition is switched on the gauge indicates the quantity of fuel in the tank. While the tank is being filled switch off the ignition to stop the engine.

Do not fill the fuel tank so that the fuel is visible in the filler intake tube. Should this be done there is a considerable risk of leakage due to expansion of the fuel when the car is left in the sun, with consequent danger from the exposed fuel. If inadvertently over-filled, make certain that the car is parked in the shade with the filler intake as high as possible.

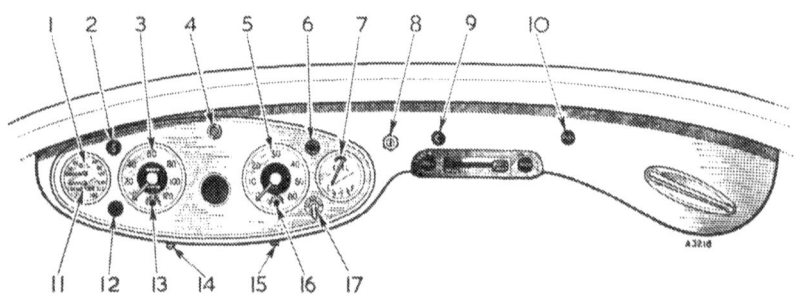

Instruments and Switches (left-hand drive)

1. Oil pressure gauge.
2. Starter switch.
3. Speedometer.
4. Flasher warning light.
5. Tachometer.
6. Lighting switch.
7. Fuel gauge.
8. Ignition switch.
9. Choke control.
10. Windshield washer control.
11. Water temperature gauge.
12. Windshield wiper switch.
13. Headlight beam warning light.
14. Trip distance setting knob.
15. Panel light switch.
16. Ignition warning light.
17. Overdrive switch.

Oil pressure gauge

The pressure of the oil in the lubricating system should be 55 to 60 lbs./sq. in. (3·87 to 4·22 kg./sq. cm.) under normal running conditions. Approximately 20 lbs./sq. in. (1·4 kg./sq. cm.) should be shown when the engine is idling. Should the gauge fail to register any pressure at all, stop the engine immediately and investigate the cause.

Water temperature gauge

The temperature of the cooling water leaving the cylinder head is indicated by this gauge and should be 185°—194°F. (85°—90°C.) when the engine is running normally. If the normal running temperature is greatly exceeded the cause must be traced and rectified immediately.

Windshield washer control

Push in the knob on the fascia to operate the windshield washer. Set the wipers in motion before using the cleaning jets.

INSTRUMENTS AND SWITCHES

Windshield wiper switch

Pull out the control marked 'WIPER' to set the wipers in motion. Push in the knob to switch off the motor and park the blades.

The windshield wipers are self-parking and can be used only when the ignition is switched on.

Ignition warning light

When the ignition is switched on the light located in the tachometer face will glow red. It will fade out again when the engine is started and the speed increased sufficiently for the dynamo to charge the battery.

Should the light still glow with increased engine speed, the cause should be investigated immediately.

Main beam warning light

A red (or blue, Export) light located in the speedometer face glows when the headlights are switched on, with the two beams in the raised poistion The light goes out when the headlights are dipped.

Direction indicator warning light

The green light located in the centre and at the top of the instrument panel flashes while the direction indicators are operating.

Seat adjustment

Each front seat is adjustable and is secured in position by a spring-loaded lever. Push the lever outwards to release the seat and move it to the desired position.

Steering column adjustment (optional)

The steering column can be adjusted to suit the driver's position. To adjust the length of the column grip the locking collar immediately behind the steering wheel hub with the hand, hold the rim of the wheel and turn the locking collar clockwise to release its clamping action.

The steering wheel may then be pushed or pulled to the desired position and locked by firmly turning the locking collar in an anti-clockwise direction.

HEATING AND VENTILATING

Heater booster switch

Pull out the knob mounted on the end of the temperature control lever to switch on the booster fan.

Air temperature control

The control moves in a quadrant and regulates the temperature of the air passing through the heater into the car interior and demister ducts.

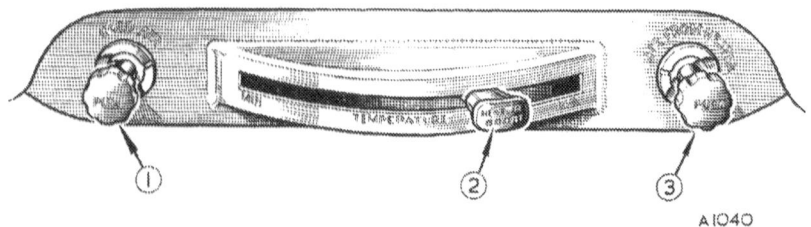

1. Air control.   2. Blower switch and temperature control.
3. Heater air control.

Heater air control

Pull out the knob on the right-hand side of the heater control panel to regulate the supply of air from the heater. When fully out the air supply is completely shut off.

In addition, a hinged shutter is provided in each air duct outlet immediately above the driver's and passenger's feet. These shutters enable the air flow to the vehicle interior to be varied.

Demisting and defrosting

Close or partly close the hinged shutters, push in the air control (3) and regulate the temperature as necessary.

Air intake control

A supply of cold air, entirely independent of the heater unit, can be admitted to the car interior for ventilation purposes by pulling out the knob on the left-hand side of the heater control panel.

OPTIONAL EXTRAS

The following additional items of equipment are available as optional fittings:

Overdrive   Heater
Adjustable steering column   Servo assisted brakes
                                        Knock-on wire wheels
Radio

B.M.C. SEAT BELTS

Description

Seat belts for the front seats of the Healey 3000 Mk. II (Part No. AHH6122) can be supplied by B.M.C. Service Ltd. Attachment points for these belts are incorporated in the construction of the body, and are located on the rear wheelarches, the rear floor and the sides of the drive shaft tunnel.

Certain body modifications are necessary if it is desired to fit seat belts to Mk. I models. A kit is available for this purpose under Part No. AHB9141.

The fitting of the seat belts to the car should only be carried out by an authorised Austin Dealer or Distributor.

Use of belts

Make sure that the short belt being used for either seat is attached to the side of the tunnel nearest to the seat, i.e. the belt must not cross the tunnel.

The seat belts in use, showing the correct position for the buckle

Adjust the short belt until the attached buckle is located just in front of the hip (see illustration). The upper part of the long belt passes diagonally across the chest; the lower part returns around the waist to the floor attachment point. The buckle tongue attached to the long belt should be approximately at belt centre.

Fasten the belt by pushing the buckle tongue into the buckle until a positive click is heard.

Adjust the long belt until the waist portion is comfortably tight and it is just possible to slide a hand between the upper part of the belt and the chest.

To release the buckle lift the buckle flap approximately 90° and exert gentle forward pressure on the belt at the same time.

Fold and stow the long belt clear of the floor area immediately after use to ensure safe exit and entry for the occupants of the car.

BODY DETAILS

Bonnet lock control

To open the bonnet pull the control handle located high behind the fascia panel on the right-hand side. The bonnet will rise an inch or so and will then be held by two spring-loaded safety catches. Insert the fingers, push back the catches simultaneously and raise the bonnet. The bonnet may be supported in the open position by releasing one end of the rod secured to the underside and engaging it in the slot on the left side of the bonnet surround.

When closing the bonnet stow the rod in the retaining clip and exert a downward pressure on the bonnet top until the locking catch is heard to engage. It is essential that the bonnet release mechanism and safety catches are adequately lubricated to ensure freedom of operation. Should any stiffness occur it might result in insecure fastening of the bonnet, with a consequent risk of the bonnet flying open when the car is in motion.

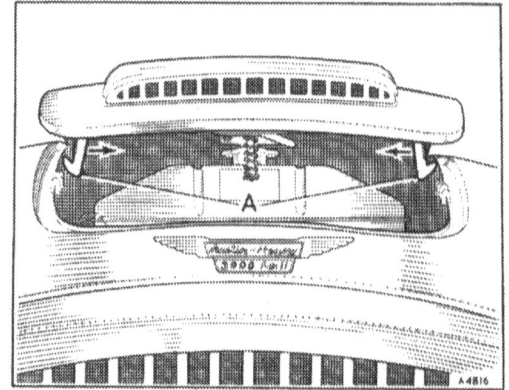

To raise the bonnet, push in safety catches 'A'.

Turn the battery master switch in a clockwise direction to immobilise the vehicle.

In the two-seater version, the switch is located on the left hand side of the compartment.

Luggage boot

The luggage boot is locked by the ignition key. Located within this compartment are the spare-wheel, tool kit and battery master switch. On four-seater models, the battery also is stowed on the right-hand side of the luggage compartment.

Remember that the spare tyre should be kept at the normal running pressure for the rear tyres

HOOD STOWAGE

2-SEATER MODEL

To lower, fold, and stow the hood, proceed as follows:—
1. Pull the rear floating stick forward to the main stick, using the loop provided.
2. Release the two buttons and the fasteners securing the hood side flaps to the outside of the body.

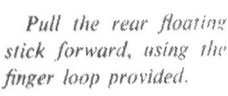

Pull the rear floating stick forward, using the finger loop provided.

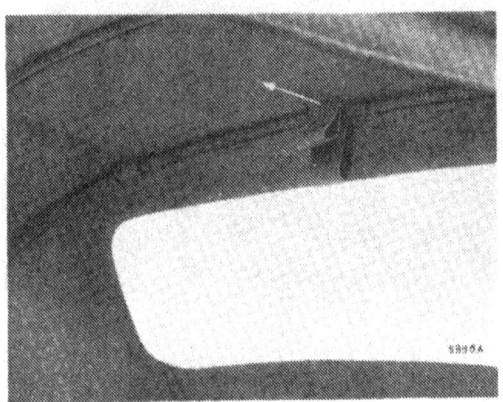

Break the cant rail hinge points and pull the front rail up to the main hood stick.

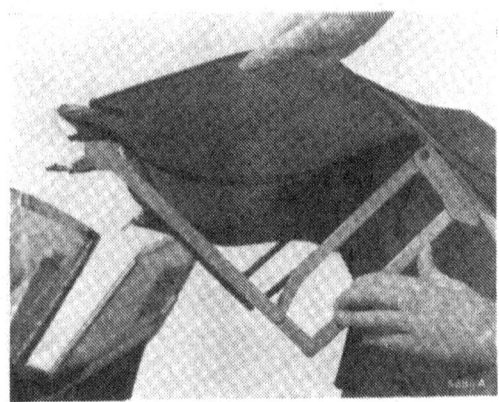

3. Remove the rear end of the hood by disengaging the securing plate from the two retainers on the rear deck panel.
4. Release the toggle catches from the top corners of the windshield.
5. Break the cant rail hinge links, and pull the front rail up to the main hood stick, ensuring that the hood covering is not trapped.

HOOD STOWAGE

6. Fold the hood onto the hood sticks with the window at the rear and the seam of the hood running along the top of the sticks. The side flaps should be folded inwards with the underneath part of the fasteners against the rear window to avoid damage.

Fold the hood onto the upright hoodsticks with the seam of the hood running along the top and the window to the rear.

Lift the hood assembly from the body sockets and stow away, passing the sticks through the retaining stirrups into the recess near the floor.

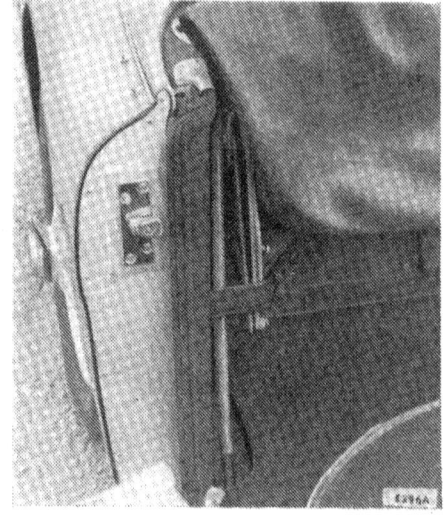

7. Lift the folded hood and sticks from the body sockets and stow away with the sticks passing through the leather covered stirrup brackets and resting in the carpet covered recesses near the floor. Ensure that the cant rail hinge links are retained by the stirrups to prevent them chafing the back of the seats when they are pushed back in their most rearward position.

HOOD STOWAGE

4-SEATER MODEL

To lower, fold, and stow the hood, proceed as follows:—
1. Break the rear stick hinge links, by upward pressure on their tabs and pull the stick forward to the main support by using the loops provided.
2. Lift the rear seat squab and open it back onto the seats.
3. Release the two buttons securing the side flaps and the fasteners along the rear deck panel.

Hood sticks and front rail in position under the rear deck panel, with the hood inverted and the first fold made.

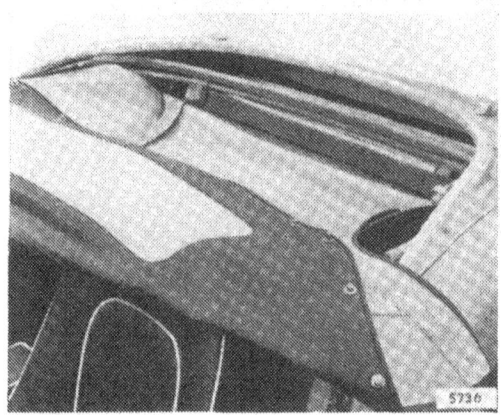

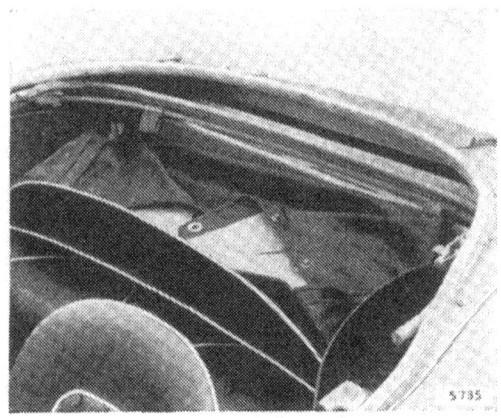

Fold the hood side flaps well over, after making the second fold in the hood.

4. Release the toggle catches from the top corners of the windshield.
5. Remove the hood from the sticks and place the front rail under the rear deck panel. Fold the sticks together and stow under the rear deck panel and over the front rail.

HOOD STOWAGE

6. Make the first fold in the hood at the seam above the window, fold again and fold the side flaps on top.
7. Loosely fold again, making sure the hood material is well clear of the seat channels. Finally replace the rear seat squab.

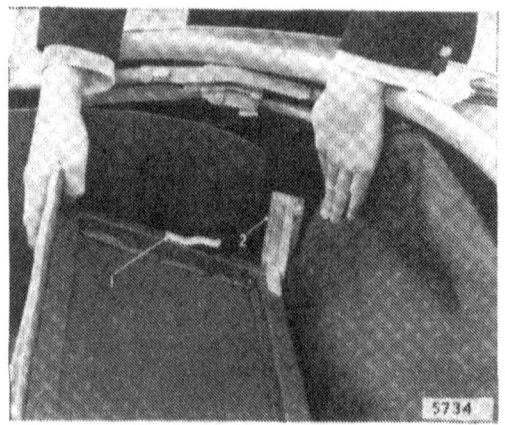

Keep the hood material clear of the rear seat squab slides '2' and securing clips '1'.

Showing a sidescreen in position secured at the front '2' and rear '1' by wing nuts.

Sidescreen removal

Release the two wing nuts clamping the sidescreen, pull the rear support clear of the stud and lift the assembly from the door.

Replace the wing nuts on to their respective studs: on the door at the rear and onto the sidescreen at the front.

Sidescreen stowage

Place the sidescreens in the tonneau cover bag and stow in the luggage compartment.

HOOD STOWAGE

Hard Top

Release the toggle catches from the top corners of the windshield and slacken off the wingnuts at the rear just sufficiently for the hooks to be pulled clear. To remove the top, lift at the rear and as the locating pins clear allow the top to move forward slightly.

When replacing position the front edge over the windshield and then locate the pins at the door post. Clamp the front end and secure at the rear.

The toggle catch securing the hard top to the windshield pillar.

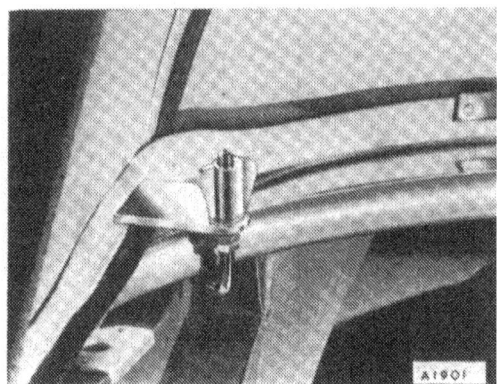

The bracket, hook, and wing nut clamping the hard top to the tonneau panel.

HOOD FOLDING

CONVERTIBLE MODEL

To lower the hood proceed as follows:
1. Pull the rear seat squab forwards from its rubber catches.
2. Release the toggle catches at each end of the windshield top rail. Pull the top of the catches downwards and then disengage the bottom of the catches from the hooks on the windshield pillars.
3. Standing beside the car, lift the front hood rail from the windshield allowing the three hood supporting rails to collapse together. Ensure that the hood material and the back window fold naturally without buckling or creasing.

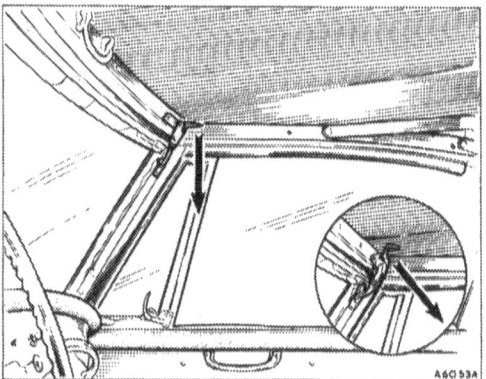

Release the toggle catches at each end of the windshield top rail. The earlier type of catch is shown inset.

Lift the front hood rail from the windshield allowing the hood supporting rails to collapse together.

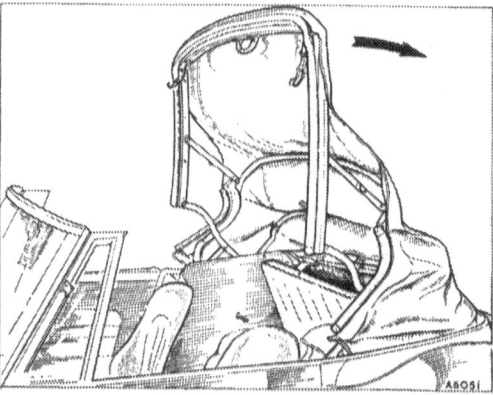

4. Push the front section of the hood backwards, inverting it in the process, and ease the hood and supporting rails into the well behind the rear seat.
5. Press the front hood rail section downwards on each side of the car in turn, making sure that the hood framework does not damage the interior trim panels.
6. Push the rear seat squab back into its retaining catches.

HOOD FOLDING

7. Fit the hood cover, securing first the two Tenax fasteners on each side of the car adjacent to the doors and then the fasteners on each interior trim panel. Press home the two fasteners on the tonneau panel and then secure the hood cover to the top of the rear seat squab with the two fasteners provided.

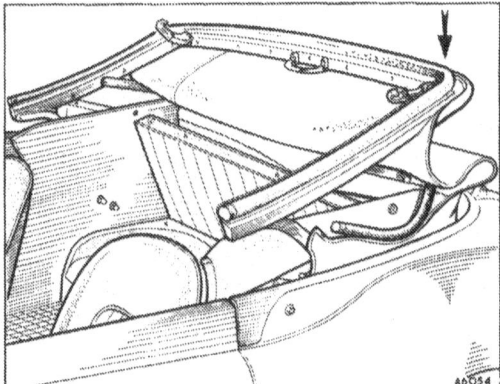

Press the front hood rail section downwards.

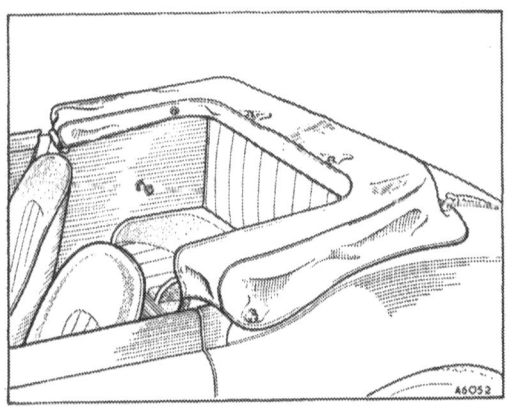

Fit the hood cover using the fasteners provided.

Raising the hood is a reversal of the above sequence. Having lifted the hood from the well behind the rear seat, sit inside the car and use the handle at the centre of the front hood rail to pull the hood down towards the top rail of the windshield. Engage the bottom of the toggle catches in the hooks on the windshield pillars and press the top of the catches firmly forwards and upwards towards the hood.

Rear window

The rear window may be folded down when extra ventilation is required with the hood in the raised position. Undo the two clips at the top of the window and release the window frame from the three metal clips on the hood frame. Fold the window panel down, avoiding creasing or buckling the transparent window material.

HOOD FOLDING

Tonneau cover (Convertible model)

To fit the tonneau cover supplied by B.M.C. Service Ltd., assemble the two sections of the cover support rail and fit it into the socket provided on each side of the car just in front of the hood frame pivot anchorage.

Lower the windows and place the cover over the car. Engage the rear edge of the cover with the fasteners on the tonneau and quarter panels, the sides with the fasteners on the doors, and the front with the fasteners on the fascia panel top.

The front of the cover may be unzipped down the centre and folded back to give access to the driver's seat, or folded back to give access to both front seats. When the cover is folded back ensure that it is placed behind the front seat, and that the front edge of the cover is folded under and the flaps provided are attached to the fasteners on the heel board below the rear seats.

Openings in the cover immediately in front of the tonneau rail permit the use of B.M.C. seat belts when the cover is in position. Lift up the press-studs securing the flap which covers the opening on the side of the car on which the belt is to be worn. Pull out the quick-release pin from the seat belt floor anchorage and detach the belt. Thread the belt, including the buckle tongue, from below the tonneau cover up through the opening. Refit the belt to the floor bracket and replace the quick-release pin.

When removing the tonneau cover, make the first fold along the central zip fastener. Stow the cover and tonneau rail in the bags provided.

RUNNING INSTRUCTIONS

Running-in Speeds

The treatment given to a new car will have an important bearing on its subsequent life, and engine speeds during this early period must be limited. The following instructions should be strictly adhered to.

During the first 500 miles (800 km.):
DO NOT exceed 45 m.p.h. (72 k.p.h.).
DO NOT operate at full throttle in any gear.
DO NOT allow the engine to labour in any gear.

Starting (hand choke control)

Before starting the engine make sure that the gear lever is in the neutral position. When starting from cold pull out the choke or mixture control (marked 'C'). Switch on the ignition and operate the starter. The crankshaft will be rotated and after a second or two the engine should start, when the control must immediately be released. It is bad practice to keep the starter operating if the engine refuses to start as the starter takes a very heavy current from the battery and may discharge it.

After the engine has run for a few minutes, or almost immediately in warm weather, the choke control should be pushed fully in. On no account must the engine be run for any length of time with this control pulled out or neat fuel will be drawn into the cylinders and considerable damage may be caused. The control should be returned to its normal position as soon as the engine is warm enough to run evenly without its use. It is not necessary and in fact is detrimental to use the mixture or choke control when starting a warm engine.

Starting (automatic choke control)

The rich mixture is controlled by a thermal switch and an auxiliary enrichment carburetter. When starting it is merely necessary to ascertain that the gear lever is in the neutral position, switch on the ignition and operate the starter switch. The crankshaft will be rotated and after a second or two the engine should start when the starter switch must immediately be released.

Warming up

Research has proved that the practice of warming up an engine by allowing it to idle slowly is definitely harmful. The correct procedure is to let the engine run fairly fast, at approximately 1,000 r.p.m., corresponding to a speed of about 20 m.p.h. (32 km.p.h.) in top gear, so that it attains its correct working temperature **as quickly as possible**. Allowing the engine to work slowly in a cold state leads to excessive cylinder wear, and far less damage is done by driving the car straight on to the road from cold than by letting the engine idle slowly in the garage.

Overdrive

Overdrive is obtainable in third or top gear by operating the small switch on the instrument panel.

The fascia switch should not be moved into the normal position at speeds in excess of the direct drive maximum.

COOLING SYSTEM

Cooling system

A pressurized cooling system is used on this vehicle and the pressure must be released gradually when removing the radiator filler cap if the system is hot. It is advisable to protect the hands against escaping steam and then turn the cap slowly anti-clockwise until the resistance of the safety stop is felt. Leave the cap in this position until all pressure is released. Press the cap downwards against the spring to clear the safety stops and continue turning until it can be lifted off.

The engine cooling system is sealed and pressurised and for that reason care must be taken when releasing the filler cap.

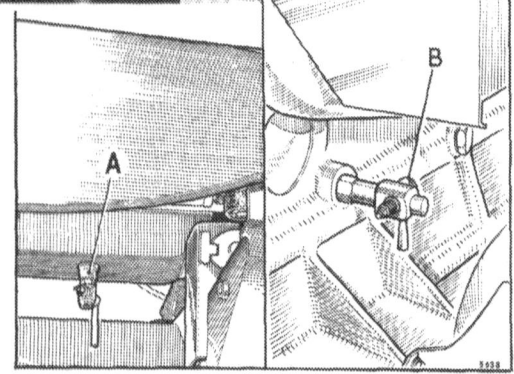

To drain the radiator and cylinder block remove the filler cap and turn the tap levers to the horizontal position. This operation will not drain the heater unit.

Draining the system

There are two drain taps; one positioned at the bottom of the radiator, and the other on the left hand side of the cylinder block. Open both taps and ascertain that the vehicle is standing on level ground while draining.

To assist in draining the system when a heater unit is fitted the temperature control lever on the heater panel should be in the right-hand or 'MAX' position.

When draining in freezing weather, do so when the engine is hot. Run the engine slowly for one minute when the water has ceased flowing to clear any water left in the pump and other places where it might collect. Finally, leave a reminder on the vehicle to the effect that the cooling system has been drained

COOLING SYSTEM

Topping-up
   This should only be necessary very occasionally to replace water lost through evaporation. Use only rain-water, if available, or clean soft water, and fill to within ½ in. (12·7 mm.) below the bottom of the filler neck.

Flushing the radiator
   To ensure efficient circulation of the coolant and to reduce the formation of scale and sediment in the radiator, the system should be periodically flushed with clean running water.
   The water should be allowed to run through until it comes out clean from the drain taps.
   A stiff piece of wire should be inserted into the taps during flushing to ensure that they are not becoming clogged with sediment.

Frost precautions
   During freezing weather an anti-freeze compound should be added to the cooling system.
   Before adding anti-freeze mixture the cooling system must be drained and flushed through by inserting a hose in the filler and allowing water to flow through until clean. The taps should be closed after allowing all the water to drain away and the anti-freeze should be poured in first, and then the water.
   To avoid wastage by overflow add just sufficient water to cover the bottom of the header tank. Run the engine until it is hot and add more water (hot) to bring the surface to the correct working level, i.e. about ½ in. (12·7 mm.) below the bottom of the filler neck.
   The correct quantities of anti-freeze for different degrees of frost resistance are:

Down to		Degrees of frost		Solution	Anti-freeze		
°C.	°F.	C.	F.		Pts.	U.S. pts.	Litres
−19	−3	19	35	20%	4	4¾	2·27
−26	−15	26	47	25%	4¾	5¾	2·69
−33	−28	33	60	30%	5¾	7	3·27

   The quantities given above are for cars equipped with heater units.
   The strength of the solution must be maintained by topping-up with anti-freeze solution as necessary. Excessive topping-up with water will reduce the degree of frost protection.
   As the cooling system is pressurized relatively high temperatures are developed in the radiator header tank. For this reason anti-freeze solutions with an alcohol base are unsuitable owing to their high evaporation rate producing a rapid loss of coolant and a consequent interruption of circulation.
   Only anti-freeze of the ethylene glycol type incorporating the correct type of corrosion inhibitor is suitable and owners are recommended to use Bluecol Anti-freeze or any anti-freeze conforming to specification BS.3151 and BS.3152.

Note.—Where a heater is fitted no provision is made for completely draining this unit. Therefore in freezing conditions anti-freeze MUST be used in the cooling system.

IGNITION EQUIPMENT

Ignition adjustment

The normal static ignition timing is given in General Data.

Adjustment is provided to enable the best setting to be obtained. The adjustment nut is indicated by the right-hand arrow in the illustration below. Turning the nut clockwise retards the ignition, turning it anti-clockwise advances the ignition.

The barrel of the screwed spindle has graduations to indicate the settings.

The range of adjustment provided by the micrometer adjuster is normally ample to deal with variations encountered.

Do not disturb the pinch-bolt at the base of the distributor unless absolutely necessary or the correct ignition timing will be lost.

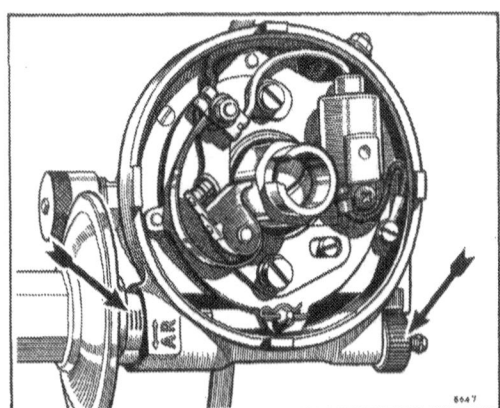

The micro-adjusting nut is indicated by the right-hand arrow, whilst the other arrow indicates the vernier scale.

The notch on the crankshaft pulley and the pointer are used to assist correct timing and indicate T.D.C.

Top dead centre

To facilitate location of the T.D.C. position of the crankshaft for Nos. 1 and 6 cylinders the rim of the crankshaft pulley has a small notch which coincides with a pointer on the timing chain case when the crankshaft is in the T.D.C. position for these two cylinders.

ELECTRICAL EQUIPMENT

Battery

Top up the cells with distilled water weekly. Do not use tap-water and do not over-fill; the correct level is **just above the top of the separators.** Do not use a naked light when examining the condition of the cells. Wipe away dirt and moisture from the top of the battery. Keep the terminals tight and well smeared with petroleum jelly. Also check the security and good electrical contact of the battery earthing clip.

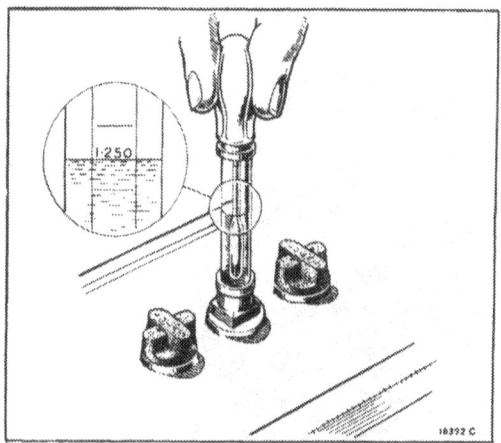

The correct use of the hydrometer.

Specific gravity

Every 6,000 miles (9600 km.) ascertain the state of charge of the battery by taking hydrometer readings from each cell. The specific gravity readings should be:—

	Home Trade and climates below 80°F. (26·6°C.)	Climates frequently above 80°F. (26·6°C.)
Cell fully charged	1·270—1·290	1·210—1·230
Cell about half discharged	1·190—1·210	1·130—1·150
Cell completely discharged	1·110—1·130	1·050—1·070

The figures given in the table are corrected to an electrolyte temperature of 60°F. (15·5°C.) and the hydrometer readings obtained must also be corrected to suit the temperature of the electrolyte:—

For every 5°F. (2·7°C.) above 60°F. (15·5°C.) — add ·002
For every 5°F. (2·7°C.) below 60°F. (15·5°C.) — subtract ·002

All cells should give approximately the same reading; if there are wide variations between the cells the battery should be examined by a Distributor or Dealer.

Never leave a battery in a discharged condition for any length of time. When the car is not in regular use have it fully charged and every fortnight give it a short refreshing charge to prevent any tendency for the plates to be permanently sulphated.

Voltage regulator

This is a sealed unit, located on the engine bulkhead, which controls the charging rate of the dynamo in accordance with the needs of the battery. It requires no attention and should not be disturbed.

ELECTRICAL EQUIPMENT

Fuses
The fuse unit is situated on the left-hand side of the engine bulkhead and contains two fuses and two spares. One 35 amp. fuse protects the accessories which work only when the ignition is switched on (e.g., stop-lights, fuel gauge, and direction flasher lights). The other fuse (50 amp.) protects those accessories which can be operated independently of the ignition. If a fuse blows, the cause of the trouble must be found before a new one is fitted.

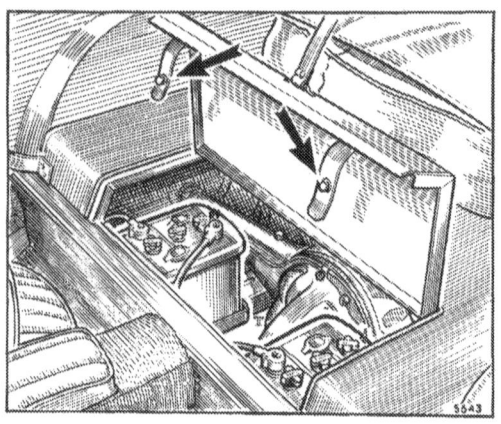

Release the two fasteners indicated by arrows to gain access to the batteries (see page 16 for battery location on four-seater models).

Spare fuses
Spare fuses are provided, and it is important to use the correct replacement. The fusing value is marked on a coloured slip of paper inside the glass tube of the fuse.

Headlamps (except European and sealed beam types)
To reach the headlamp bulb remove the rim after extracting the retaining screw from the under side, push the lamp reflector and glass assembly inwards against the springs, turn it anti-clockwise until the locating screws register with the enlarged ends of the slots, and withdraw the light unit. Depress the back-shell and turn it to release the bulb. When replacing the bulb ensure that the slot on the bulb flange engages the keyway in the holder.

To replace the back-shell push it home against the spring pressure and turn it clockwise to engage the bayonet attachment. Replace the dust-excluding rubber and refit the front rim, locking it in position with the retaining screw.

Headlamp (European type)
These lamps are fitted with special front lenses and bulbs giving an asymmetrical light beam. Access to the bulb is gained in the same manner as that described above, but the bulb is released by withdrawing the three-pin socket and pinching the two ends of the retaining clip to clear the bulb flange. When replacing the bulb, make certain the rectangular pip on the bulb flange engages the slot in the reflector seating. Replace the spring clip with its coils resting in the base of the bulb flange and engaging the retaining lugs on the reflector.

ELECTRICAL EQUIPMENT

Headlamp (North American sealed beam)

To change a sealed beam light unit, remove the retaining screw from the bottom face of the lamp rim, lift the bottom of the rim forwards and upwards and detach the rim. Slacken the three Phillips screws securing the light unit retaining rim and rotate the rim anti-clockwise to remove, supporting the lens at the same time. Pull off the three-pin plug from the rear of the light unit.

The light unit must be renewed when necessary as a complete assembly.

To reassemble the lamp, reverse the above procedure, ensuring that the registers moulded on the rear edge of the light unit engage in the slots in the back shell.

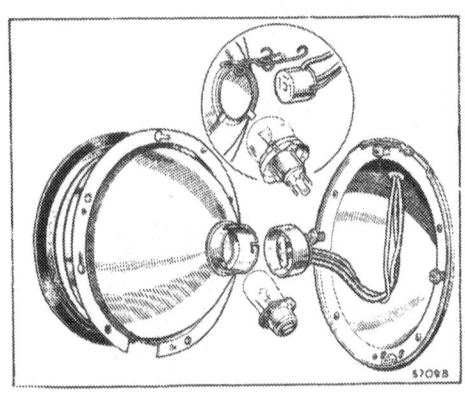

The headlamp light unit removed to show the bulb holder and back shell, etc., with the European type lamp shown inset.

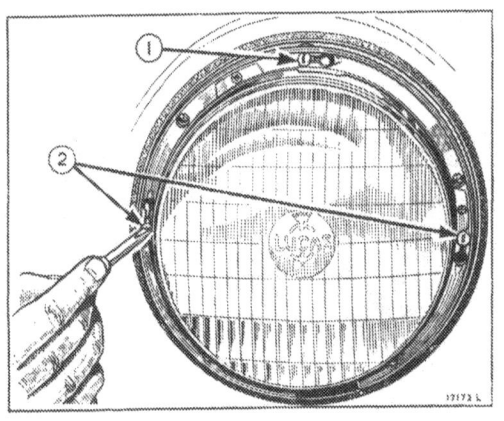

The method of setting the headlight beams:
1. The vertical setting adjusting screw.
2. The horizontal setting adjusting screws.

Setting headlamps

The lamps should be set so that the main driving beams are parallel with the road surface or in accordance with the local regulations.

ELECTRICAL EQUIPMENT

Adjust by means of the screws shown on page 31. Vertical adjustment is made by turning the screw at the top, and horizontal adjustment by those at the sides. The sealed beam headlamp has only one horizontal adjusting screw.
Always set the beams with a normal load on the car.
Do not set the beams above the horizontal as they would then dazzle oncoming traffic and give inferior road illumination.

Pilot, tail and indicator lamps
Move back the rubber lip, insert a coin or screwdriver blade under the glass retaining collar and gently lever the collar out from the lamp body. This will enable the lamp glass to be removed completely, leaving the bulb accessible in its socket.

Rear number plate lamp
The lamp is situated inside the bumper. Remove the screw and lift off the cover to gain access to the bulb.

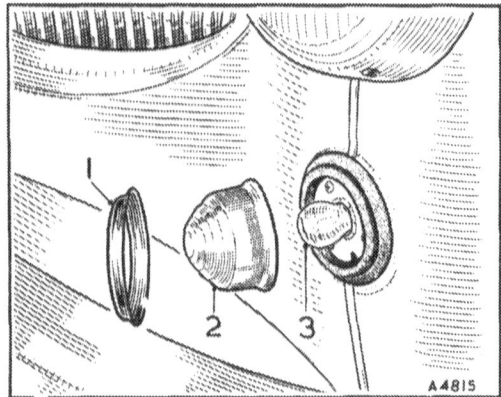

Front pilot and indicator lamp.
1. Rim.
2. Glass.
3. Bulb.

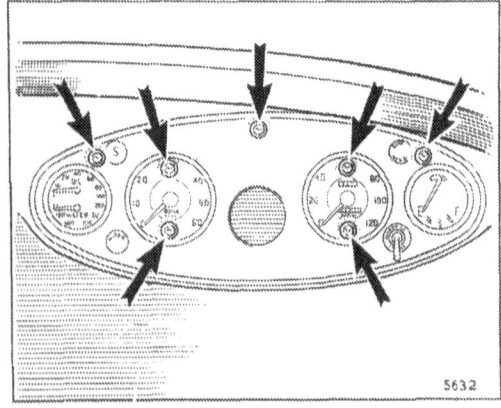

The location of the panel and warning light bulbs: the bulb holders are reached from behind the instrument panel.

Panel lights
The holders can be pulled from their fittings at the back of the instrument panel and the bulbs are then easily removed.

ELECTRICAL EQUIPMENT

Ignition, headlamp main beam and indicator warning lights
The bulbs can be unscrewed from their holders when pulled out from the back of the panel.

Windshield wiper blades
Should it be necessary to reposition the wiper arms on their spindles, they can be withdrawn by holding back the small retaining spring clip, which locates in a register in the spindle, and withdrawing the arm. Replace the arm on the required spline, pushing it hard down on the spindle until retained by the spring clip.

To fit a new rubber, pull the blade away from the windshield and withdraw the old rubber from its carrier. Fit the new rubber in the locating pins.

Starter motor
Should the starter pinion become jammed with the flywheel ring it can usually be freed by turning the squared end of the armature with a spanner after removing the protecting cap.

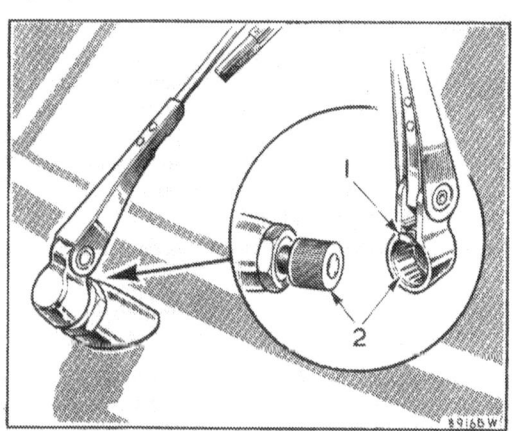

To re-position the wiper arm raise the spring clip (1), withdraw the arm and refit on another spline (2).

Replacement bulbs

Headlamps:	Watts	B.M.C. Part No.
R.H.D.—left dip	50/40	BFS 414
L.H.D.—right dip	50/40	BFS 415
R and L.H.D. Europe (except France)	45/40	BFS 410
France only (yellow)	45/40	BFS 411
Combined Pilot and Flasher Lamps	21/6	BFS 380
Combined Stop, Tail and Flasher Lamps	21/6	BFS 380
Number Plate Illumination Lamp	6	BFS 989
Panel and Warning Lights	2.2	BFS 987

Fuel pump
Fuel is delivered to the carburetters by means of an electrically operated S.U. pump, LCS type. The pump is located on the left-hand side of the car and is reached through the hinged portion of the spare wheel floor (two-seater models) or by removing the left-hand seat pan (four-seater models).

On later cars (two- and four-seater models) the fuel pump and fuel lines are located on the right-hand side.

WHEELS AND TYRES

Care of tyres

In order to obtain maximum mileage from the tyres the following points should be kept in mind:—
1. Maintain recommended pressures, not forgetting the spare wheel.
2. Change the wheels around diagonally to regularize wear.
3. Incorrect wheel alignment will cause excessive wear.

Remember that vicious braking and accelerating shortens the life of tyres.

Flints and other sharp objects should be removed with a penknife or similar tool. If neglected they may work through the cover.

Any oil or grease which may get onto the tyres should be cleaned off by using fuel sparingly. Do not use paraffin (kerosene), which has a detrimental effect on rubber.

Checking pressures

For accurate results, pressures should be checked when the tyres are cold, otherwise an allowance must be made for the increase in pressure resulting from the heat generated during running. Pressures should never be reduced in warm tyres where increases above the recommended figures are due to temperature. A tyre that loses more than three to four pounds per square inch in a week should be suspected of a slow puncture, but first make sure that the valve is not the cause.

The recommended tyre pressures for speeds up to 110 m.p.h. (177 km.p.h.) are:

Front .. 20 lb./sq. in. (1·4 kg./cm.^{2}).
Rear .. 25 lb./sq. in. (1·76 kg./cm.^{2}).

It should be noted that when driving at maximum performance speeds inflation pressures for both front and rear tyres must be increased by 5 lb./sq. in (·35 kg./cm.^{2}).

Maintain the correct pressures by checking with an accurate tyre gauge at least once a week, and inflating if necessary.

Any unusual pressure loss must be investigated. Under-inflation causes rapid tyre wear, and even more serious is the possibility of damage to the fabric of the tyre owing to the excessive flexing of the tyre walls.

Valves and caps

See that the valve caps are screwed down firmly by hand. Do not use tools as too much force will damage the rubber seating. The cap prevents the entry of dirt into the valve mechanism and forms an additional seal on the valve, preventing any leakage if the valve core is damaged.

Jacking

A screw type jack is supplied in the tool kit. To lift the front wheels the lifting platform of the jack should be placed across the outer rim of the spring

WHEELS AND TYRES

lower plate, so that the lipped end projects into the recess in the spring plate, and the flat end is between the two bottom wishbone links. There is a recess across the jack lifting platform, which allows the strengthening ring on the spring plate to locate.

To lift the rear wheels, place the lifting platform across the lowest spring leaf to the rear of the axle, with the lipped end on the outside of the spring end up against the spring 'U' bolt; this prevents any turning movement.

Changing a wheel

To remove a pressed steel type wheel, apply the hand brake. Remove the plated hub cover from the wheel with the tool provided and slacken the wheel nuts. Jack up the car at the appropriate point and completely unscrew the wheel nuts. Remove the wheel.

When replacing the wheel locate its centre on the hub wheel studs. Tighten the nuts lightly with the wheelbrace, ensuring that the coned ends of the nuts face the wheel. Lower the jack and fully tighten the nuts. Imagining the nuts to be numbered 1 to 5, the recommended tightening sequence is 1, 3, 5, 2, 4. Refit the plated hub cover.

When removing a wire wheel (optional equipment) the 'knock-on' type hub cap concerned should be loosened by using a mallet on the cap wings before the car is jacked up. Hub caps fitted to right-hand side hubs have left-hand threads, left-hand hubs have right-hand threads. The direction for turning is clearly marked on each cap.

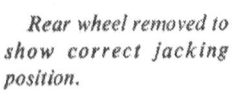

Rear wheel removed to show correct jacking position.

Once the cap is loosened, the car should be jacked in the manner previously described and the hub cap screwed right off. The wheel can then be pulled off the splined hub.

Refitting the wire wheel is simply a reversal of this removal procedure, but the splines of both hub and wheel are so fine that care must be taken to engage them correctly and avoid jamming. Before refitting, lightly smear the splines and cone faces with grease

WHEELS AND TYRES

Tyre removal

Remove the valve interior to deflate the tyre completely and push both cover edges into base of rim at the point diametrically opposite to the valve, then lever the cover edge near the valve over the rim. Continue round the tyre until the bead on one side is completely free. Stand the tyre and wheel upright, keeping the remaining bead in the well-base of the wheel rim, this permits the valve to be pushed through the hole in the rim and the withdrawal of the inner tube.

Lever the tyre bead at the top of the wheel over the rim flange, and at the same time push the wheel away from the cover.

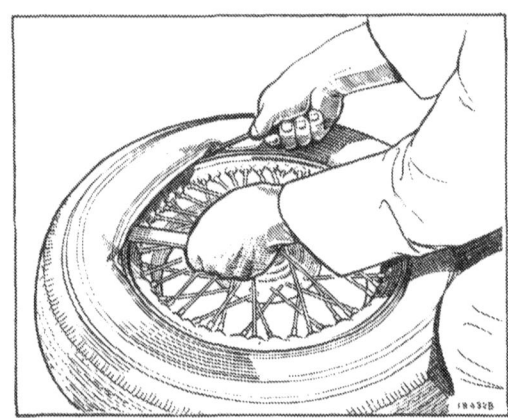

The cover edge can be levered over the rim close to the valve position.

Tyre replacement

A similar technique has to be employed when replacing the tyre, keeping the beaded edge in the well-base of wheel rim and carefully levering the tyre edge over the wheel rim on the opposite side. Great care must be exercised to avoid damage to the tyre bead and the tyre levers used must be in good condition.

It is important when replacing the tube and outer cover to make sure that their coloured balance spots coincide. These coloured spots indicate the lightest point of the tyre, and should be fitted in line with the tyre valve to ensure the best wheel balance and good steering.

Changing position of tyres

To obtain the best tyre mileage and to suppress the development of irregular wear on the front tyres it is essential that the wheels are interchanged diagonally with the rear wheels and the spare wheel every 3,000 miles (4800 km.)

Impact fractures

Excessive local distortion as a result of striking a kerb, a loose brick, a deep pot-hole, etc., may cause the casing cords to fracture. Every effort should be made to avoid such obstacles.

CARBURETTERS

Carburetter slow running adjustment (Mk.I)
After the first 500 miles (800 km.) or so when the engine is fully run in, the slow running adjustment may need attention. The adjustment should be made only after the engine has reached its normal running temperature.

Before attempting to adjust the slow-run valves, make sure that the throttles are closed and that the throttle shaft interconnecting clips are secure.

Turn the slow-run valve adjusting screw on one carburetter in a clockwise direction until it 'bottoms' and then screw it back 2¼ turns. Adjust the screw on the other carburetter in a similar manner making certain that the screw is returned exactly the same amount. The slow-running speed should now be approximately correct, but if any further adjustments are required it is essential to remember that **the adjustments on each carburetter must be identical.**

Turning the slow-run valve screws in a clockwise direction reduces the engine speed, whilst turning in an anti-clockwise direction increases it.

NOTE.—It is necessary to retain a small clearance between the fast-idle adjusting screw and the anvil beneath it. This clearance should always be in evidence except when the mixture control is in use.

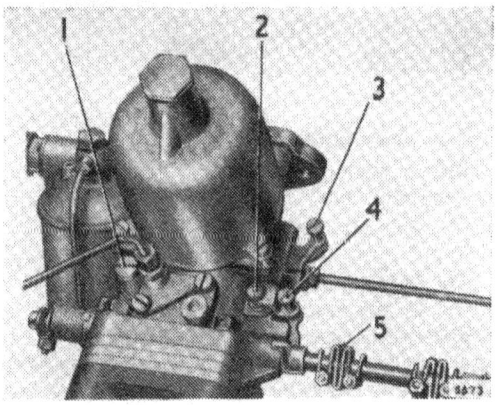

Carburetter adjustments.
1. Slow-run valve.
2. Top plate securing screw.
3. Jet adjusting screw.
4. Fast idle adjusting screw.
5. Throttle shaft inter-connection clip.

Nos. 2 and 4 are not fitted to automatic choke carburetters.

Mixture adjustments
Run the engine until it attains its normal running temperature and adjust the slow-running as detailed above. The strength of the mixture is regulated by the jet adjusting screws. Turning the screws in a clockwise direction enriches the mixture; both screws must be turned equally. Turn the screws in the appropriate direction until the engine idles evenly, firing on all cylinders evenly and running at its best speed.

Check the setting by raising each carburetter piston with the pin provided beneath the dashpot flange. If the speed increases momentarily the setting is correct. If the engine stalls the setting is too weak and if the speed increases permanently it is too rich. Final adjustment to the slow running may be required and should be made on the slow-run screws. It must be remembered that these screws must be turned the same amount.

CARBURETTERS

Models fitted with Thermo carburetters (automatic choke control)

To assist in cold starting the carburation is automatically enriched by the Thermal Electric Choke, thereby doing away with the manually operated mixture control. This device is brought into operation upon starting from cold and enriches the mixture until the engine reaches the pre-set cut-off temperature of the thermo switch.

The screw indicated by the arrow adjusts the mixture strength when the choke or mixture control is operated.

Tuning and adjustment

Before attempting to adjust the auxiliary enrichment device, the main carburetters must be correctly adjusted for mixture and slow running.

The only adjustment provided is the needle 'stop screw' which limits the travel of the needle. With the engine at its normal running temperature energise the solenoid when the mixture should become distinctly rich (exhaust gases are black in colour and with the engine running regularly). To enrich the mixture turn the stop screw anti-clockwise, and turn clockwise for the opposite effect.

In order to energise the solenoid when the thermostatic switch has broken the circuit merely short-circuit the switch to earth. The stop-screw is located on top of the auxiliary carburetter, the setting adjustment being located by a spring finger.

CARBURETTERS

The carburetters fitted to the Healey 3000 Mk. II are triple S.U. type HS4.

Slow running adjustment and synchronization

After the first 500 miles (800 km.) or so when the engine is fully run in, the slow running may require adjustment. This must only be carried out when the engine has reached its normal running temperature.

As the needle size is determined during engine development, tuning of the carburetters is confined to correct idling setting. Slacken the actuating arms on the throttle spindle inter-connection. Close all throttles fully by unscrewing the throttle adjusting screws, then open each throttle by screwing down each idling adjustment screw one turn.

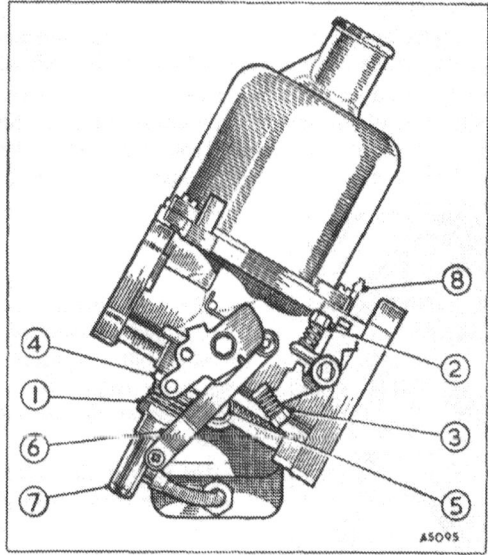

The HS4 type carburetter showing:
1. *Jet adjusting nut.*
2. *Throttle adjusting screw.*
3. *Fast idle adjusting screw.*
4. *Jet locking nut.*
5. *Float chamber securing nut.*
6. *Jet link.*
7. *Jet head.*
8. *Ignition vacuum control take-off.*

Remove the pistons and suction chambers, and disconnect the jet control cables. Screw the jet adjusting nuts until each jet is flush with the bridge of its carburetter, or as near to this as possible (all jets being in the same relative position to the bridge of their respective carburetters). Replace the pistons and suction chamber assemblies, and check that the pistons fall freely on to the bridge of the carburetters (by means of the piston lifting pins). Turn down the jet adjusting nuts two complete turns each (12 flats).

Re-start the engine, and adjust the throttle adjusting screws to give the desired idling speed, by moving each throttle adjusting screw an equal amount. By listening to the hiss in the intakes, adjust the throttle adjusting screws until the intensity of the hiss is similar on all intakes. This will synchronize the throttles.

When this is satisfactory, the mixture should be adjusted by screwing each jet adjusting nut up or down by the same amount, until the fastest idling speed is obtained consistent with even firing. During this adjustment, it is

CARBURETTERS

necessary that the jets are pressed upwards to ensure that they are in contact with the adjusting nuts.

As the mixture is adjusted the engine will probably run faster, and it may therefore be necessary to unscrew the throttle adjusting screws a little, each by the same amount, to reduce the speed.

Now check the mixture strength by lifting the piston of the front carburetter by approximately $\frac{1}{32}$ in. (.75 mm.) when if:

(a) the engine speed increases, the mixture strength of the front carburetter is too rich.

(b) the engine speed immediately decreases, the mixture strength of the front carburetter is too weak.

(c) the engine speed momentarily increases very slightly, the mixture strength of the front carburetter is correct.

Repeat the operation at the centre and rear carburetters, and after adjustment re-check the front carburetter, since all carburetters are inter-dependent.

When the mixture is correct the exhaust note should be regular and even. If it is irregular with a splashy type of misfire and colourless exhaust, the mixture is too weak. If there is a regular or rythmical type of misfire in the exhaust beat together with a blackish exhaust, then the mixture is too rich.

The carburetter linkage with a feeler behind the throttle shaft stop, and the pin at the bottom of the clearance in the forked lever.

The throttle, fast idling and choke cable securing screws are also indicated.

Linkage adjustment

The carburetter throttle on each carburetter is operated by a lever and pin, with the pin working in a forked lever attached to the throttle spindle. A clearance exists between the pin and fork, which must be maintained when the throttle is closed and the engine idling, to prevent any load from the accelerator linkage being transferred to the throttle butterfly and spindle.

To set this clearance: with the throttle shaft levers free on the throttle shaft, put a .012 in. (.305 mm.) feeler between each throttle shaft stop (2) at the top and the carburetter heat shield. Move each throttle shaft lever downwards in turn until the lever pin rests lightly on the lower arm of the fork in the carburetter throttle lever. Tighten the clamp bolt of the throttle shaft lever at this position. When all three carburetters have been dealt with, remove the feelers. The pins on the throttle shaft levers should then have clearance in the forks.

CARBURETTERS

Re-connect the choke cables, ensuring that the jet heads return against the lower face of the jet adjusting nuts when the choke control is pushed fully in.

Pull out the mixture control knob on the dash panel to its maximum movement without moving the carburetter jets (about ⅝in.; 15.87 mm.) and adjust the fast idle cam screws to give an engine speed of about 1000 r.p.m. when hot.

CARBURETTERS

The Austin-Healey 3000 Mk. II Sports Convertible is equipped with twin S.U. carburetters, type HS6.

Slow running and synchronization

The construction of the HS6 carburetter is basically similar to that of the HS4 type fitted to the Austin-Healey 3000 Mk. II Series BN7 and BT7.

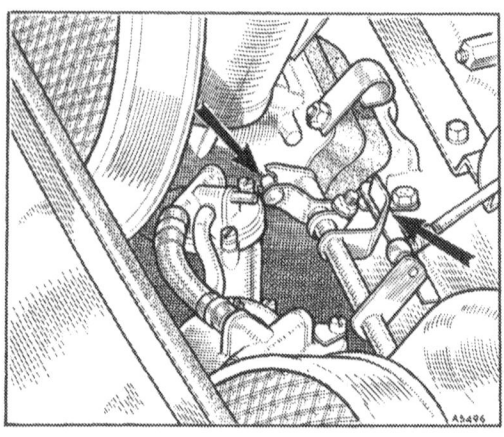

The carburetter linkage with a feeler below the throttle shaft stop, and the pin at the bottom of the clearance in the forked lever.

Linkage adjustment

The throttle on each carburetter is operated by a lever and pin, with the pin working in a forked lever attached to the throttle spindle. A clearance exists between the pin and fork which must be maintained when the throttle is closed and the engine idling, to prevent any load from the accelerator linkage being transferred to the throttle butterfly and spindle.

To set this clearance, with the throttle shaft levers free on the throttle shaft, put a ·012 in. (·305 mm.) feeler between the throttle shaft stop and its abutment on the inlet manifold. Move each throttle shaft lever downwards in turn until the lever pin rests lightly on the lower arm of the fork in the carburetter throttle lever. Tighten the clamp bolt of the throttle shaft lever at this position. When both carburetters have been dealt with, remove the feeler. The pins on the throttle shaft levers should then have clearance in the forks.

Re-connect the choke cables, ensuring that the jet heads return against the lower face of the jet adjusting nuts when the choke control is pushed right in.

Pull out the mixture control knob on the dash panel to its maximum movement without moving the carburetter jets, i.e. about ⅝ in. (16 mm.). With the control in this position, adjust the fast idle cam screws to give an engine speed of approximately 1000 r.p.m. when hot.

KEY TO RECOMMENDED LUBRICANTS

Component	A Engine and Air Cleaner			B			C Water Pump Grease Points	D Oilcan and Carburetter	E Upper Cylinder Lubrication
	Tropical and temperate down to 32° F. (0° C.)	Extreme cold down to 10° F. (−12° C.)	Arctic consistently below 10° F. (−12° C.)	Gearbox and Overdrive	Steering Gearbox and Rear Axle (Hypoid Gears) All conditions down to 10° F. (−12° C.)	Arctic consistently below 10° F. (−12° C.)			
Climatic conditions									
CASTROL	Castrol X.L.	Castrolite	Castrol Z	Castrol X.L.	Castrol Hypoy	Castrol Hypoy Light	Castrolease L.M.	Castrolite	Castrollo
ESSO	Esso Extra Motor Oil 20W/30	Esso Extra Motor Oil 20W/30	Esso Motor Oil 10	Esso Extra Motor Oil 20W/30	Esso Gearoil G.P. 90	Esso Gearoil G.P. 80	Esso Multipurpose Grease H	Esso Extra Motor Oil 20W/30	Esso Upper Cylinder Lubricant
MOBIL	Mobiloil A	Mobiloil Arctic	Mobiloil 10W	Mobiloil A	Mobilube G.X. 90	Mobilube G.X. 80	Mobilgrease M.P.	Mobiloil Arctic	Mobil Upperlube
BP ENERGOL	Energol S.A.E. 30	Energol S.A.E. 20W	Energol S.A.E. 10W	Energol S.A.E. 30	Energol E.P. S.A.E. 90	Energol E.P. S.A.E. 80	Energrease L.2.	Energol S.A.E. 20W	Energol U.C.L.
SHELL	Shell X—100 30	Shell X—100 20W	Shell Rotella 10W	Shell X—100 30	Shell Spirax 90 E.P.	Shell Spirax 80 E.P.	Shell Retinax A	Shell X—100 20W	Shell Upper Cylinder Lubricant
FILTRATE	Filtrate Medium 30	Filtrate Zero 20/20W	Filtrate Sub-Zero 10W	Filtrate Medium 30	Filtrate Hypoid Gear 90	Filtrate Hypoid Gear 80	Filtrate Super Lithium Grease	Filtrate Zero 20/20W	Filtrate Petroyle
STERNOL	Sternol W.W. 30	Sternol W.W. 20	Sternol W.W. 10	Sternol W.W. 30	Ambroleum E.P. 90	Ambroleum E.P. 80	Ambroline L.H.T.	Sternol W.W. 20	Sternol Magikoyl
DUCKHAM'S	Duckham's NOL Thirty	Duckham's NOL Twenty	Duckham's NOL Ten	Duckham's NOL Thirty	Duckham's Hypoid 90	Duckham's Hypoid 80	Duckham's L.B. 10 Grease	Duckham's NOL Twenty	Duckham's Adcoid Liquid

KEY TO LUBRICATION CHART

DAILY
1. ENGINE. Check the oil level with the dipstick, and top up if necessary with oil to Ref. 'A'.

EVERY 3,000 MILES (4800 Km.)
2. ENGINE. Drain off the old oil and refill with fresh oil to Ref.'A'.
3. GEARBOX AND OVERDRIVE. Check the oil level with the dipstick, and top up if necessary with oil to Ref. 'A'.
4. REAR AXLE. Check the oil level, and top up if necessary with oil to Ref. 'B'.
5. STEERING GEARBOX. Check the oil level, and top up if necessary with oil to Ref. 'B'.
6. STEERING IDLER. Check the oil level, and top up if necessary with oil to Ref. 'B'.
7. STEERING JOINTS. Give three or four strokes of the grease gun filled with grease to Ref. 'C' to the nipples on the steering joints. (Later Mk. II cars have sealed ball joints which are not equipped with nipples and do not require greasing.)
8. PROPELLER SHAFT. Give the nipples on the sliding and universal joints three or four strokes of the grease gun filled with grease to Ref. 'C'.
9. HANDBRAKE CABLE. Give the cable nipple three or four strokes of the grease gun filled with grease to Ref. 'C'.
10. HANDBRAKE COMPENSATOR. Give the nipple three or four strokes of the grease gun filled with grease to Ref. 'C'.
11. HANDBRAKE LINKAGE. Lubricate with an oil can filled with oil to Ref. 'D'.
12. REAR SPRING SHACKLES. Give the nipples three or four strokes of the grease gun filled with grease to Ref. 'C'.
13. CARBURETTERS. Remove the caps from the top of the suction chambers, and top up the piston dampers if necessary with oil to Ref. 'D'.
14. AIR CLEANERS. Remove each cleaner, wash in fuel, drain, moisten with oil to Ref. 'A', and refit.
15. STEERING COLUMN (early cars). Add a few drops of oil to Ref. 'D' through the hole at the top of the column.

EVERY 6,000 MILES (9600 Km.)
16. OIL FILTER. Wash the bowl in fuel and fit a new element.
17. GEARBOX & OVERDRIVE. Remove both drain plugs, drain off the old oil, and refill with fresh oil to Ref. 'A'.
18. REAR AXLE. Drain off the old oil and refill with fresh oil to Ref. 'B'.
19. DISTRIBUTOR. Withdraw the rotor arm and add a few drops of oil to Ref. 'D' to the cam bearing, to the advance mechanism through the gap around the cam spindle, and also one spot to the contact breaker pivot pin. Smear the cam with grease to Ref. 'C'.
20. DYNAMO. Add two drops of oil to Ref. 'D' to the hole in the end of the dynamo bearing.

EVERY 12,000 MILES (19200 Km).
21. ENGINE. Drain off the old oil, flush the engine, using one of the recommended flushing oils, and refill with fresh oil to Ref. 'A'. (At 24,000 miles remove engine sump and oil pump strainer. Clean the sump, oil pump strainer, and crankcase internally, reassemble and refill with fresh oil.)
22. WATER PUMP. Remove the plug and add a small amount of grease to Ref. 'C'. Replace the plug.
23. DISTRIBUTOR. Give the drive shaft bearing grease cap one half-turn.

MULTIGRADE MOTOR OILS

In addition to the recommended lubricants listed, we approve the use of these motor oils, as produced by the oil companies shown, for all climatic temperatures unless the engine is in poor mechanical condition.

LUBRICATION CHART

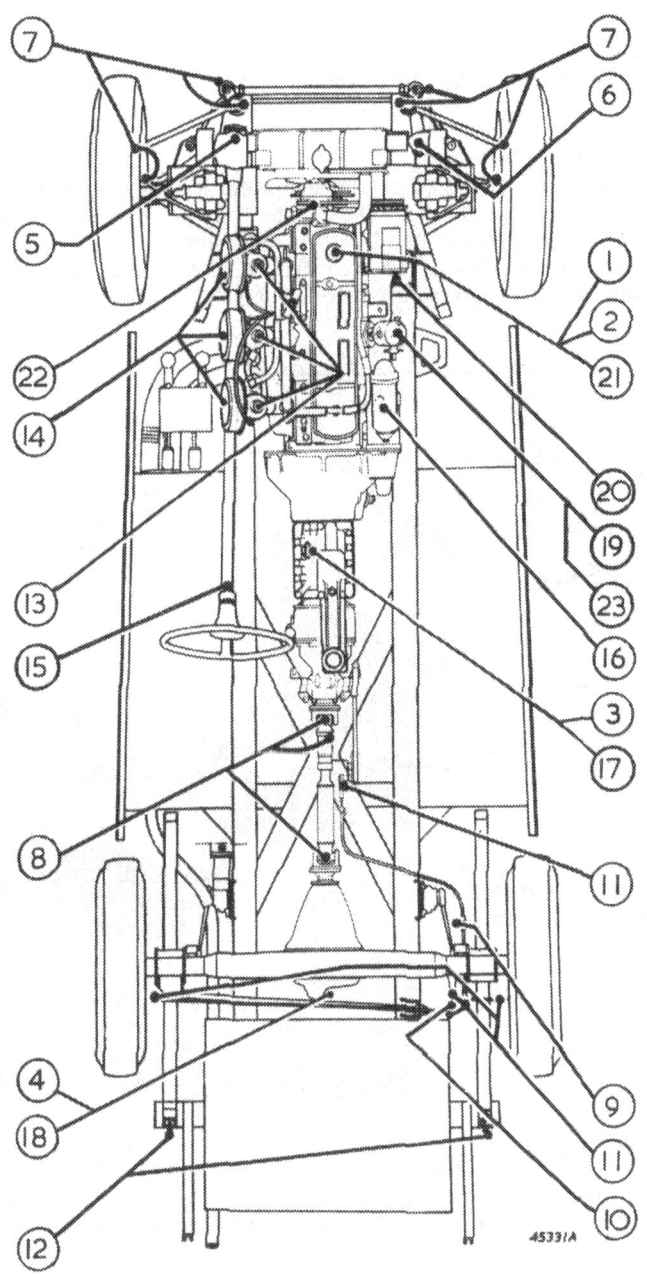

MAINTENANCE ATTENTION

DAILY

Radiator
Check the level of water in the radiator and top up if necessary

Engine oil level
Check the level of the oil in the sump and top-up if necessary to the "MAX." mark on the dipstick. The oil filler is in the valve rocker cover and the dipstick is on the right hand side of the engine.
After adding oil, allow a few seconds to elapse for the oil to reach the sump from the valve rocker cover before checking the level.

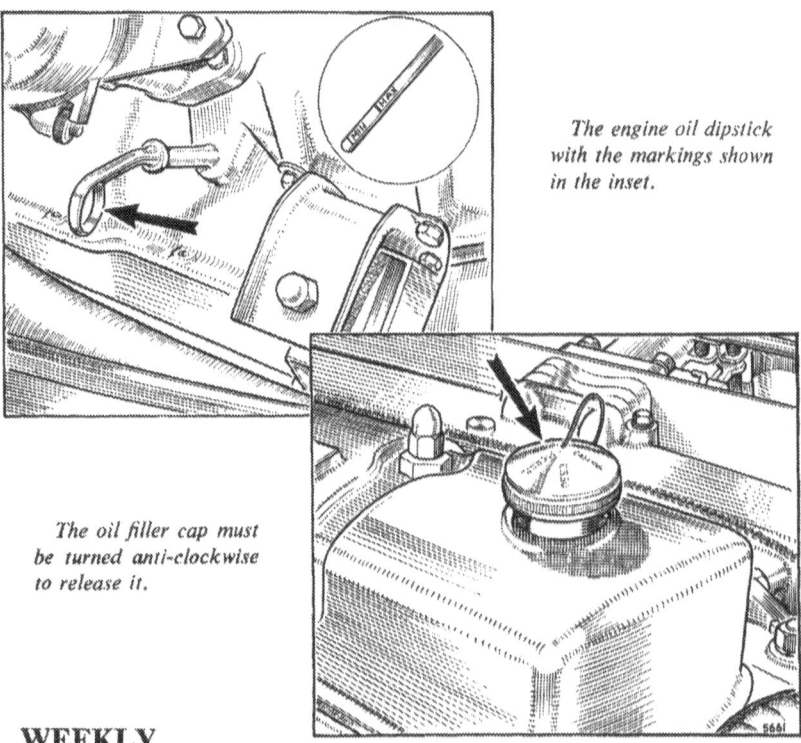

The engine oil dipstick with the markings shown in the inset.

The oil filler cap must be turned anti-clockwise to release it.

WEEKLY

Tyre pressures
Check all tyre pressures with a tyre gauge, and inflate or deflate if necessary, to the recommended pressures. Ensure that the valves are fitted with screw caps, inspect the tyres for possible damage, and wipe off any oil or grease.

Battery
Check electrolyte level and top up if necessary

EVERY 3,000 MILES (4800 Km.)

Draining the sump
The drain plug is located on the right-hand side of the sump. Remove the plug and allow the engine oil to drain. Clean the plug thoroughly, replace, screw up tightly and refill the sump with one of the recommended oils. This operation is best carried out when the oil is warm and fluid.

Refill the sump with fresh oil to Ref. 'A' (page 229).

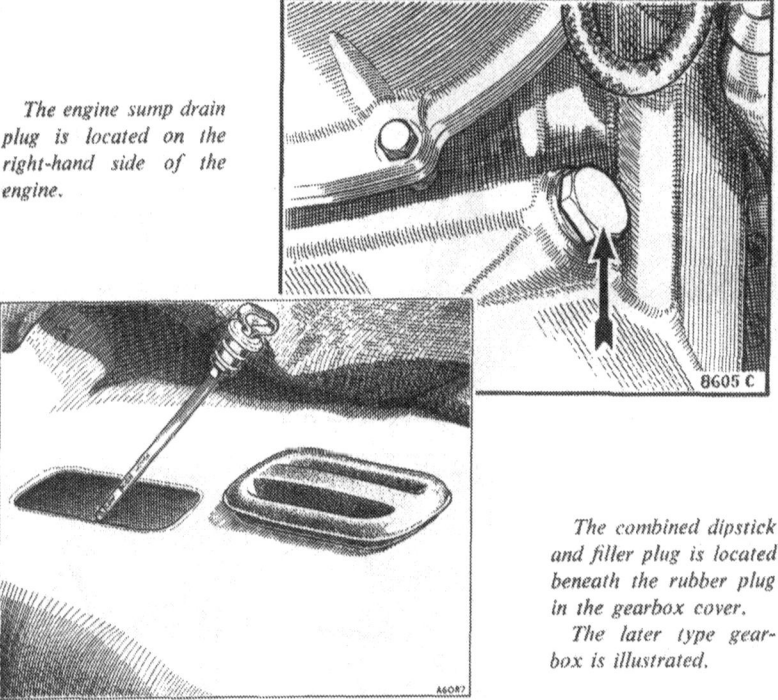

The engine sump drain plug is located on the right-hand side of the engine.

The combined dipstick and filler plug is located beneath the rubber plug in the gearbox cover.

The later type gearbox is illustrated.

Gearbox and Overdrive
Check the oil level and top up if necessary. For access take out the inspection panel in the top right-hand side of the gearbox cover when the filler plug will be accessible.

On later gearboxes with the shorter centrally mounted gear lever, the combined filler plug and dipstick is situated on the left-hand side of the gearbox in front of the gear lever.

Remove the combined dipstick and filler plug, and fill up to the correct level.

EVERY 3,000 MILES (4800 Km.)

Rear axle

Check the oil level and replenish if necessary. The correct grade of oil should be injected into the axle casing from underneath.

The plug also serves as an oil level indicator. Therefore do not replace the plug at once, but give the oil time to run out if too much has been injected. This is most important because if the rear axle is overfilled the lubricant may leak through to the brakes and render them ineffective. Wipe away excess oil from the casing.

IMPORTANT.—Use only Hypoid oil in the rear axle

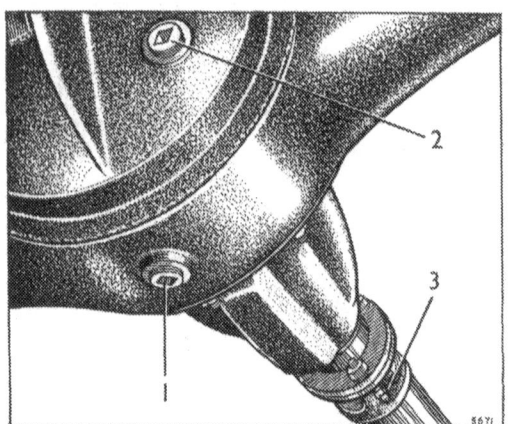

1. *The drain plug.*
2. *Filler and level plug.*
3. *Grease nipple for propeller shaft universal.*

Use a square ended spanner to remove the plugs.

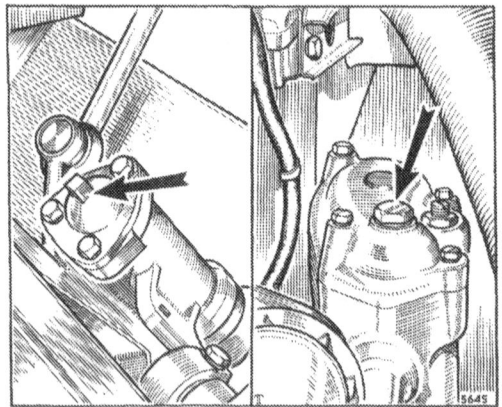

The steering gearbox and steering idler filler plugs. The correct level is flush with the bottom of the filler holes.

Steering gearbox

The steering gearbox should be topped up with oil, using an oil gun. Take out the hexagon plug on the top of the steering gearbox to inject the oil. Make certain that grit does not enter the casing during the operation, and wipe away any excess oil.

EVERY 3,000 MILES (4800 Km.)

Steering idler
Check the level of oil in the steering idler and top up if necessary.

> NOTE.—On no account should the steering idler be overlooked, as lack of lubricant in this component may cause a serious breakdown due to the additional load imposed on the steering gearbox.

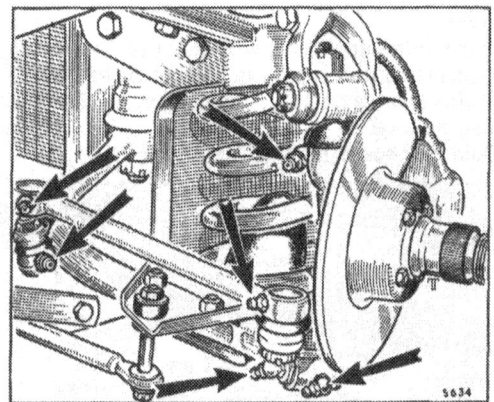

Front suspension and steering lubrication points.

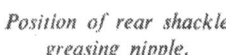

Position of rear shackle greasing nipple.

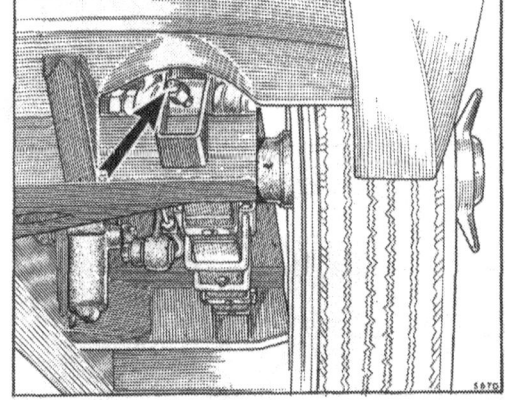

Lubrication points
Nipples are situated at the points listed below and should receive several strokes of the gun filled with grease to Ref. 'C' (page 229).
(1) Front suspension outer fulcrum pins (one nipple on each side).
(2) Swivel pins (two nipples on each side). This is best done when the car is partly jacked up as the grease is then able to penetrate properly around the bushes.
(3) Steering track-rod and tie-rod ball joints (one on each joint—six in all). Later 3000 Mk. II cars have sealed ball joints without nipples and do not require greasing.
(4) Propeller shaft (two universal **joint nipples** and one nipple on the sliding joint).

EVERY 3,000 MILES (4800 Km.)

(5) Rear spring shackles (one nipple on each side).

(6) Hand brake cable (one nipple on right-hand side) and hand brake compensator (one nipple on right-hand side of axle casing).

Linkages

Lubricate all the hand brake and carburetter control joints with an oil can filled to Ref. 'D' (page 229).

Brake and Clutch fluid reservoirs

Check the fluid level in the hydraulic supply reservoir mounted on the side of the engine bulkhead, and replenish if necessary with Castrol Girling Brake and Clutch Fluid Crimson. If this is not available a fluid which conforms to specification S.A.E.70R3 should be used.

Maintain the level of the fluid just below the filler neck.

The reservoir for the brake and clutch master cylinders; maintain the fluid at the correct level.

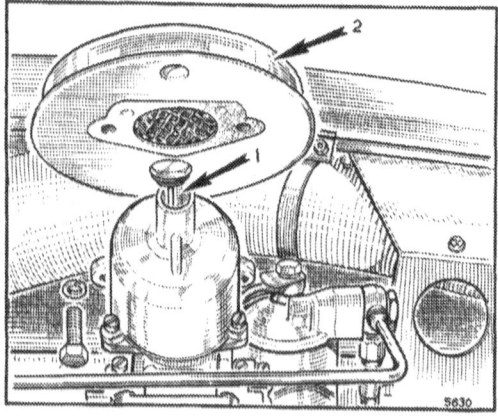

1. Unscrew the top of the suction chamber to top up the damper.
2. The air cleaner removed for cleaning with the securing bolt shown.

Carburetter dampers

Unscrew the oil cap at the top of each suction chamber and withdraw the cap with its attached plunger. Top up to within ½″ (12·7 mm.) from the top of the hollow piston rod, with oil to Ref. 'D'(page 229).The function of this piston damper unit is to provide an appropriate degree of enrichment for acceleration, and also to improve cold starting.

EVERY 3,000 MILES (4800 Km.)

Air cleaners
   The air cleaners should be removed, but in especially dusty conditions more frequent attention may be needed. Wash each cleaner in paraffin, drain, immerse in engine oil and drain again before refitting.

Fan belt
   The fan belt must be sufficiently tight to prevent slip at the dynamo and water pump, yet it should be possible to move it laterally about half an inch each way.
   To make any necessary adjustment, slacken the bolt securing the slotted link and the two bolts on which the dynamo pivots and raise or lower the dynamo until the desired tension of the belt is obtained. Then securely lock the dynamo in position again.

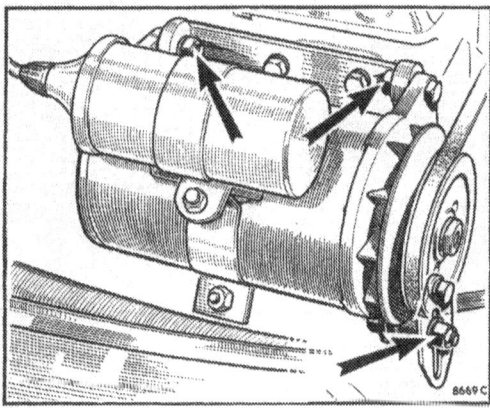

Slacken the bolts indicated by arrows to move the dynamo in order to adjust the tension of the belt.

Body
   Lubricate door locks, door hinges, bonnet lock and operating mechanism, and safety catches with oil to Ref. 'D'. Lightly smear dovetails and striking plates with grease to Ref. 'C' (page 229).

Braking system
   The system employs hydraulically operated disc brakes at the front and drum brakes at the rear with a dual purpose internal expander unit for the rear shoes, enabling them to be operated hydraulically or mechanically.
   The handbrake is mounted between the seats and operates the mechanical linkage to the rear brakes, while the pedal operates hydraulically on all four wheels.

Front brake adjustment
   Wear on the front disc brake friction pads is automatically compensated during braking operations, manual adjustment is therefore not required. In order to maintain peak braking efficiency and at the same time obtain the maximum life from the friction pads, they should be examined, and if the wear on one pad is greater than the other their operating positions should be changed over.
   This work should be undertaken by an Authorised Austin Distributor or Dealer.

EVERY 3,000 MILES (4800 Km.)

Rear brake adjustment

Firmly chock one of the front wheels and then jack the vehicle until the wheel to be adjusted is clear of the ground. Adjustment is made by turning the square-ended adjuster on each rear brake backing plate in a clockwise direction as far as it will go. The brake shoes are then hard on, and the adjuster should be turned back two full notches to give the shoes the correct clearance from the drum. This operation automatically adjusts the handbrake.

After adjustment the brake pedal should be applied hard two or three times to centralise the brake shoes in their drums.

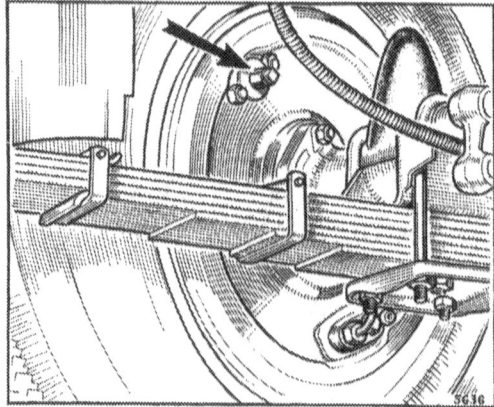

The square headed brake-shoe adjusting bolt, on the rear brake back plate.

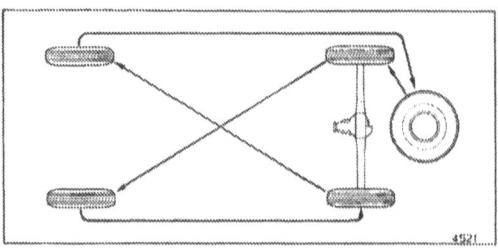

Change the wheels round diagonally and bring the spare into use as shown in this illustration.

Tyres

Change the running position of the tyres and bring the spare wheel into use as shown in the illustration. This will equalize the tyre wear of the front and rear wheels and prolong the life of the tyres.

Check the tyre pressures after the wheels have been changed round

Inspect the tyres frequently and remove any pieces of flint, stone or glass which may have become embedded in the covers.

EVERY 6,000 MILES (9600 Km.)

Distributor

Remove the distributor cap and add a few drops of oil to Ref. 'D'*through the hole in the contact breaker base through which the cam passes.

Lubricate the distributor cam bearings by withdrawing the rotor arm from the top of the distributor spindle and carefully adding a few drops of oil to Ref. 'D'*around the screw exposed to view. Take care to refit the rotor arm correctly by pushing it on to the shaft and turning until the key is properly located.

Apply a trace of grease to Ref. 'C'*to the distributor cam. Be careful not to let any oil or dirt reach the contact breaker points. (* see page 229)

Apply a drop of oil to Ref. 'D'*to the contact breaker pivot.

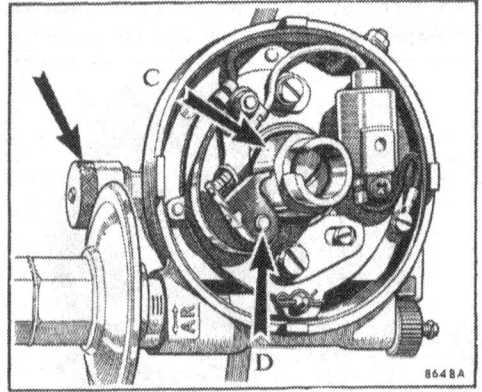

The distributor cam, drive shaft and contact breaker pivot lubricating points.

The distributor cam bearing and automatic advance mechanism lubricating points.

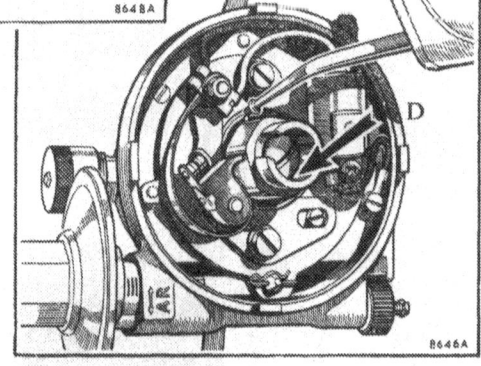

Contact breaker points

Clean the contact breaker points with a fine carborundum stone or with very fine emery-cloth. Cleaning the contacts is made easier if the contact breaker lever carrying the moving contact is removed. To do this, remove the nut, insulator and wire terminals from the terminal post and lift off the spring. Before replacing smear the pivot on which the contact breaker works with clean oil. Check the contact breaker setting and re-set if necessary.

EVERY 6,000 MILES (9600 Km.)

To adjust the contact breaker points, turn the crankshaft until the contacts are fully open. Slacken the fixed contact plate securing screws. Move the plate with the eccentric adjusting screw until the gap gauge is a sliding fit between the contacts (·014—·016 in. or ·356—·406 mm.) and then fully tighten the securing screws. Finally re-check the gap and replace the rotor arm. Before replacing the distributor cap wipe the inside and outside with a soft dry cloth, taking care not to disturb the seals of water-repellent Silicone grease at the points of entry of the ignition leads into the cap. Adequate sealing at these points is vital, since otherwise water may in extreme circumstances penetrate into the cap down the outside of the leads and cause ignition failure. Make sure that the small carbon brush on the inside of the cap works freely in its holder and that the terminals are secure.

If the leads are at any time removed from the cap, the holes which receive them should be filled with Silicone grease and the leads then pushed into position, watching in the process that the displaced surplus grease exudes evenly all round the leads to form a perfect seal. Care should be taken to leave an adequate surplus on the surface of the cap at the lead entry points.

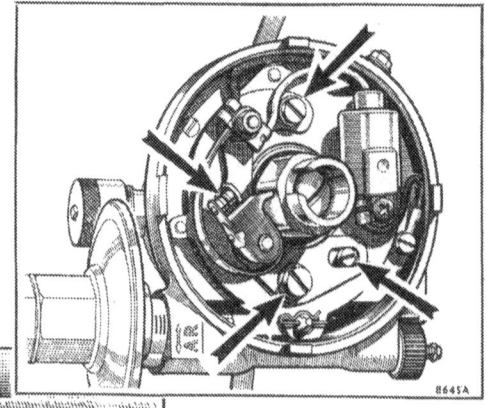

The distributor points, contact plate securing screws, and the eccentric adjuster.

Add a few drops of oil to the dynamo end bearing.

Dynamo bearing
Apply a few drops of oil to Ref. 'D'* to the commutator end dynamo bearing via the oil hole provided in the bearing housing. (* page 229)

Avoid over-lubrication.

EVERY 6,000 MILES (9600 Km.)

Gearbox
A drain plug is provided on the under side of the gearbox. Drain when the oil is warm after a run, and refill to the level indicated on the filler plug dip stick with new oil

Overdrive
The unit has no separate filler plug. When draining the gearbox, the overdrive drain plug must be withdrawn. Remove the overdrive oil pump filter and clean the gauze by washing in fuel. The filter is accessible through the drain plug hole and is secured by a central set bolt.

For oil capacity see General Data

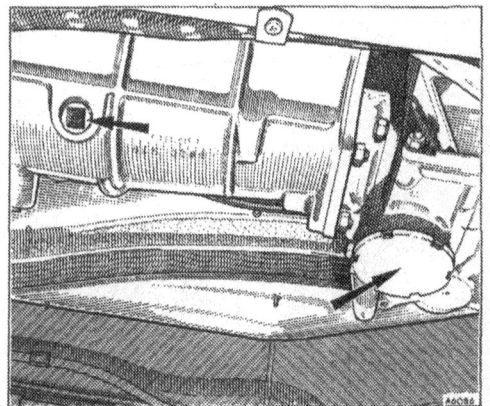

Remove both the overdrive and gearbox drain plugs and remove the overdrive pump filter to clean. Earlier overdrive units have a hexagonal drain plug.

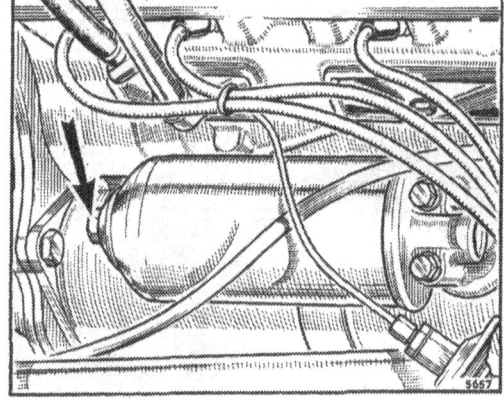

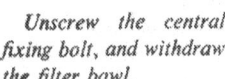

Unscrew the central fixing bolt, and withdraw the filter bowl.

Renewing oil filter element
Remove the centre fixing bolt and support the container by hand to allow the oil to drain away. Remove the casing and discard the filter element. Wash out the casing with fuel and clean thoroughly. Insert a new element in the container and holding the centre fixing bolt in position against the bottom of the container, locate it in the head casting and tighten just sufficiently to make an oil tight joint.

EVERY 6,000 MILES (9600 Km.)

Rear axle
Drain when the oil is warm after a run, and refill to the level of the filler plug with new oil.
For capacity see General Data

Carburetter filters (Mk. I)
To ensure a free flow of fuel to the float chambers the filters should be removed and thoroughly cleaned with a stiff brush and clean fuel. Never use rag. The filters are situated behind the banjo union at the junction of the fuel pipe with each float-chamber lid.

When reassembling the inlet unions, make certain that the two washers are correctly positioned each side of the flange and tighten very carefully.

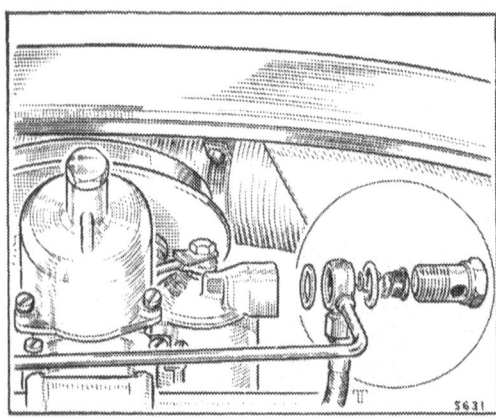

The carburetter filters must be replaced with their open ends outwards.

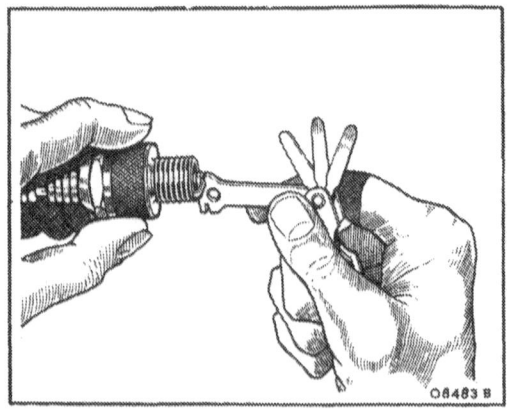

Use a special Champion sparking plug gauge and setting tool and move the side electrode: never the centre electrode.

Sparking plugs and leads
The sparking plugs should be cleaned and tested, preferably by a service garage with a special 'air-blast' service unit.

The gaps should be set at ·024—·026 in. (·61—·66 mm.).

Use a special Champion sparking plug gauge and setting tool and move the side electrode on the plug, never bend the centre electrode.

EVERY 6,000 MILES (9600 Km.)

Valve rockers

The clearance between the valve rockers and valves should be ·012 in. (·3 mm.) when the engine is hot.

Remove the two nuts and washers and lift the valve rocker cover from cylinder head taking care not to damage the cork seal.

To check the clearance between each rocker arm and valve stem, turn the crankshaft until the valve concerned is fully closed, and insert a feeler gauge, which should be a sliding fit.

Showing (1) feeler gauge inserted between the (2) rocker pad and valve stem whilst the clearance is adjusted with a spanner holding the (3) locknut and a screwdriver on the adjusting screw (4).

Adjustments must be made with the tappet on the back of the cam; testing and adjustments should be carried out in the following order:

No. 1 valve with No. 12 fully open	No. 12 valve with No. 1 fully open
No. 7 ,, ,, No. 6 ,, ,,	No. 6 ,, ,, No. 7 ,, ,,
No. 9 ,, ,, No. 4 ,, ,,	No. 4 ,, ,, No. 9 ,, ,,
No. 2 ,, ,, No. 11 ,, ,,	No. 11 ,, ,, No. 2 ,, ,,
No. 5 ,, ,, No. 8 ,, ,,	No. 8 ,, ,, No. 5 ,, ,,
No. 10 ,, ,, No. 3 ,, ,,	No. 3 ,, ,, No. 10 ,, ,,

To adjust the clearance slacken the adjusting screw locknut on the opposite end of rocker arm, rotate the screw clockwise to reduce clearance or anti-clockwise to increase it. Re-tighten the locknut when the clearance is correct, holding the screw against rotation with a screwdriver.

Always re-check the clearance in case adjustment has been disturbed during the process of tightening the locknut.

As there is no provision for a starting handle, the crankshaft can be turned by putting the car in top gear and pushing the car slowly forward whilst observing the rise and fall of the push rods. An alternative method of crankshaft turning is possible by using a **spanner** on the crankshaft pulley nut.

EVERY 6,000 MILES (9600 Km.)

Battery
Ascertain the state of charge of the battery (batteries) by taking hydrometer readings

Front wheel alignment
Excessive or uneven tyre wear is usually caused by faulty wheel alignment and since checking entails the use of a special gauge, this work should be entrusted to an Authorised Austin Dealer.

Toe-in taken along a horizontal line at centre height using wheel rims as data points, should be from $\frac{1}{16}$—$\frac{1}{8}$ in. (1·59—3·18 mm.).

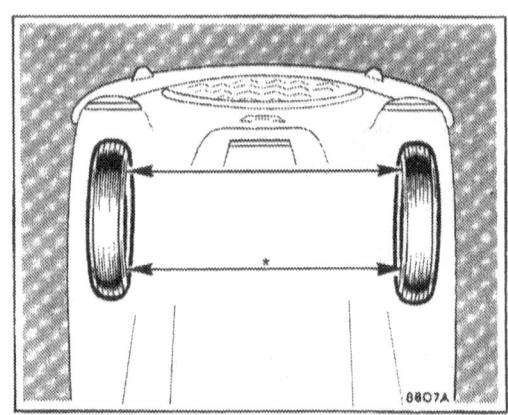

The dimension between the front wheel rims should be greater at the rear*by $\frac{1}{16}''$—$\frac{1}{8}''$ (1.59—3.18 mm.) when the wheels are in the straight ahead position.

EVERY 12,000 MILES (19200 Km.)

Water pump

Remove the plug on the water pump housing and inject a small amount of grease Ref. 'C'.* Lubricate sparingly, otherwise grease will run past the bearings onto the face of the carbon sealing ring and impair its efficiency.

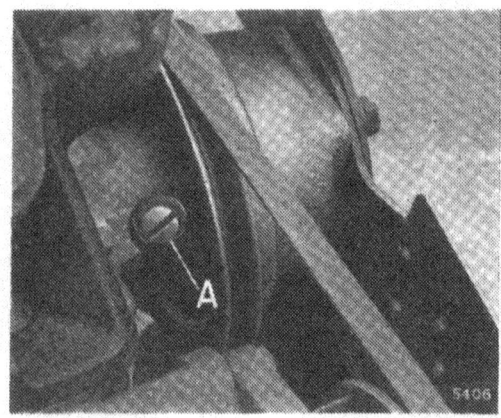

Water pump lubrication plug 'A' located on the pump body.

Carburetter pistons

Clean the suction chamber and piston of each carburetter. Dealing with each suction chamber in turn, remove the piston damper and unscrew the three suction chamber securing screws.

Withdraw the suction chamber, piston return spring, and piston, taking care not to damage the jet needle.

Using a clean rag moistened with fuel, clean the main inside bore of the suction chamber and the periphery of the piston.

Lubricate the piston rod only with a few drops of oil to Ref. 'D'*

and reassemble, ensuring that the locating groove on the lower portion of the piston engages the key in the carburetter body. (* page 229).

Refill the piston damper reservoir

Sparking Plugs

To maintain peak sparking plug performance new plugs must be fitted. Use Champion N3 for high speed motoring, changing over to Champion N5 for town running. This will reduce plug fouling to the minimum. Ensure that they are set to the correct gap

Distributor shaft

Give the lubricator on the side of the distributor body one half turn in a clockwise direction, to lubricate the distributor drive shaft.

EVERY 12,000 MILES (19200 Km.)

Front and rear dampers

Check the fluid levels and top up if necessary. The correct level is just below the filler plug threads. Carefully clear away all road dirt and grit from the vicinity of the filler plugs before removal.

Removal of the appropriate road wheel greatly facilitates access to the filler plug.

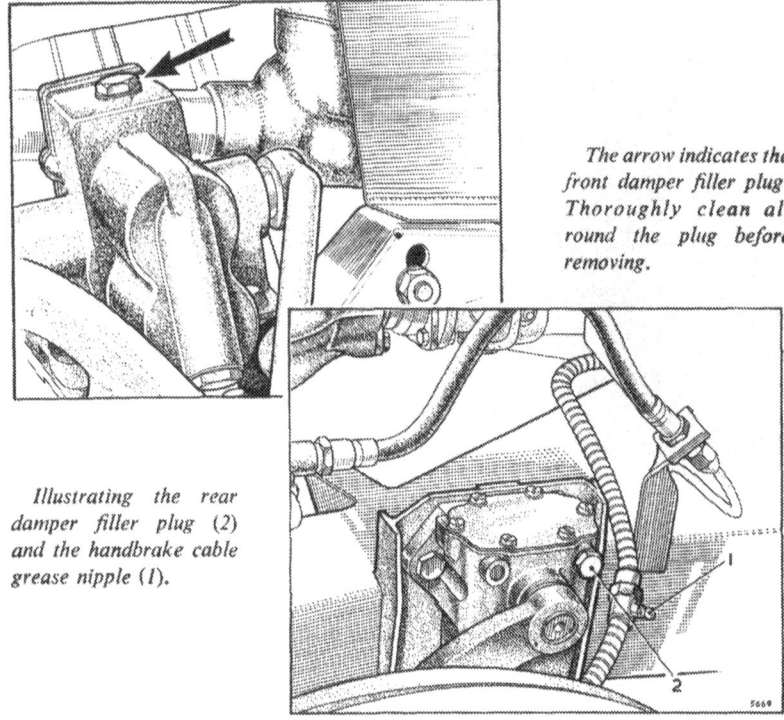

The arrow indicates the front damper filler plug. Thoroughly clean all round the plug before removing.

Illustrating the rear damper filler plug (2) and the handbrake cable grease nipple (1).

The use of Armstrong Super (thin) Shock Absorber Fluid is recommended for use in the dampers. If this fluid is not available a good-quality mineral oil conforming to Specification S.A.E. 20/20W may be used. This alternative is not suitable for low temperature operation.

No means of adjustment is provided on the dampers.

Headlamps

The headlight beam setting should be checked and reset if necessary

This work is best entrusted to your Distributor or Dealer who will have the equipment necessary to ensure the accurate setting of the beams.

Radiator

Open the radiator and cylinder block drain taps and flush out the radiator and cylinder block. Refill with water (preferably soft) or one of the recommended anti-freeze solutions

EVERY 12,000 MILES (19200 Km.)

Engine flushing
Remove the engine sump drain plug and allow the old oil to drain completely.
Replace the plug and pour flushing oil in through the engine filler cap to approximately half engine capacity
A flushing oil supplied by one of the recommended lubricant manufacturers should be used. Run the engine at fast tick-over for 2½–3 minutes. After stopping the engine special care must be taken to ensure complete drainage of the flushing oil.
Replace the sump drain plug and fill the engine with oil to Ref. 'A' (page 229).

EVERY 24,000 MILES (38400 Km.)

Engine sump
Remove the engine sump and oil pick-up strainer, clean thoroughly, and reassemble.
Refill the sump with engine oil to Ref. 'A' (page 229).

This work should be entrusted to your Distributor or Dealer.

SUPPLEMENTARY TOOL KIT

To supplement the tool kit, a roll containing the following is obtainable from all Distributors. Part No. 97H524 should be quoted.

4 spanners: $\frac{5}{16}$ in. × $\frac{3}{8}$ in. A.F.
$\frac{7}{16}$ in. × $\frac{1}{2}$ in. A.F.
$\frac{9}{16}$ in. × $\frac{5}{8}$ in. A.F.
$\frac{11}{16}$ in. × $\frac{3}{4}$ in. A.F.

1 pair 6 in. pliers.
1 7 in. adjustable spanner.
1 ½ in. × $\frac{9}{16}$ in. A.F. tubular spanner.
1 ⅜ in. diameter tommy bar.
1 Phillips screwdriver.

BODYWORK

Coachwork, wings, and windshield

Regular attention and care to the body finish are necessary if the new appearance of the car exterior is to be maintained against the effect of air pollution, rain, and mud. Frequent washing of bodywork is recommended. Large deposits of mud must be softened with water before using a sponge. When clean, dry the surface of the car with a damp chamois-leather. Any damaged parts should immediately be covered with paint and a complete repair effected as soon as possible. When 'touching-in' light scratches and abrasions with paint ensure that all traces of wax polish are removed from the affected area beforehand.

Methylated spirits (denatured alcohol) should be used to remove spots of grease or tar from the bodywork, windshield, and bright parts of the car.

The application of a good-quality liquid polish is recommended to give added lustre to the paintwork and any Distributor or Dealer will advise you of the one most suitable for your car. Do not allow silicone- or wax-based polishes to come into contact with the windshield; they have been known to have a detrimental effect on the wiper blades and are difficult to remove.

Should the windshield become contaminated with silicone-based polish, due to the indiscriminate use of a polish-impregnated duster, remove the contamination by the use of a mild domestic abrasive or by washing with a strong solution of detergent and hot water. If the latter method is used ensure that no solution is allowed to get onto the paintwork.

Bright trim

Metal polish must not be used to clean chromium, plastic, stainless steel, or anodized aluminium bright parts. Wash them frequently with soap and water, and when the dirt has been removed polish the surface with a clean, dry cloth or chamois-leather until bright. Never use an abrasive.

A slight tarnish may be found on stainless steel which has not been washed regularly, and this can be removed with impregnated wadding such as is used on silverware.

Surface deposits on chromium parts may be removed with a chromium cleaner.

An occasional application of wax polish or light oil to metal trim will help to preserve the finish, particularly during winter, when salt has been applied to the roads, but these protectives should not be used on plastic finishers.

Interior

Clean the carpets in the car, preferably before washing the outside, by using a stiff brush or a vacuum cleaner. The leather or leathercloth cushions and door trim may be cleaned periodically by wiping over with a damp cloth. Dust and dirt, if allowed to accumulate too long, will eventually work into the pores of the leather, giving it a soiled appearance that is not easily remedied. A little neutral soap may be used, but detergents, caustic soaps, petrol, or spirits of any kind must not be used.

A razor blade should be used to remove the transfers from the window glass.

MAINTENANCE SUMMARY

Regular servicing, as proved by presentation of completed voucher counterfoils, could well enhance the value of your vehicle in the eyes of a prospective buyer.

ALL MATERIALS CHARGEABLE TO THE CUSTOMER.

Daily
Check oil level in crankcase. Top up if necessary.
Check water level in radiator. Top up if necessary.

Weekly
Test tyre pressures, and regulate if necessary.
Check battery electrolyte level and top up if necessary.

3,000 miles (4800 km.) service

1. *Engine*
    Top up carburetter piston dampers.
    Lubricate carburetter controls.
    Clean and re-oil air cleaners.
    Check fan belt tension.
    Check water level in radiator and top up if necessary.

2. *Clutch*
    Check level of fluid in hydrulic clutch supply tank and top up if necessary.

3. *Brakes*
    Check brakes and adjust if necessary.
    Make visual inspection of brake lines and pipes.
    Check level of fluid in hydrulic brake supply tank and top up if necessary.
    Inspect disc brake friction pads and report if attention is required.

4. *Body*
    Lubricate locks, hinges, bonnet lock and operating mechanism, and safety catches.
    Lightly smear dovetails and striking plates with suitable grease.

5. *Electrical*
    Check battery electrolyte level and top up if necessary.

6. *Lubrication*
    Change engine oil.
    Top up oil levels in gearbox, rear axle, steering gearbox, and steering idler.
    Lubricate all grease nipples.

7. *Wheels and tyres*
    Change road wheels round diagonally (including spare) to regularise tyre wear.
    Check tyre pressures.

MAINTENANCE SUMMARY

6,000 miles (9600 km.) service

1. *Engine*
   Top up carburetter piston dampers.
   Lubricate carburetter controls.
   Clean carburetter filters (if applicable).
   Clean and re-oil air cleaners.
   Check fan belt tension.
   Check valve rocker clearances and adjust if necessary.
   Check water level in radiator and top up if necessary.

2. *Ignition*
   Check functioning of automatic advance and retard mechanism.
   Lubricate all distributor parts as necessary.
   Check and adjust if necessary distributor contact points.
   Clean and adjust sparking plugs.

3. *Clutch*
   Check level of fluid in hydraulic clutch supply tank and top up if necessary.

4. *Brakes*
   Check brakes and adjust if necessary.
   Make visual inspection of brake lines and pipes.
   Check level of fluid in hydraulic brake supply tank and top up if necessary.
   Inspect disc brake friction pads and report if attention is required.

5. *General*
   Check rear road spring seat bolts.

6. *Body*
   Lubricate locks, hinges, bonnet lock and operating mechanism, and safety catches.
   Lightly smear dovetails and striking plates with suitable grease.

7. *Electrical*
   Check battery cell specific gravity readings and top up to correct level.
   Lubricate dynamo bearing.
   Check all lamps for correct functioning.

8. *Lubrication*
   Change oil in engine, gearbox, rear axle, and overdrive (when fitted).
   Fit new oil filter element.
   Lubricate all grease nipples.
   Top up oil levels in steering gearbox and steering idler.

9. *Wheels and tyres*
   Change road wheels round diagonally (including spare) to regularise tyre wear.
   Check tyre pressures.
   Check front wheel alignment and adjust if necessary.

10. *Test*
    Road test car and report.

MAINTENANCE SUMMARY

9,000 miles (14400 km.) service

Carry out the 3,000 miles (4800 km.) service.

12,000 miles (19200 km.) service

1. *Engine*
   Remove carburetter suction chambers and pistons, clean, reassemble, and top up dampers.
   Lubricate carburetter controls.
   Clean carburetter filters (if applicable).
   Clean and re-oil air cleaners.
   Check fan belt tension.
   Check valve rocker clearances and adjust if necessary.
   Lubricate water pump sparingly.

2. *Ignition*
   Check functioning of automatic advance and retard mechanism.
   Lubricate distributor drive shaft by one half-turn of grease cap and all parts as necessary.
   Check and adjust if necessary distributor contact points.
   Fit new sparking plugs.

3. *Clutch*
   Check level of fluid in hydraulic clutch supply tank and top up if necessary.

4. *Steering*
   Check steering and suspension moving parts for wear.

5. *Brakes*
   Check brakes and adjust if necessary.
   Make visual inspection of brake lines and pipes.
   Check level of fluid in hydraulic brake supply tank and top up if necessary.
   Inspect disc brake friction pads and report if attention is required.

6. *Hydraulic dampers*
   Examine all hydraulic dampers for leaks and top up if necessary.

7. *Radiator*
   Drain, flush out, and refill radiator.

8. *General*
   Check rear road spring seat bolts.

9. *Body*
   Lubricate locks, hinges, bonnet lock and operating mechanism, and safety catches.
   Lightly smear dovetails and striking plates with suitable grease.

MAINTENANCE SUMMARY

10. *Electrical*
    Check battery cell specific gravity readings and top up to correct level.
    Lubricate dynamo bearing.
    Check all lamps for correct functioning.
    Check headlight beam setting and adjust if necessary.

11. *Lubrication*
    Drain engine, flush out, and refill with fresh oil.
    Change oil in gearbox, rear axle, and overdrive (when fitted).
    Fit new oil filter element.
    Lubricate all grease nipples.
    Top up oil levels in steering gearbox and steering idler.

12. *Wheels and tyres*
    Change road wheels round diagonally (including spare) to regularise tyre wear.
    Check tyre pressures.
    Check front wheel alignment and adjust if necessary.

13. *Test*
    Road test car and report.

24,000 miles (38400 km.) service
Carry out the **12,000 miles (19200 km.) service**, with the following amendment:

11. *Lubrication*
    Remove engine sump and pick-up strainer, clean, and re-assemble, filling with fresh oil.

WIRING DIAGRAM (R.H.D. and L.H.D.)

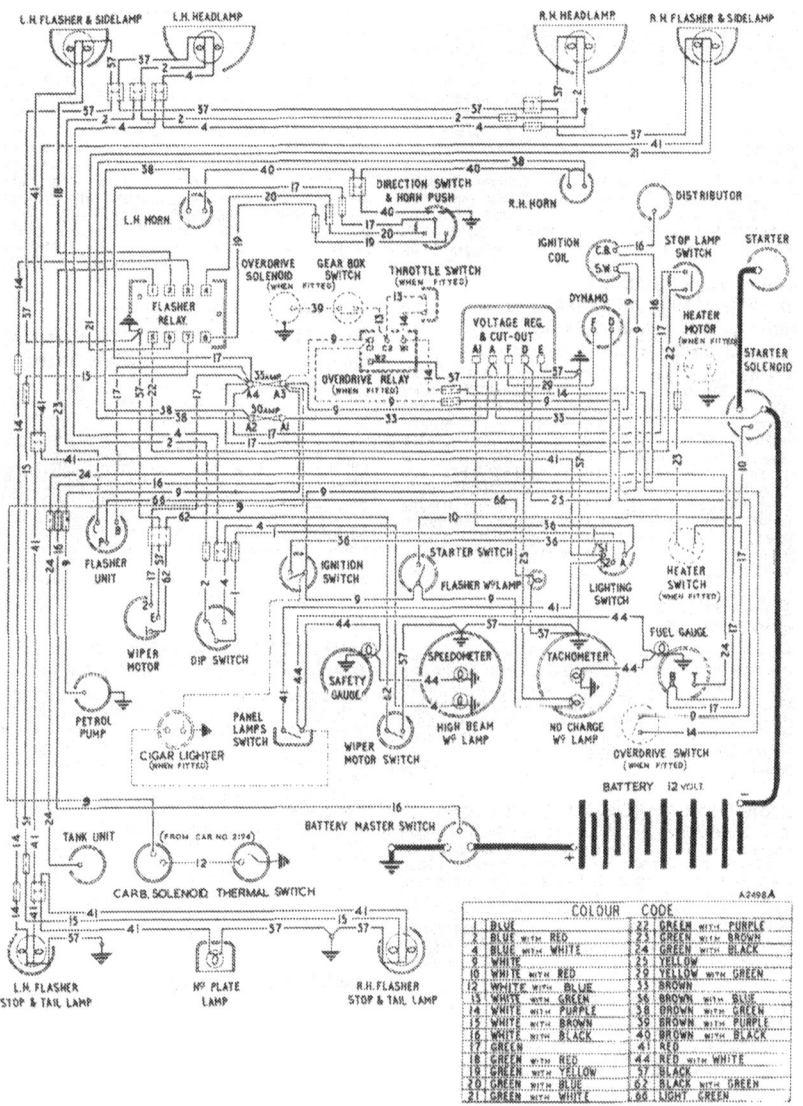

OTHER BOOKS CURRENTLY AVAILABLE FROM

www.VelocePress.com

CHECK OUR WEBSITE OR CONTACT YOUR DEALER FOR

AVAILABILITY & PRICING

AUTOBOOKS SERIES OF WORKSHOP MANUALS

ALFA ROMEO GIULIA 1750, 2000 1962-1978 WORKSHOP MANUAL
AUSTIN HEALEY SPRITE, MG MIDGET 1958-1980 WORKSHOP MANUAL
BMW 1600 1966-1973 WORKSHOP MANUAL
FIAT 124 1966-1974 WORKSHOP MANUAL
FIAT 124 SPORT 1966-1975 WORKSHOP MANUAL
FIAT 500 1957-1973 WORKSHOP MANUAL
FIAT 850 1964-1972 WORKSHOP MANUAL
JAGUAR E-TYPE 1961-1972 WORKSHOP MANUAL
JAGUAR MK 1, 2 1955-1969 WORKSHOP MANUAL
JAGUAR S TYPE, 420 1963-1968 WORKSHOP MANUAL
JAGUAR XK 120, 140, 150 MK 7, 8, 9 1948-1961 WORKSHOP MANUAL
LAND ROVER 1, 2 1948-1961 WORKSHOP MANUAL
MERCEDES-BENZ 190 1959-1968 WORKSHOP MANUAL
MERCEDES-BENZ 230 1963-1968 WORKSHOP MANUAL
MERCEDES-BENZ 250 1968-1972 WORKSHOP MANUAL
MG MIDGET TA-TF 1936-1955 WORKSHOP MANUAL
MINI 1959-1980 WORKSHOP MANUAL
MORRIS MINOR 1952-1971 WORKSHOP MANUAL
PEUGEOT 404 1960-1975 WORKSHOP MANUAL
PORSCHE 911 1964-1969 WORKSHOP MANUAL
RENAULT 8, 10, 1100 1962-1971 WORKSHOP MANUAL
RENAULT 16 1965-1979 WORKSHOP MANUAL
ROVER 3500, 3500S 1968-1976 WORKSHOP MANUAL
SUNBEAM RAPIER, ALPINE 1955-1965 WORKSHOP MANUAL
TRIUMPH SPITFIRE, GT6, VITESSE 1962-1968 WORKSHOP MANUAL
TRIUMPH TR2, TR3, TR3A 1952-1962 WORKSHOP MANUAL
TRIUMPH TR4, TR4A 1961-1967 WORKSHOP MANUAL
VOLKSWAGEN BEETLE 1968-1977 WORKSHOP MANUAL

OTHER WORKSHOP MANUALS, MAINTENANCE & TECHNICAL TITLES

BMW ISETTA FACTORY REPAIR MANUAL
FERRARI 250/GT SERVICE AND MAINTENANCE
FERRARI GUIDE TO PERFORMANCE
FERRARI OPERATING, MAINTENANCE AND SERVICE HANDBOOKS 1948-1963
FERRARI OWNER'S HANDBOOK
FERRARI TUNING TIPS & MAINTENANCE TECHNIQUES
MASERATI OWNER'S HANDBOOK
OBERT'S FIAT GUIDE
PERFORMANCE TUNING THE SUNBEAM TIGER

MOTORCYCLE WORKSHOP MANUALS, MAINTENANCE & TECHNICAL TITLES

ARIEL MOTORCYCLES WORKSHOP MANUAL 1933-1951
BMW MOTORCYCLES FACTORY WORKSHOP MANUAL R26 R27 (1956-1967)
BMW MOTORCYCLES FACTORY WORKSHOP MANUAL R50 R50S R60 R69S R50US R60US R69US (1955-1969)
NORTON MOTORCYCLES FACTORY WORKSHOP MANUAL 1957-1970
NORTON MOTORCYCLES WORKSHOP MANUAL 1932-1939
TRIUMPH MOTORCYCLES FACTORY WORKSHOP MANUAL NO. 11 (1945-1955)
TRIUMPH MOTORCYCLES WORKSHOP MANUAL 1935-1939
TRIUMPH MOTORCYCLES WORKSHOP MANUAL 1937-1951
VINCENT MOTORCYCLES MAINTENANCE AND REPAIR 1935-1955

CLASSIC AUTO TITLES & REFERENCE BOOKS

ABARTH BUYERS GUIDE
DIALED IN ~ THE JAN OPPERMAN STORY
FERRARI 308 SERIES BUYER'S AND OWNER'S GUIDE
FERRARI BERLINETTA LUSSO
FERRARI BROCHURES & SALES LITERATURE 1946-1967
FERRARI SERIAL NUMBERS PART I ~ STREET CARS TO SERIAL # 21399 (1948-1977)
FERRARI SERIAL NUMBERS PART II ~ RACE CARS TO SERIAL # 1050 (1948-1973)
FERRARI SPYDER CALIFORNIA
IF HEMINGWAY HAD WRITTEN A RACING NOVEL ~ THE BEST OF MOTOR RACING FICTION 1950-2000
LE MANS 24 ~ WHAT THE MOVIE COULD HAVE BEEN
MASERATI BROCHURES AND SALES LITERATURE ~ POSTWAR THROUGH INLINE 6 CYLINDER CARS

www.ingramcontent.com/pod-product-compliance
Lightning Source LLC
Chambersburg PA
CBHW020122240426
43673CB00038B/564